Lecture Notes in Economics and Mathematical Systems

476

Springer
Berlin
Heidelberg
New York
Barcelona
Hong Kong
London
Milan
Paris
Singapore
Tokyo

Roland Demmel

Fiscal Policy, Public Debt and the Term Structure of Interest Rates

 Springer

Author

Dr. Roland Demmel
Institute of Public Finance
University of Saarland
P.O. Box 151150
D-66041 Saarbrücken, Germany

Cataloging-in-Publication Data applied for

Die Deutsche Bibliothek - CIP-Einheitsaufnahme

Demmel, Roland:
Fiscal policy, public debt and the term structure of interest rates /
Roland Demmel. - Berlin ; Heidelberg ; New York ; Barcelona ;
Hong Kong ; London ; Milan ; Paris ; Singapore ; Tokyo : Springer,
1999
   (Lecture notes in economics and mathematical systems ; 476)
   Zugl.: Saarbrücken, Univ., Diss., 1998
   ISBN 3-540-66243-X

ISSN 0075-8442
ISBN 3-540-66243-X Springer-Verlag Berlin Heidelberg New York

© Springer-Verlag Berlin Heidelberg 1999
Printed in Germany

Typesetting: Camera ready by author

"Gedruckt mit Unterstützung der Deutschen Forschungsgemeinschaft"

As "Habilitationsschrift" printed by recommendation of Fakultät für Wirtschafts-
wissenschaften of the University of Munich with the support of Deutsche Forschungsgemeinschaft.

SPIN: 10699835   42/3143-543210 - Printed on acid-free paper

Acknowledgments

This book is based on my Ph.D. thesis submitted to and accepted by the University of Saarland in Saarbrücken, Germany. First of all, I want to thank the members of my thesis committee Jürgen Eichberger, Robert Holzmann, Christian Keuschnigg and Klaus Schindler for fruitful discussions and helpful criticism. Second, I owe lots of thanks to many colleagues of the Department of Economics at the University of Saarland and to the participants of the department research seminar, particularly Yves Hervé, Holger Meinhardt, Gesa Miehe-Nordmeyer and Katarzyna Zukowska-Gagelmann who have also become good friends of mine. A big share of thanks goes to many colleagues (economists, mathematicians, finance theorists etc.) who I have had the pleasure to meet and talk to intensively on many conferences and workshops during the last four years. Their number, however, is too large to list all of them. Last but absolutely not least, I want to thank my parents, my brother and my nonacademic friends for having been extremely patient with me all the time throughout writing my thesis. They truly constitute the essence which makes live worth living.

Roland Demmel

Saarbrücken, Germany

April 8, 1999

Acknowledgements

Contents

1 Introduction

The introduction of the thesis consists of four parts: first, we motivate our chosen macroeconomic setting by looking at some real world phenomena. For a better understanding of these phenomena, we argue that the mutual dynamic interactions between fiscal policy and financial markets need to be closely examined in a macroeconomic framework. Second, we review different strands of the economic literature in order to show that most of the literature has so far exclusively concentrated either on financial market dynamics or on fiscal policy issues. We conclude that a more integrated model setting is called for in order to explain the dynamic interactions observed in reality. Third, we discuss at length the economic assumptions underlying our model. This avoids multiple repetition later on. Finally, we outline the structure of the thesis and the objectives we pursue in the different chapters.

1.1 Motivation

Fiscal policy and financial market reactions are increasingly receiving world-wide attention. The most recent examples are the Maastricht criteria about fiscal control, the South-East Asia financial crisis and the resulting IMF policy stance, the high level of public debt in developed and developing countries and the effect on interest rates and economic growth. In contrast to the still underdeveloped theoretical literature on these dynamic links, finding empirical evidence that supports the existence of these links is not a very hard task. Looking back at the respective time series data for the then twelve member countries of the EU in the 1980s, Dornbusch/Draghi (1991, Chapter 1) pointed out that, with the exception of the United Kingdom and Luxembourg, debt and deficit ratios rose remarkably during this decade. A similar upward movement was observed for real interest rates [1]. Dornbusch/Draghi claimed that three main reasons were responsible for the rise in debt ratios: the rise in interest rates, lower growth rates than ex ante expected and too low primary budget surpluses. This seems a sensible

---

[1] See Appendix 1.1 for the corresponding data of selected European countries.

2

explanation only at first sight. Several questions are left open: is the suggested causality, namely that interest rates, growth rates and primary budget deficits drive public debt, always so clear? Are there no dynamic economic links between interest rates, growth rates and primary budget deficits? Do changing debt ratios not trigger repercussions on growth, interest rates and future deficits? A problem with most macroeconomic models is that they usually eliminate any possible feedback effects between fiscal policy, public debt, growth and interest rates by treating at least one of these variables as exogenous. However, it is well conceivable that rising deficits that have to be financed via issuing government bonds drive up interest rates. This, in turn, could affect portfolio investment decisions of financial market actors. Since productive capital is one kind of financial asset, there may be a long run effect on GDP and growth which, in turn, is likely to affect fiscal policy. The circle is closed. Hence, it seems highly desirable to develop macroeconomic models that take such feedback mechanisms into consideration.

Further empirical evidence calling for an integrated model concerns the supposed link between fiscal policy on one side and the term structure of interest rates on the other side. One of the most prominent examples is the situation on US-American bond markets in 1980 [2]: starting in January and February with a real yield curve that was hump-shaped for short-term maturities and slightly inverse for medium and long-term maturities, the term structure began to turn in spring and reached a normal slope which lasted the whole summer. Simultaneously, the level of the real yield curve dropped substantially. During September and October, the term structure began to turn again. In November and December, it reached an even sharper hump-shaped/inverse slope than at the year's beginning. It was accompanied by an increase in the level of the yield curve. When we recall that just in fall the presidential campaign between Carter and Reagan came into its decisive phase (the election took place in November) and that both candidates had quite different ideas about future fiscal policy, then it is only a short step to recognize that expectations and the final realization of Reagan's victory

---

[2] Appendix 1.2 contains the respective real yield curves in monthly frequency during 1980.

associated with a tremendous change in fiscal policy may have been an important reason for the changes in the real yield curve in 1980 [3]. More recent evidence for a link between fiscal policy and the term structure of interest rates comes from the situation on German bond markets in the aftermath of German Reunification (where the term structure changed to an inverse slope) and from bond markets in former centrally planned economies of Central and Eastern Europe [4].

The last point on our motivation agenda has to do with the European Monetary Union (EMU). The Maastricht Treaty, more or less explicitly, pins down fiscal 'stability criteria' for EMU membership. The rationale behind these criteria is that the 'fathers' of the Maastricht Treaty thought that they are necessary to contain eventual negative spillovers resulting from too high fiscal deficits and public debt. The main negative externality hereby is judged to be the default on the debt service of a bankrupt government which would oblige others to proceed with a costly bailout [5]. Critics have argued that, given the no-bailout provisions of the Maastricht Treaty [6], financial market sanctions in the form of risk premia on interest rates would be sufficient to discipline governments and prevent them from pursuing unsustainable debt policies (Bishop/Damrau/Miller (1989)). That the fiscal criteria were imposed nonetheless is a clear indicator that the 'fathers' of the Treaty themselves did not believe in the credibility of the no-bailout rules[7].

---

[3] We are aware of the fact that, in October 1979, the new chairman of the Fed, Paul Volcker, began to change US monetary policy by replacing the old interest rate target with a new money supply target. This policy change already induced lower inflation rates during the considered year and may have also been influential for the real yield curve, possibly via existing covariances between nominal and real financial market variables.

[4] For an analysis of the term structure on Russian bond markets, see Schöbel/Yakovlev (1996).

[5] Another frequently cited externality is a general increase in interest rates due to excessive deficits. Buiter/Corsetti/Roubini (1993) object by pointing on the 'pecuniary externality' aspect of an interest rate increase: in their view, the interest rate increase simply constitutes a relative price adjustment on a perfectly competitive financial market.

[6] Art. 104 forbids a monetary bailout by the ECB, Art. 104b forbids a fiscal bailout by the EU, i.e. the member states.

[7] The underlying reasoning could be the following: consider a member country (or a coalition of member countries) that decides to default on its debt due to unsustainable fiscal policy. Any bank holding a significant part of its portfolio in bonds of this government could go bankrupt. Via a systemic crisis, the whole financial system could

4

Independently which side of the dispute one tends to, the arguments presented and the choice of the criteria (a 3% ceiling on the deficit ratio of GDP, a 60% ceiling on the debt ratio) have revealed that the interaction between fiscal policy decisions, financial market reactions and real sector developments is still considered as a black box in economic policy circles. One source of uncertainty is clearly the default issue. Why, when and to what degree countries default for purely fiscal reasons remains largely unknown, though it increasingly constitutes an issue of theoretical research (first steps were taken in several chapters of Dornbusch/Draghi (1991)). At least as important in our view, but nearly totally neglected up to now, is the following issue: how does volatility on financial markets that is unrelated to default issues affect economic growth, interest rate and public debt dynamics?

Since they implicitly deem the no-bailout rules to be time-inconsistent, the proponents of the Maastricht fiscal provisions also deem fiscal policies' impact on interest rates to be rather negligible. But what about other aspects? Critics have correctly attacked the arbitrariness the 3% and 60% ceilings rules that do not take into account country specificities. The debt and deficit ceilings are based on pure budgetary arithmetic: given expected nominal growth rates of 5%, keeping the budget deficit permanently at 3% implies a debt ratio converging to 60%. If the debt level is considered to be the main problem, however, debt ratio stabilization at 60% allows for much higher deficit ratios in countries with higher growth rates. On the other hand, the deficit ceiling should be reduced for lower growth countries. While the fiscal rules have been correctly criticized for this arbitrariness that is hard to justify economically, the more important point is probably the following: there is apparently only a vague understanding regarding the link between public debt and economic growth that determines future public deficits.

The same qualitative critique can be addressed to those who believe that financial markets alone will be sufficient to ensure sustainable fiscal policies.

---

break down. Faced with the costs of such a breakdown, it would not be time consistent for the remaining governments to stick to the no-bailout rules. Anticipating this, financial markets are unlikely to sanction unsound fiscal performance in the first place. This, in turn, reduces the costs of pursuing unsound fiscal policies. For a complete and detailed discussion of these issues, see Holzmann/Hervé/Demmel (1996).

They anticipate interest rate reactions, but only in response to default risk. They do not anticipate large interest rate reactions in case of the absence of default risk. They largely ignore how interest rate developments will affect the time path of the public debt via feedback effects on growth and tax revenues.

To summarize: understanding the dynamic interplay of important fiscal variables like public deficits and debt in an economic framework of growth, especially in interaction with financial markets, is a key prerequisite for addressing related policy questions properly. Though it completely ignores the issue of debt default, we hope and believe the model framework which will be developed here constitutes a significant methodological step in the exploration of this yet rather unknown territory.

1.2 Brief review of the literature

The innovative part of the thesis will deal with theoretically modeling the interactions between fiscal policy and financial markets in a dynamic general equilibrium framework under risk. The three main questions are:

- How does fiscal policy influence short-term interest rate dynamics and hence the term structure of interest rates in general?

- How is economic growth affected by fiscal policy and financial market behavior?

- How does the fiscal stance of the model economy evolve given financial market behavior?

Before embarking on introducing our model ideas, we will briefly review the recent literature that has dealt with each of these problems. Doing so, one discovers that all questions together have never before been theoretically discussed and analyzed in a continuous-time general equilibrium framework with risk [8].

---

[8] We emphasize that the following literature review is far from being complete but represents just the main achievements as we see them.

1.2.1 Review of the literature on interest rate dynamics and the term structure of interest rates

In the traditional literature on interest rates and term structure of interest rates, one usually distinguishes between three main historical approaches:

- The 'expectations hypothesis' by Fisher (1896), Hicks (1939), Lutz (1940), Malkiel (1966) and Roll (1970, 1971)

- The 'liquidity preference theory' by Hicks (1939)

- The 'theory of preferred habitats' (or: 'market segmentation theory') by Culbertson (1957) and Modigliani/Sutch (1966)).

The earliest work in this respect stems from the great Irving Fisher and dates back to the last century, namely 1896. It is fair to say that Fisher's work marked the beginning of contemporary term structure of interest rate theory. It took then remarkably long, namely more than 40 years, until Hicks (1939) put up the question again and deepened the approach of Fisher [9]. Their approach is commonly known as the 'expectations hypothesis'. It states that the shape of the yield curve [10] emerges through and thus reflects the expectations of market participants. Assume that bonds of all maturity sell at the same yield-to-return and that investors believe that future interest rates will rather be lower than higher. Then they will 'bet' on long-term bonds instead of short-term bonds because, if expectations materialize, prices of long-term bonds will go up, whereas short-term bonds will probably already have expired. Thus long-term bonds yield capital gains. As a result of these expectations, investors with such beliefs are willing to bid up today's prices of long-term bonds and sell off short-term bonds. The consequence are sinking prices for these bonds. In turn, short-term yields rise and long-term

---

[9] This long time range can certainly be better understood when one recalls that during that time the economic problems caused by World War I and its aftermath as well as the question of unemployment and hyperinflation linked to the Great Depression stood high on the agenda of economists thereby leaving less time and interest to other questions.

[10] Burton G. Malkiel (1989, pp. 265, line 1-3) defines what term structure of interest rates is all about: „The term structure of interest rates concerns the relationship among the yields of default-free securities that differ only with respect to their term to maturity. The relationship is more popularly known as the shape of the yield curve...". In this spirit, we will further use 'term structure of interest rates' and 'yield curve' synonymously to denote the same concept: the time to maturity dependency of interest rates.

yields fall. A falling yield curve (in terms of rising maturity) emerges which is called 'inverse yield curve'. The expectations hypothesis hence explains inverse term structures by expectations of sinking interest rates in the future. Accordingly, a 'normal' term structure (i.e. a rising yield curve in terms of increasing time to maturity) is explained by future expectations of increasing interest rates. Under the assumption of perfect foresight and in the absence of transaction costs and any other form of friction, one gets a strict formal relation between short-term and long-term interest rates. Long-term rates are then an average of current and expected future short-term rates.

Hicks (1939) extended this hypothesis to the 'liquidity preference hypothesis' by introducing uncertainty. In a world of uncertainty, Hicks argues, investors prefer short-term to long-term bonds because the short-term bonds are more liquid. If the interest rates develop unsatisfactorily for an investor, he/she looses less money holding short-term bonds than long-term bonds. Thus, a premium for holding long-term bonds has to be paid: the liquidity premium. This explains the frequently observed 'normal' (i.e. increasing) character of yield curves. Inverse term structures can still be explained by the expectations argument as in the expectation hypothesis, but the normal term structure is the usual case.

From these still not very mathematical roots laid down by Fisher and Hicks emerged a lot of work during the 1940s to 1960s. A special development of the term structure theory criticizing the existing theories, the 'theory of preferred habitats' (or: 'market segmentation theory'), was spread out by Culbertson (1957) and Modigliani/Sutch (1966). They argue that investors do not have a general preference for liquidity as claimed by Hicks but have to be distinguished according to their institutional and business characteristics. Life insurers, for example, are claimed to have an interest to invest into long-term bonds, whereas commercial banks have rather a preference for short-term bonds. As a consequence, the whole bond market should be seen, according to this theory, as being segmented into a short-term and a long-term market. The corresponding yields result from the supply and demand characteristics on each market alone.

Looking at the interest rate literature that has evolved over the last two decades, one notices inevitably two strands that have diverged more and more: the mathematical finance literature on the one hand and the macroeconomic literature dealing with term structure questions on the other hand. The former was initiated by a major methodological breakthrough which happened in the late 1970s: mathematically stringent dynamic 'factor models' regarding the term structure of interest rates were developed. Vasicek (1977), Richard (1978) and Brennan/Schwartz (1979), among others, are the most prominent proponents of early work in this area. This work built upon the methodological revolution in finance which was pioneered by Fischer Black, Myron Scholes and Robert C. Merton at the beginning of the 1970s using the tools of stochastic calculus [11]. The principle idea these papers have in common is to assume that the price of a default-free zero-coupon bond depends only on time to maturity of the bond and on an arbitrary number of 'factors'. In most papers, one or two factors are assumed to exist and are usually identified as the short- and long-term real interest rate. The evolution of these factors is introduced by assuming ad-hoc functional forms of diffusion processes characterized by stochastic differential equations. The choice of these functional forms is mainly based on the desire to obtain simple closed-form solutions and to enable econometricians to estimate the dynamics easily. The authors then build up portfolios using bonds of different maturity along the lines of Black/Scholes (1973) and end up with a second-order partial differential equation that resembled the one of Black/Scholes with one exception: there is an additional term in this equation, the so-called 'market price of risk' [12]. In order to parameterize the market price of risk, special mathematical expressions depending on the factors and time to maturity are assumed to be exogenously given. The valuation equation can then be solved according to the well-known theory of linear partial differential equations. This approach has the obvious weakness that the arbitrary choice of the market price's functional

---

[11] The importance of the work of Black, Scholes and Merton became finally visible when the latter two were awarded the Nobel Price in Economics in 1997. The reason why Fischer Black was not honored is that he died in 1995 and Nobel prices are usually not awarded posthumously (the only exemption so far has been the Secretary General of the U.N., Dag Hammarskjöld, in 1961).

[12] This 'market price of risk' appears in the valuation equation since the 'underlying assets', short- and long-term interest rate, are not tradable per definition. In the

form is crucial for the bond price and thus for the term structure [13]. Dothan (1978) and especially Cox/Ingersoll/Ross (1985 a, b) took a different approach: they introduced a representative investor facing an intertemporal saving-investment problem given the stochastic evolution of the prices of so-called 'productive investment opportunities'. In principle, the solution of this problem leads to a set of demand equations for the different assets giving, at least in the Cox/Ingersoll/Ross framework, the short-term interest rate as well as the bond prices in equilibrium. In their approach, the market price of risk is derived endogenously. It became clear that specific choices for the market price of risk in former papers were in sharp contrast to the endogenously determined market price of risk in a general equilibrium setting. The reason for this contrast lies in the fact that the exogenous introduction of specific forms of market risk can lead to arbitrage opportunities which cannot occur in a general equilibrium setting.

Most of the recent approaches in modeling the term structure are founded on the work of Harrison/Kreps (1979) and Harrison/Pliska (1981). These authors showed that, in an environment of dynamically complete financial markets where information resolution is driven by semimartingale processes, present equilibrium asset prices must have the martingale property. This property means that expected future prices given today's information must be equal to today's price. Calculating present prices in the 'traditional' way, namely as the expected value of future cash flows discounted by the riskless interest rate, where the expectation is carried out using the probability measure generated by the original stochastic factor dynamics, would therefore lead to prices for which arbitrage opportunities may exist. In order to calculate asset prices correctly, one needs to change the original probability measure into a measure that guarantees the martingale property of asset prices. Such probability measures are called 'equivalent martingale measure' (short: EMM). The stochastic analysis tool which provides the required probability measure transformation is the theorem of Girsanov (1960). Moreover, Harrison, Kreps and Pliska showed that under some

---

Black/Scholes framework the underlying asset, the stock, is tradable so that no 'market price of risk' term is involved in their valuation equation.
[13] For a detailed overview as well as a criticism of this approach, see Vetzal (1994).

technical conditions imposed on the stochastic dynamics driving the factors on such markets, the EMM exists and is unique. In order to value arbitrary derivatives (the term structure can be viewed as such a derivative 'written' on a pre-specified set of factors), it is hence sufficient to find such an EMM of probabilities and use it to calculate whatever asset prices one is interested in. The most prominent example of this presently leading approach in term structure modeling is the work of Heath/Jarrow/Morton (1992). They introduced the dynamics of a continuum of factors, namely the forward rates, as stochastic differential equations and derived the term structure using the EMM approach. Recent theoretical work goes towards generalizing the assumptions of the EMM approach to allow for incompleteness of financial markets (be it owing to the presence of transaction costs, stochastic volatility or just a too low number of traded assets in view of the number of 'sources' of riskiness) and more general formulations of stochastic factor dynamics (compare, for example: Delbaen/Schachermayer (1994), Björk/Di Masio/Kabanov/Runggaldier (1997) and Björk/Kabanov/Runggaldier (1997)). All these recent term structure models have given up any explicit, microeconomically founded decision-making of financial market actors. The researchers in this field consider this an advantage over the older methods since it provides practitioners with formulas that avoid arbitrary assumptions of functional forms for the market price of risk (like in Vasicek (1977), Richard (1978) or Brennan/Schwartz (1979)). Moreover, 'practitioner-confusing' parameters like preferences of the representative investor (like in Dothan (1978) and Cox/Ingersoll/Ross (1985 a, b)) are no longer part of the valuation formulas using the EMM approach.

In contrast to the mathematical finance literature, the traditional macroeconomic literature on the determination of interest rates and term structure tried to identify and model the channels through which government policy influences interest rates. This was mainly accomplished by assuming very crude financial market settings where the actors usually form rational expectations without considering risk or even uncertainty. A reason for this shortcoming may be that macroeconomists are usually interested only in qualitative instead of quantitative analysis and results. Hence they abstained from employing the advanced tools from stochastic analysis for a long time.

Accordingly, their approach implies that financial markets are assumed to have perfect foresight. This yields the strong equality of returns on assets that are perfect substitutes. Constant interest rates as well as flat term structure curves are the consequence. Given empirical observation of financial markets, it is definitely out of question that financial markets produce such simple outcomes. Papers representing this kind of deterministic financial market approach are Blanchard (1981), Turnovsky/Miller (1984), Turnovsky (1989) or Fisher/Turnovsky (1992), to mention just the most prominent papers. Fisher (1995) extended this approach to a small country setting where disturbances of the world interest rate on the term structure of the small country are studied. An interesting exception from the deterministic financial market papers was a discrete time stochastic model with a representative agent by Lee (1991). Since the main goal of this paper was to test the Ricardian equivalence hypothesis empirically, the model was hence consciously kept simple and did not concentrate on deriving the term structure.

More recently, Turnovsky/Grinols (1993, 1994, 1996) in a series of important papers implemented financial markets in a continuous-time macroeconomic setting with risk. They were among the first to introduce a more realistic picture of financial markets into dynamic macroeconomic models by modeling the household decision problem as an intertemporal discounted utility maximization problem under risk. Their setting yielded more interesting economic conclusions than all the preceding deterministic models. However, these models had not the purpose to develop a complete derivation of the term structure of interest rates via, for example, the one- or multi-factor line of argumentation used by Vasicek (1977) and all his followers.

1.2.2 Review of the macroeconomic literature on fiscal policy, public debt and economic growth

The second main topic of the thesis regards the question of how economic growth and the fiscal stance (i.e. public debt and deficits) of an economy are dynamically influenced by stochastic financial market behavior. The recent macroeconomic literature has analyzed public deficits and debt in a dynamic growth framework. Earlier papers dealing with public debt had their main focus on short-run macro-stabilization and not on long-run economic growth. These models were pretty much rooted in the old Keynesian fashion. They viewed the government as a controller acting against a 'structurally fixed economic nature' who tries to fine-tune the economy by fiscal demand management. The collapse of the Bretton Woods system and the oil price shock at the beginning of the 1970s plunged the post-war Keynesian way of macroeconomic thinking into a deep intellectual crisis since the old recipes did no longer work.

Although rational expectations had already been introduced to economics by Muth (1961), it was this crisis that paved the road for the macroeconomic breakthrough of the rational expectations hypothesis by Lucas (1972, 1973, 1976). The core message of Lucas was that private agents endowed with rational expectations will foresee the effects of government policy and hence react on it by adjusting their own consumption and saving decisions. As a consequence, the 'economic nature' does no longer remain structurally fixed. There remains much less leeway for the controller to influence the economy according to his preferences.

At almost the same time, Barro (1974) revived the old question whether or not Ricardian equivalence holds, i.e. whether a shift in public expenditure financing away from taxation and towards more bond financing and hence public indebtedness has an impact on consumption, savings and output or whether it is neutral. The work of Lucas and Barro made clear that there are indeed conditions so that fiscal policy falls flat without any of the effects predicted by Keynesians economists. For both theoretical reasons as well as empirical findings, many economists, even if they are proponents of rational expectations, still disagree whether Ricardian equivalence should be seen as a good approximation to reality or just as a theoretical but completely unrealistic benchmark[14].

---

[14] According to Romer (1996, p. 67), „The relevant question, however, is not whether it (Ricardian equivalence) is exactly correct, but whether there are large departures from it." Judd (1987, p. 51) discusses possible departures from Ricardian equivalence by extending Barro's model to a continuous-time deterministic setting and reaches the conclusion:

As a consequence, a whole branch of the macroeconomic literature dealing with possible interactions of public indebtedness and growth has evolved, either assuming a positive or a normative view of fiscal policy. Since it is well-known that in a deterministic growth setting with representative households there is no need for public debt when the government has access to lump-sum taxation, models representing the normative standpoint introduced public debt as a mean to redistribute tax distortions over time when only distorting taxes can be implemented. Examples for work in this direction are Barro (1979), Lucas/Stokey (1983), or Chamley (1985, 1986). Zhu (1992) and Aiyagari/McGrattan (1994) substantially deepened the analysis by introducing both risk and capital accumulation into the optimal taxation framework.

There has also been significant work committed to a positive view of fiscal policy in a dynamic growth setting. Some examples are Eaton (1981), who was one of the first to introduce stochastic continuous-time dynamics into macroeconomics, Aschauer (1988), or Baxter/King (1993). They all assumed specific forms of fiscal policy in terms of taxation, expenditure and deficit financing. They then analyzed the effects of these policies on capital accumulation or public indebtedness. Welfare considerations thus did not play any role. The model environment we will present in our thesis is closely related to this strand of literature, with the extension that we include a risky financial market setting.

A different positive approach, namely a political-economic one, was proposed by Alesina/Tabellini (1990), among others. They argued that normative models cannot explain observed large variations in debt policies among different countries with similar economic structure. Their opinion stands in sharp contrast to the view that governments act like benevolent dictators and is hence quite similar to the opinion professed by proponents of the public choice school: governments should be seen as self-interested agents. The work of Aghion/Bolton (1991) is pretty much in the same spirit, although their main intention is to explain the possibility of default on public

---

„Hence, the impact of debt is an empirical issue and Ricardian neutrality appears to be a reasonable benchmark." Thus, Ricardian equivalence should be seen as a theoretical benchmark but it is certainly not a strict paradigm.

debt instead of the emergence of debt dynamics. Very recently, Velasco (1997 a, b) contributed to this branch of literature by assuming that government resources are a common pool from which different interest groups can extract resources according to their own personal objectives. This setting allows him to explain emerging deficit and debt dynamics even though there is no inherent need for intertemporal smoothing through indebtedness. Additionally, he examines the effect on delayed fiscal reforms based on the framework of Alesina/Drazen (1991). Though this branch of the literature seems quite promising in explaining real phenomena regarding public indebtedness, the picture would be more clear cut when taking into consideration the stochastic environment of financial markets.

Independently from the normative or positive view, the question of time inconsistency of optimal fiscal and/or monetary policy was raised by Kydland/Prescott (1977) and Calvo (1978), to mention just the pioneering papers. Time inconsistency means that announced governmental policy may, after the other agents in the economy have made their decisions based on the announcement which leads to a new state of the economy, no longer be optimal for the government given this new state. As Feichtinger/Hartl (1986, 537-540) pointed out, time inconsistency almost always takes place if the government acts as a Stackelberg leader in an open-loop optimization problem (open-loop implies that optimal policies do depend on the initial state and time only). In a Nash equilibrium between private and public sector or in case that policies are feedback policies depending only on the actual state of the economy, time inconsistency does not appear. Since a Stackelberg open-loop environment frequently yields better results in terms of welfare than the other strategic settings, the question appears whether time consistency in a Stackelberg open-loop situation can be guaranteed. This will be the case if sound pre-commitment devices can be found that oblige the government to stick to pre-announced policies [15]. In our model, the time consistency problem is eliminated since we introduce permanent fiscal policy rules.

---

[15] For example, a country's constitution could be thought of being such a device. For a detailed discussion of the subject, see Persson/Tabellini (1990).

1.2.3 Résumé

All contemporary mathematical finance models abstract from any other perspective than the financial market one. Influences of fiscal policy, for example, on interest rates cannot be accounted for. Their objective was clearly a different one: the construction of a consistent theory for the valuation of interest rate dependent derivatives in view of the obvious needs of financial market practitioners. Sticking only to this strict financial market point of view, however, has the obvious disadvantage that this ignores that financial markets are nothing else than one knot in a network of dynamic interactions on an economy's macroeconomic level. Especially in times where the whole economic environment is subject to drastic changes, the ad-hoc postulated factor dynamics in mathematical finance models may deliver essentially misleading results since their parametrization does not make visible the inherent links with important macroeconomic variables. When one believes that fiscal policy matters for interest rates dynamics, one has to extend these models correspondingly by embedding them into a fully-fledged macroeconomic setting.

In contrast, most macroeconomic papers dealing with fiscal policy and public debt solely did not include a reality-oriented description of the financial market dynamics. This is unproblematic if one believes (as the authors apparently did) that financial markets do not play an essential role in explaining public debt or economic growth. More likely, the mathematical finance literature was then still developing its own methodology so that it was just too young to spread out as a useful tool for macroeconomists. In addition, the rigorous stochastic-analytical foundation of mathematical finance has in the meantime gone so far that mathematicians, statisticians and probability theorists with less interest in economics dominate the field. Since the application of stochastic analysis in macroeconomics is still in its very infancy, the main reason for today's strict separation between both fields seems to lie in the divergence of the methodological basis of the fields.

As Section 1.1 should have made clear, the consideration of the complex interactions between financial markets and macroeconomic dynamics is important for a better understanding of the dynamic behavior of fiscal and financial variables as well as economic growth. A mathematical finance perspective alone cannot account for the influence of fiscal policy on asset prices in a satisfying way. On the other hand, general equilibrium macroeconomic models without a realistic embedding of financial markets neglect the repercussion of asset prices on capital accumulation and public deficits which, in turn, hampers a better understanding of economic growth and public indebtedness. The main objective of our thesis is to provide an analytical framework that enables us to simultaneously examine the term structure of interest rates, the dynamics of fiscal variables and economic growth. To achieve this, we will explicitly include financial markets into a continuous-time macroeconomic model that overcomes the deficiencies of both approaches. Since the main emphasis of the work lies in the analysis of the above-mentioned dynamic links, we use the simplest descriptions of production (a linear technology depending on capital only) and fiscal policy (exogenously given policy rules). This work does hence not per se contribute to important macroeconomic research topics like sources of endogenous growth, optimal fiscal policy, political-economic policy making etc. Extensions towards these directions are highly desirable, but prior to such extensions we need to gain some understanding of the possibly nonlinear feedback effects between financial markets and fiscal policy in their simplest form. This is also the main reason why we do not carry out an empirical analysis of our model [16]. In view of the whole literature on mathematical finance as well as on macroeconomics, our work should hence be seen as a step towards melting financial market modeling in the tradition of mathematical finance into dynamic macroeconomics from a general equilibrium perspective. Based on such a foundation, the model can be enriched by economically more interesting and more realistic 'building blocks' in future work leading to dynamic results that bear large potentials for successful empirical work.

---

[16] A minor problem is that a very advanced soft- and hardware equipment is needed in order to estimate the model dynamics.

1.3 General discussion of the basic model assumptions

Throughout this thesis, we use a dynamic general equilibrium model of a real, closed economy with a private sector, a public sector and a financial market. Time is assumed to evolve continuously [17]. An important argument for continuous-time comes from our desire to study the term structure of interest rates which requires the development of a yield curve formula. Since the yield curve is parameterized by the variable 'time to maturity' and there is no reason to assume that this variable shall be discrete, it is straightforward to use continuous time [18].

The reason for the closed economy assumption is that it allows us to derive the interest rate dynamics endogenously. This is not possible in a small open economy where prices and interest rates are usually determined on world markets and taken as given by the economy. An alternative could be a two country model, but then the number of state variables increases essentially and complicates the analysis significantly. Such a model framework can be interesting for future work but is presently beyond the scope of this thesis.

Regarding the private sector, we will use a representative agent approach with an infinitely long living household endowed with rational expectations. The main reason for this choice is that it is the simplest and simultaneously most tractable analytical way to model dynamic, forward-looking behavior of the private sector. Moreover, the use of a standard overlapping generations model (OLG model) with each generation living for two periods cannot address satisfactorily the term structure issue. Even an expansion to an OLG

---

[17] Doing so poses the basic question: should one use discrete or continuous time to formulate macroeconomic models? Proponents of discrete time models have often argued that nature evolves on a discrete time scale. Even more important is their argument that individuals as the subjects of any economy receive and operate information in discrete time and not continuously. Their conclusion is that models should be formulated in discrete time. We agree to the extent that the models should then use the 'natural time unit of individual information processing' as the proper distance between discrete time points. Although nobody seems to know what the appropriate time unit of human information processing is, most people would agree that such a natural time unit lies certainly in the range of seconds instead of days, weeks, months or even years. Continuous-time modeling is hence certainly a better approximation of reality than using monthly or longer time units in discrete-time modeling.

[18] Doing so is additionally in the tradition of term structure modeling in mathematical finance.

model with many periods and cohorts (for instance, in the spirit of Auerbach/Kotlikoff (1987)) would not be helpful. In order to have enough periods for an interesting discussion of the term structure, we would have to introduce too many cohorts to get analytically tractable results [19]. An alternative to the representative agent approach could be a continuous-time OLG model in the tradition of Blanchard/Fischer (1989, Chapter 3.3). It has the advantage that there is heterogeneity among households in contrast to the representative agent model. Such heterogeneity is certainly a helpful device when one wants to model fiscal policy more realistically. Heterogeneity among households allows to introduce redistribution among different types of households as a goal of fiscal policy. However, it is not our goal to examine the dynamic macroeconomic consequences of redistributive fiscal policy in this work. For our purpose, it is sufficient to choose the simplest meaningful representation of fiscal policy possible. Another deficiency with the heterogeneous agent setting is that the aggregation in a stochastic environment could cause severe technical problems.

The representative household is assumed to maximize (expected) discounted life-time utility. This yields consumption and asset demand functions. Utility stems from consumption alone. The utility function is assumed to be time-separable with instantaneous utility being characterized by a constant elasticity of substitution (CES) function. Such specifications are quite common in the dynamic macroeconomic literature. We are aware that there are several problems involved with such a specification. In an important empirical work, Mehra/Prescott (1985) pointed out that the excess volatility of equity returns over safe bond returns given equity's predicted return can only be reconciled with the use of such time-separable utility functions if highly unrealistic utility parameter values are chosen. This critique certainly calls for the use of more complicated, time-inseparable utility functions when one wants to explain the equity risk premium observed on financial markets in reality. As Constantinides (1990) showed, habit formation could probably explain this result. However, using 'more realistic' utility functions (see, for

---

[19] One should, however, emphasize that the Auerbach/Kotlikoff framework is highly recommendable in case one wants to do simulations in order to study dynamic behavior of macroeconomic variables. A recent successful demonstration of the strength of this framework is Altig et al. (1997).

example, Duffie/Epstein (1992) or Obstfeld (1994)) would ultimately lead to very difficult hence unsolved problems in terms of getting closed-form solutions for the household's optimization problem. It is not the equity premium puzzle we aim to explain. In order to reach our theoretical objective, we need to work out solutions in the most explicit way to allow for economic interpretation. Hence, we sacrifice more realistic utility functions and use common CES-utility.

The household maximizes utility subject to its own dynamic budget constraint. This budget constraint describes the (stochastic) evolution of private wealth which is the state variable for the household's optimization problem. Private wealth consists of private capital, public debt in form of short-term bonds and private bonds of arbitrary maturity. Starting with a positive initial endowment of wealth, the household chooses its consumption stream as well as its different holdings of available assets. This determines the accumulation of wealth. In doing so, the household takes all asset prices as parametrically given and does not take the government's budget constraint into account. This corresponds to the view that the representative household represents a large number of atomistic agents that do not perceive the aggregate effects of their behavior, neither on the government budget constraint nor on the determination of prices in equilibrium.

Output in this one-sector model is produced via a linear production technology where capital is the only input factor. The factor labor is thus excluded and the returns arising from holding the different assets are the only source of income in this economy. The main reason why we have excluded labor is that we want to focus on the dynamic interrelation between financial markets, public indebtedness and economic growth. This does not require the incorporation of labor markets [20]. The stock of capital increases immediately with investment [21] and goes down owing to capital depreciation. There are

---

[20] If, however, one recognizes that taxes on labor income play an important role for the overall amount of tax revenues in most countries, then it becomes clear that the labor-leisure choice should be included in future work in order to get a better 'picture' of taxation and dynamic composition of public deficits.

[21] As Kydland/Prescott (1982) point out, this assumption is an unpleasant one when one wants to tackle the problem of matching observed business cycle data with model-

no additional costs for carrying out investment. This type of production function is the simplest conceivable form and it may lead to endogenous growth (see for example Turnovsky (1995) or Barro/Sala-i-Martin (1995)).

The structure of the financial market is characterized by three types of assets: capital, government bonds and private bonds. Additionally, we assume that trading may happen continuously without friction. Continuous trading without transaction costs seems to be a hard assumption given reality, but these standard assumptions are necessary conditions for the financial market to be dynamically complete in the sense of Harrison/Kreps (1979) and Harrison/Pliska (1981). This completeness guarantees uniqueness of the financial market equilibrium later on. Apart from these technical arguments, it is still an open question whether financial market frictions affect macroeconomic dynamics significantly. This is definitely an avenue for future research.

Both types of bonds are assumed to be default-free. They are held only by the private households, at least in principle [22]. This means that the aggregate stock of private bonds has to be zero in equilibrium. Private bonds are hence said to be in net-zero supply.

The public sector is introduced by exogenously given rules determining the evolution of taxes and public expenditures. Although the taxation and spending rules are exogenous, their dynamic evolution is completely endogenous since the bases for these rules are endogenous variables. Taxation is modeled as a proportional tax on private wealth in the tradition of Turnovsky/Grinols (1993). It is the simplest form of an aggregate distortionary tax [23]. We thus abstract from income and consumption taxes

---

generated data. Since this is not our main concern here, we abstract from the fact that in reality investment decisions need time to add to the existing capital stock.

[22] We note that the stock of public bonds can also become negative. In such a case (for example, in Chapter 2), the government is a creditor to the private sector.

[23] Of course, the question is whether we should not introduce lump-sum taxation, especially since this form of taxation is known to be welfare-superior to all other tax rules. The answer is that distortionary taxation reflects reality much better than lump-sum taxation. An example for the practical difficulty to introduce lump-sum taxes goes back to the 1980s in the United Kingdom. Prime Minister Margaret Thatcher tried to introduce a lump-sum tax called 'poll tax' and failed owing to the 'pressure of the street' although she had a comfortable majority in parliament. This is clear evidence that the introduction of

although we are conscious that these distortionary taxes account for the lion share of most countries' tax revenues [24]. The consequence of our taxation rule is that Ricardian equivalence does not hold (see Turnovsky (1995, p. 243) for a summary of necessary conditions for validity of Ricardian equivalence) [25].

Regarding public expenditure [26], we assume it to be a fixed percentage of overall production. In view of empirical data for many European Union members over the last decade, this assumption is not a bad approximation of reality [27]. Such a linear rule has the additional advantage that government expenditure will never exceed production which would be a contradiction to our closed economy assumption.

In our model, government expenditure is unproductive, i.e. it can be interpreted as pure public consumption. It does not affect the utility of the private sector and can be understood to exist for public choice reasons out of the model [28]. We are not interested in the motives for public expenditure, we are purely interested in how existing public expenditure affects macroeconomic dynamics. Nevertheless, the analysis of our model will show that, despite of the waste-of-resources character of government expenditure, they will have some stabilizing effects in a stochastic environment.

---

lump-sum taxes in a democracy is hard to push through. It is particularly true when there are large groups of the people having strong preferences for 'social justice'. Such distributional aspects are neglected by lump-sum taxes.

[24] Taxes on stocks like wealth are less frequently found in literature although they are part of many countries tax code. The reason for this is that they constitute only a small share of tax revenues compared to the taxes on flows.

[25] This is not per se harmful since Ricardian equivalence is still hotly debated among economists as we have already mentioned in section 1.2.2. We therefore view our departure from Ricardian equivalence as justified since the theoretical analysis will yield important insights in how far fiscal policy impacts on the economy in our model.

[26] When we talk about government expenditure now or later, then we always mean all public expenditure except for interest payments, i.e. primary expenditure.

[27] See Appendix 1.3 for the relevant time series data of government consumption ratios for France, Germany, Luxembourg and the United Kingdom from 1980-1989.

[28] Examples for the literature that views government expenditure as either productive input or utility-enhancing 'good' for the private households are Aschauer (1988), Aschauer/Greenwood (1985), Barro (1981, 1989, 1990), Barro/King (1984), Baxter/King (1993), Turnovsky/Fisher (1995) and Hervé (1998). See also Turnovsky (1995, chapter 9 and 13) for a general discussion of the motives for the different assumptions made about government expenditure in dynamic macroeconomic models.

For the given expenditure and tax policy rules, the government budget constraint determines the accruing deficit. We assume that the financing of deficits occurs in the form of short-term government bonds only [29]. The government is not necessarily always in a debt position. A series of budget surpluses could finally drive the stocks of public debt to zero and even to negative values, i.e. the government would become a creditor of the private sector. In consequence, the stock of public debt varies endogenously. The stock of public debt is not tied to capital, output or money as in many dynamic macroeconomic models. Although the authors of these models rationalize their assumptions by economic arguments, a main motive for doing so seems to lie in the fact that such assumptions eliminate a state variable and avoid nonlinear reduced-form dynamics. As will be seen later on, the incorporation of a more reality-oriented description of financial markets dynamics together with our innocent-looking assumption regarding the financing of accruing deficits leads almost automatically to a model in two state variables. Nonlinear feedback effects between interest rates, fiscal variables and capital accumulation are generated. The interesting model variables (like short-term interest rate, private capital, public deficit and debt) are hence characterized by quite complicated nonlinear stochastic dynamics which are very likely to explain observed data much better than previous models. This should contribute to a better theoretical understanding of the interactions between fiscal policy, financial markets and growth.

1.4 Structure of the thesis

The structure of the thesis is as follows: in Chapter 2, the whole macroeconomic model setting will be deterministic. This provides an easily understandable benchmark against which to compare the results in a

---

[29] One economic justification for allowing only short-term government bonds could be an inherent distrust of the private sector concerning the soundness of fiscal policy. Thus, the private sector is only willing to lend its resources for extremely small amounts of time in order to be able to get them back as early as possible to decide then again what to do next with the resources. Such a situation happened, for example, in Italy in the early 1980s when average time to maturity of public debt shrunk from a usual value of six years to hardly one year (see Dornbusch/Draghi (1991) and therein especially Alesina/Prati/Tabellini (1991)).

stochastic setting derived in the subsequent chapters. It will only then become clear how dramatically the introduction of risk affects economic outcomes. As a result, the reduced form of the model in Chapter 2 is easily solvable and the results are clear-cut. We will see that the short-term interest rate and the whole term structure are constant and independent of fiscal policy. We then derive and interpret conditions to be imposed on fiscal policy to prevent the economy from collapsing. Subsequently, we derive the time paths of capital and public debt. They are used to calculate growth rates and debt ratios. The influence of different model parameters on these variables is scrutinized and interpreted. In contrast to the financial market variables, economic growth will be seen to be influenced by fiscal policy.

In Chapter 3, we will introduce risk into the production function: productivity is modeled by a geometric Brownian motion. The household's decision problem then contains a risky asset allocation decision between capital, public bonds and private bonds. In equilibrium, the asset price processes are determined. The short-term interest rate is shown to be a nonlinear function of the state variables private capital and public debt. The reduced-form of the model consists of two stochastic differential equations which jointly describe the accumulation of capital and public debt. We will show that the short-term interest rate dynamics can be represented by an autonomous nonlinear stochastic differential equation, an unprecedented feature in finance literature. In contrast to Chapter 2, interest rates in Chapter 3 do not remain constant but float all the time in a quite nonlinear fashion that reflects the influence of fiscal policy. Using these dynamics, we will derive conditions for the fiscal policy parameters so that viability of the model is maintained. This is achieved by conducting a boundary behavior analysis of the diffusion process driving the short-term interest rate. Moreover, we will show that the fiscal policy constraints ensure the existence of a stochastic steady-state of the interest rate dynamics. This steady-state is characterized by a stationary probability density associated with the short-term interest rate. Finally, we will analyze the short as well as long run effects of fiscal policy on the interest rate dynamics and interpret the results.

Chapter 4 is devoted to the analysis of the term structure of interest rates. Using the financial market equilibrium for private bonds from Chapter 3, we will develop a partial differential equation whose solution describes the price of private bonds of arbitrary maturity. Given this price function, the yield-to-return function which characterizes the term structure of interest rates can be easily derived. Since the partial differential equation for the private bond price cannot be solved explicitly in closed-form, we will use an approximation scheme to derive an explicit solution for the yield curve that characterizes the term structure relation. This approximation scheme has the feature that the level of the yield curve is determined by the short-term interest rate only, whereas the structure of the yield curve is solely influenced by the model parameters. Equipped with these results, we will examine analytically how fiscal policy changes quantitatively (and not only qualitatively as in most macromodels) affect the term structure. We explicitly work out parameter conditions under which the term structure remains invariant for specific changes in fiscal policy. In order to clarify the results, we also do some numerical calculations. Finally, we try to give the results an economic interpretation by identifying the channels through which the yield curve is affected by fiscal policy.

In Chapter 5, we will focus on economic growth. The economic growth process will be shown to depend primarily on the evolution of the capital output ratio. Since its equilibrium dynamics turn out to be nonlinear and interest rate dependent, we have to apply advanced tools from the theory of diffusion processes in order to study the qualitative features of the dynamics. These features include stability of equilibrium points, attainability of certain areas and boundary behavior. We will show that there is an unstable equilibrium for economic growth so that the growth process never stops. Additionally, two regions for economic growth are identified: a lower-growth and a higher-growth region. Once the lower-growth region is reached, it can never be left again. It will also be shown that the growth process can always reach the region of lower-growth, thereby exhibiting an average long-run tendency to converge to lower levels. We will link these properties of the growth process to the model parameters and give economic interpretations. Finally, we examine the short and long run dependency of the growth process on the fiscal policy parameters and the short-term interest rate. An economic explanation of these effects closes the chapter.

Chapter 6 deals with the analysis of public debt dynamics. We take the debt ratio as the appropriate variable to characterize the fiscal stance of the public sector. We first employ the public bond market equilibrium condition to show that the sign of the debt per output ratio depends on the short-term interest rate, whereas its magnitude is influenced by the capital output ratio. Thus, we conclude that the interest rate dynamics is mainly responsible for the question whether debt stabilization (i.e. convergence to an area of low values) is possible or not. We then show under which conditions the debt ratio remains locally bounded which rules out the possibility of explosions. Furthermore, we show that under some special parameter constellation debt stabilization is a very likely feature of the model. Finally, we consider short and long run effects of changes in fiscal policy parameters and interest rate values on the debt ratio and interpret the economic meaning of these effects.

In Chapter 7, we summarize, assess and comment upon the findings of the different chapters. Finally, we outline future research possibilities.

At the end of the work, we will eventually present three general, mathematical appendices that aim at helping the reader get a feeling for the advanced mathematical methods necessary to study optimizing behavior and dynamic analysis within a stochastic environment in continuous-time. The first general appendix deals with Brownian motion and stochastic integration. The second appendix discusses some important concepts and methods of stochastic differential equations and diffusion processes. The third appendix is meant to briefly introduce into the Bellman method of dynamic programming.

Appendix 1.1: Real interest rates, general government deficit and debt per GDP ratios for UK, France, Luxembourg and Germany 1980-1989

The deficit and GDP data depicted in the following figures were taken from several editions of the Government Financial Statistics (GFS) Yearbook published by the International Monetary Fond (IMF). The debt data stem from the OECD except for the Luxembourg debt data which were taken from the International Financial Statistics CD-ROM 09/1997 [30]. The monthly real interest rate time series data were principally calculated by subtracting the inflation rate from the nominal interest rate. As proxy for the inflation rate we took monthly reported changes in the consumer price index from the IMF International Financial Statistics CD-ROM 09/97. As proxy for the nominal interest rate, we took the monthly reported government bond yield data from the same source. Although the treasury bill rates are usually supposed to be the better proxy, we did not take them for they were not at hands for all countries so that comparability would have been lost.

The data confirm the observations of Dornbusch/Draghi with one exception: Germany's deficit ratio experienced a slight reduction during the 80s and dropped substantially at the end of the decade. However, in the aftermath of German Reunification in 1990 the deficit ratio rose again to levels similar to those faced in the beginning of the 80's.

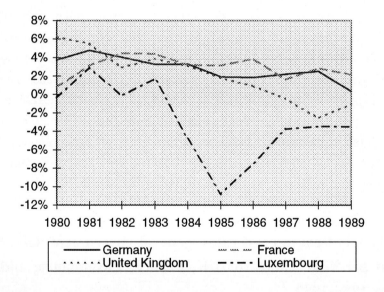

Figure 1.1: Annual deficit per GDP ratios.

---

[30] We are well aware of the fact that the IFS data in contrast to the GFS data use the central government concept instead of the general government. However, in the case of Luxembourg both concepts almost coincide so that comparability of Luxembourg's debt data with the general government debt data of the three other countries is guaranteed.

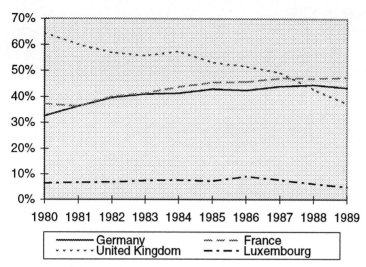

Figure 1.2: Annual debt per GDP ratios.

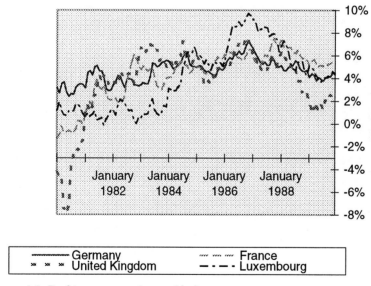

Figure 1.3: Real interest rates in monthly frequency.

28

Appendix 1.2: Real yields to return for the US zero-coupon bond market in 1980

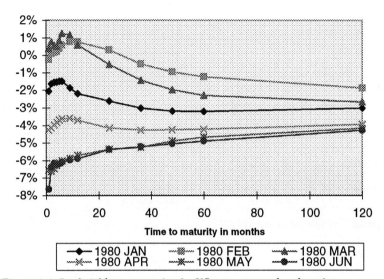

Figure 1.4: Real yields to return for the US zero-coupon bond market.

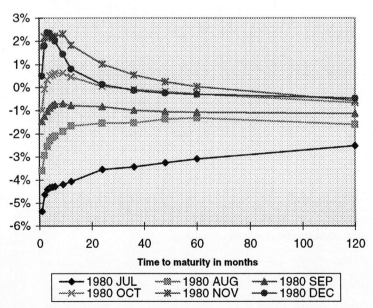

Figure 1.5: Real yields to return for the US zero-coupon bond market.

The nominal yield-to-return data were taken from the data appendix by McCulloch in Shiller (1990). We calculated the real yields by subtracting the monthly reported changes in consumer prices, which we take as proxy for inflation rates, from the nominal data. The monthly reported price data were taken from IMF International Financial Statistics CD-ROM 09/97.

Appendix 1.3: Government consumption ratios for France, Germany, Luxembourg and the United Kingdom

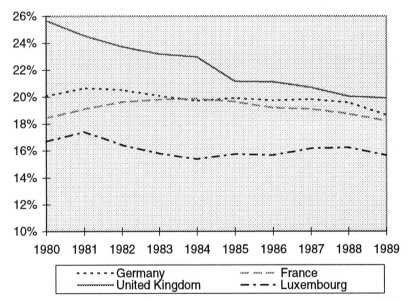

Figure 1.6: Annual government consumption ratio for France, Germany, Luxembourg and the United Kingdom from 1980 - 1989.

The government consumption data stem from annual time series reported in the IMF International Financial Statistics CD-ROM 09/97, the GDP data were taken from several editions of GFS yearbooks. We took the consumption ratios as proxy for the expenditure ratios since public investment spending data necessary to calculate expenditure ratios were not at hand. The almost constant values seem to confirm our model assumption of constant expenditure ratios.

2 The basic deterministic macroeconomic model

2.1 Introduction

The main purpose of this chapter is to build and explore a benchmark macro-model in a deterministic setting of financial markets. Although this model exhibits highly unrealistic features like a constant short-term interest rate and thus a flat term structure of interest rates, it has nevertheless some merits: first of all, the income and debt dynamics are linear so that we can calculate and analyze the time paths of these variables explicitly. This delivers clear-cut results with regard to economic growth and public indebtedness. Second, the stochastic macro-model to be developed later on converges to this deterministic version when risk disappears. We can check the correctness of the reduced-form dynamics of our stochastic model by simply looking at the deterministic model. Third, by comparing the outcomes of the stochastic version with the deterministic one, we can discern the qualitative effects brought about by the introduction of risk.

The structure of the chapter is the following: in Section 2, we briefly describe the economic setting of the model by presenting production and financial market structure. In Section 3, we derive and solve the household's consumption/saving problem and give interpretations of the relevant relations. In Section 4, we introduce fiscal policy rules regarding taxation and public spending. Section 5 is devoted to the calculation of equilibrium prices and derivation of conditions that guarantee optimality of the household's problem. In Section 6, we compute the solution of the time path of capital and hence output. We further derive conditions under which the stock of capital never reaches zero. Moreover, we study how economic growth evolves over time and how it depends on fiscal policy and the economy's initial conditions. Section 7 is devoted to an examination of the evolution of public deficits and debt. We concentrate especially on the public debt per output ratio as a prominent measure characterizing the fiscal stance of the public sector. Section 8 closes the chapter by summarizing the main results.

2.2 Basic structure of the economy and the financial market

The homogeneous good in our economy can be both consumed and invested without any adjustment costs. It is assumed to be produced according to the following linear A-K technology[1]:

$$(2.1) \quad Y = \alpha_K \cdot K$$

Y stands here for output, K for the stock of capital and α_K is an exogenously given fixed parameter denoting the marginal product of capital [2]. We abstract from labor as a possible input. The only production factor is hence capital which can be broadly interpreted (including, for example, machines, buildings, licenses, telecommunication networks etc.). Since we assume that capital is only possessed by the private sector (i.e. by the representative household), we view capital as an asset traded on the financial market. Its price in terms of output units is denoted P_K. The relative change in price equals the rate of return r_K by definition[3]:

$$(2.2a) \qquad \frac{\dot{P}_K}{P_K} \equiv r_K$$

As soon as r_K is determined in equilibrium, the whole time path of P_K is given by (2.2a).

The second asset in the economy are short-term government bonds. We assume that these bonds are default-free, meaning that they are paid back with certainty. By short-term we mean that these bonds, when issued at time t, are paid back with interest (i.e. the short-term interest rate r_D) at time t +

---

[1] Barro/Sala-i-Martin (1995, Chapter 1.3 and 4.1) call this production function 'A-K technology'. They also show that this type of production function is the simplest one that generates endogenous growth.

[2] We have omitted the time index and will continue to do so mainly for notational convenience. The reader should note that all variables in this chapter are described by capital letters and are functions of time.

[3] From now on dots on variables denote derivatives with regard to time.

dt [4]. The price of government bonds P_D and its rate of return r_D is now related as follows:

$$(2.2b) \qquad \frac{\dot{P}_D}{P_D} \equiv r_D$$

The rate of return on short-term government bonds is identical to the short-term interest rate which will be determined in equilibrium later on. We can already conjecture that the rate of return on both assets, capital and government bonds, will be the same. The reason is that in absence of transaction costs and risk, both assets will be perceived to be perfect substitutes.

The third asset 'class' consists of private bonds of arbitrary maturity that are only held by private households. In the aggregate over all households, the holdings of this asset 'nets out' to zero. We say that this asset is in net-zero supply. Its price P_F and rate of return r_F is given as:

$$(2.2c) \qquad \frac{\dot{P}_F}{P_F} \equiv r_F$$

In the following section, the intertemporal decision problem of the representative household will be described, solved and interpreted.

2.3 Decision problem of the representative household

Wealth W (in terms of output units) of the representative household consists of its holdings of the available assets: capital K, government bonds (i.e. public debt) D and private bonds F. Denoting the number of 'pieces' of capital, public and private bonds held by the household with n_K, n_D and n_F,

---

[4] Government debt in form of short-term bonds can hence be thought to be rolled over continuously. We abstract from the issue of government default because every specification of a possible default of the government would be arbitrary and thus ad-hoc if we did not model government behavior endogenously.

then $n_i \cdot P_i$ denotes the wealth associated with asset i. We can write the static wealth identity in the following form:

(2.3a)
$$W = K + D + F$$
$$\Rightarrow W = n_K \cdot P_K + n_D \cdot P_D + n_F \cdot P_F$$

The dynamic budget constraint of the representative private household can now be derived by simply taking derivatives with respect to time t:

(2.3b)
$$\dot{W} = \underbrace{\dot{n}_K \cdot P_K + \dot{n}_D \cdot P_D + \dot{n}_F \cdot P_F}_{\text{voluntary wealth change}} + \underbrace{n_K \cdot \dot{P}_K + n_D \cdot \dot{P}_D + n_F \cdot \dot{P}_F}_{\text{involuntary wealth change}}$$

The change in wealth consists of two parts: a voluntary part and an involuntary part. The voluntary change in wealth is caused by the households own asset holding decisions for given asset prices. The involuntary part is due to price changes for a given structure of asset holdings. Of course, the household is subject to a constraint: outlays for consumption and tax payments have to be financed by the voluntary wealth change. This constraint is called 'financing condition'. If we assume taxation to be given by a proportional tax on wealth (see equation (2.8)), we will obtain the following financing condition:

(2.3c)
$$\underbrace{\dot{n}_K \cdot P_K + \dot{n}_D \cdot P_D + \dot{n}_F \cdot P_F}_{\text{voluntary wealth change}} = -(\tau \cdot W + C)$$

Plugging (2.3c) into (2.3b) and using (2.2a-c) and (2.3a) delivers:

(2.3d)
$$\dot{W} = n_K \cdot P_K \cdot \frac{\dot{P}_K}{P_K} + n_D \cdot P_D \cdot \frac{\dot{P}_D}{P_D} + n_F \cdot P_F \cdot \frac{\dot{P}_F}{P_F} - \tau \cdot W - C$$
$$\Rightarrow \dot{W} = (r_K - r_D) \cdot K + r_D \cdot W + (r_F - r_D) \cdot F - \tau \cdot W - C$$

(2.3d) is the dynamic budget constraint of the representative household in form of an ordinary differential equation. It states that the time change in wealth is made up by the sum of the rates of returns earned on all different assets minus taxes and consumption. The household's decision upon consumption and asset holdings influences the development of its private wealth, which then determines future consumption and asset allocation possibilities. Consequently, the state variable for the decision problem of the household is private wealth W. The decision or control variables are the holdings of capital and private bonds as well as the consumption flow [5]. Since we assume that the household has rational expectations, it will choose the whole time path of its control variables given asset prices in order to maximize its intertemporal utility function.

We use a setting where the household represents a dynastic family with an infinite planning horizon. The utility function of the representative household is time-separable with ρ denoting the rate of time preference. The instantaneous utility function is a CES-type function with $\gamma \in (1, \infty)$. γ denotes the elasticity of substitution. Now, the optimization problem of the representative household can be summarized as problem (2.4):

$$(2.4) \qquad \max_{C,K,F} \int_0^\infty e^{-\rho \cdot t} \cdot \frac{C^{1-\gamma}-1}{1-\gamma} \cdot dt$$

subject to: $\qquad \dot{W} = (r_K - r_D) \cdot K + r_D \cdot W + (r_F - r_D) \cdot F - \tau \cdot W - C$

$$W(0) = W_0, W(t) > 0 \text{ for } t \in [0, \infty)$$

(2.4) is a typical example of a dynamic control problem. It will be solved using the celebrated Maximum Principle of Pontryagin et al. [6]. Applying this principle requires the set-up of the so-called Hamilton function:

$$(2.5) \quad H(C,F,K,W,\lambda) = e^{-\rho \cdot t} \cdot \frac{C^{1-\gamma}-1}{1-\gamma} + \lambda \cdot \left(\begin{matrix} (r_K - r_D) \cdot K + r_D \cdot W \\ + (r_F - r_D) \cdot F - \tau \cdot W - C \end{matrix} \right)$$

---

[5] Note from (2.3a) that any pair of stocks of the three assets could be thought to be control variables since by choosing two stocks the third stock is determined via (2.3a) given the stock of wealth.

[6] The original reference is Pontryagin et al. (1962). Books including economic examples of how to use this Maximum Principle are Kamien/Schwartz (1991), Chiang (1992), Léonard/Van Long (1992) and Takayama (1993).

λ is the so-called co-state variable. It plays a role similar to the Lagrange parameter in static constrained optimization problems. Assuming that there is an interior solution, Pontryagin's Maximum Principle yields a set of first-order conditions [7]:

(2.5a) $$\frac{\partial H(C,F,K,W,\lambda)}{\partial C} = 0 \Rightarrow e^{-\rho \cdot t} \cdot C^{-\gamma} = \lambda$$

(2.5b) $$\frac{\partial H(C,F,K,W,\lambda)}{\partial F} = 0 \Rightarrow r_F = r_D$$

(2.5c) $$\frac{\partial H(C,F,K,W,\lambda)}{\partial K} = 0 \Rightarrow r_K = r_D$$

(2.5d) $$\dot{\lambda} + \frac{\partial H(C,F,K,W,\lambda)}{\partial W} = 0 \Rightarrow \frac{\dot{\lambda}}{\lambda} = \tau - r_D$$

(2.5e) $$\lim_{t \to \infty}(\lambda \cdot W) = 0$$

(2.5a) states that in optimum the marginal utility of consumption has to equal the co-state variable λ. λ can thus be interpreted as the 'shadow price of wealth' since it measures how much discounted marginal utility an incremental unit of wealth yields. This means that at any point in time the additional utility arising from consuming an infinitesimally small amount more of the homogenous good has to equal the opportunity cost of not investing this small amount into wealth the opportunity cost of which is measured by λ.

(2.5b-c) state that the rates of return on all three assets have to be equal. These conditions can be interpreted as no-arbitrage conditions for there is no inherent risk in this model and the assets are perfect substitutes. If (2.5b) or (2.5c) was violated, the household would demand the 'too cheap' asset in infinitely large amounts financing it by corresponding short-sells of the 'too

---

[7] We do not consider the second-order condition here since it is extremely easy to see that it holds as long as γ is positive.

expensive' asset. In the absence of transaction costs, all arbitrage opportunities will hence be fully exploited such that an arbitrage-free equilibrium with strict equality of asset returns results.

Equation (2.5d) states the time-path of the co-state variable (shadow price of wealth). The growth rate of λ equals the tax rate minus the short-term interest rate. Since this shadow price is a scarcity measure of wealth, an increase in the tax rate increases the future shadow price of wealth. The reason is that taxing away more resources drives short the remaining resources available for wealth accumulation and increases their scarcity. On the other hand, an increase in the short-term interest rate drives the future shadow price down. If wealth yields higher returns, the resources available for wealth accumulation increase which cuts the shadow price of wealth.

Finally, (2.5e) is the usual transversality condition. It states that at the end of the planning horizon either the stock of private wealth or the shadow price of wealth has to be zero. If the shadow price is not zero at the end of the time horizon, then positive wealth can still provide utility. Not using up wealth completely would be a waste of resources under these circumstances. On the other hand, if the shadow price is zero than wealth does no longer yield utility. It can be left over without violating the transversality condition.

Using condition (2.5a) and (2.5d), we can now solve for the time path of optimal consumption. For this purpose, we differentiate (2.5a) with respect to time t and plug the result together with (2.5a) into (2.5d). This yields the so-called Keynes-Ramsey-Rule orEuler-equation:

(2.6)
$$\frac{\dot{C}}{C} = \frac{r_D - \tau - \rho}{\gamma}$$

(2.6) shows that the growth rate of consumption equals the short-term interest rate r_D minus the tax rate τ and the rate of time preferences ρ divided by the elasticity of substitution γ. The influence of these parameters on consumption growth are as expected: a higher rate of time preferences and higher elasticity of substitution decrease consumption growth since they imply future consumption to be less appreciated than today's consumption. A higher tax rate has the same effect. It withdraws more resources from the household so that less resources are available for future consumption. Higher short-term interest rates have a positive effect on consumption growth since they enable the household to create more wealth as a source for future consumption.

2.4 Fiscal policy

In this section, we introduce the behavioral equations characterizing fiscal policy. We make three assumptions regarding taxation, public expenditure and deficit financing. We will begin with primary government expenditure G which is assumed to be given by a constant fraction z of output:

(2.7) $$G = z \cdot Y \Rightarrow G = z \cdot \alpha_K \cdot K$$

This assumption may not seem obvious at first sight but a look at the data presented in Appendix 1.3 suggests that it is not a too bad approximation of reality in many countries. Moreover, this linear expenditure rule has the convenient feature that government expenditure cannot become bigger than output which would constitute a bad inconsistency in a closed economy model. De facto, government expenditure in our model constitutes a waste of private resources.

As already mentioned above, tax revenues result of a wealth tax where the tax rate $\tau \in (0, 1)$ is constant over time:

(2.8) $$T = \tau \cdot W$$

Using (2.7), (2.8) and (2.3a), the public deficit accrues as:

(2.9) $$\begin{aligned} \text{Def} &= G - T + r_D \cdot D \\ &\Rightarrow \text{Def} = (z \cdot \alpha_K - r_D) \cdot K + (r_D - \tau) \cdot W - r_D \cdot F \end{aligned}$$

(2.9) says that the public deficit consists of interest payments on old bonds plus primary public expenditure minus tax revenues. If the sign of the deficit becomes negative, then we speak of a public surplus. In order to close the model, we have to specify how the government finances the accruing deficit. We assume that this is accomplished by issuing new short-term bonds. We implicitly assume that the government has unlimited access to the domestic financial market. Of course, it seems implausible at first sight that the financing of deficits has to be carried out only by use of short-term bonds. This implies that governments have to roll over their complete debt all the time. Including long-term bonds in form of consols would not be a conceptional problem and would allow us to generate any maturity structure of government debt. The introduction of government bonds with different maturity, however, would complicate the analysis in such a way that we decided to abstract from it.

Assuming the public bond market in equilibrium, the evolution of public debt (i.e. the stock of short-term bonds) is described by the following first-order differential equation:

(2.10) $$\dot{D} = (z \cdot \alpha_K - r_D) \cdot K + (r_D - \tau) \cdot W - r_D \cdot F$$

Like the consumption growth equation (2.6), debt accumulation still depends on the price of public bonds contained in r_D.

2.5 General equilibrium

We have four markets in our economy: the capital, goods, private bond and public bond market. By Walras' Law, equilibrium on three markets implies equilibrium on the fourth if prices are allowed to adjust infinitely fast.

The goods market equilibrium for the closed economy, where savings equal investment, states that output Y equals investment I plus consumption and government expenditure. Government consumption is given by government expenditure G in our model. Using output equation (2.1) and government expenditure equation (2.7), we obtain the goods market equilibrium:

(2.11) $$I = (1 - z) \cdot \alpha_K \cdot K - C$$

The capital market equilibrium is given by:

(2.12a) $\dot{K} + \delta \cdot K = I$

Investment is used to replace the depreciated stock of capital $\delta \cdot K$ and to install new capital $\dot{K}$. The depreciation rate δ is a fixed positive parameter between 0 and 1. Inserting the good market equilibrium condition (2.11) into (2.12) yields the new capital market equilibrium condition:

(2.12b) $\dot{K} = \left((1-z) \cdot \alpha_K - \delta\right) \cdot K - C$

The private bond market equilibrium requires that the representative household's holding of private bonds has to be zero since private bonds are in net-zero supply. The equilibrium condition for the private bond market is hence $F = 0$. Due to the static wealth equation (2.3a), this implies:

(2.13) $F = 0 \Rightarrow W = K + D \Rightarrow \dot{W} = \dot{K} + \dot{D}$

Equilibrium on the private bond market thus implies that (changes in) private wealth consists of (changes in) capital and public bonds only. Plugging (2.5b-c) into the private household's budget constraint (2.3d) and using this equation together with the capital market equilibrium (2.12b) in order to eliminate $\dot{W}$ and $\dot{K}$ from (2.13a), we obtain:

(2.14) $\dot{D} = (r_D - \tau - (1-z) \cdot \alpha_K + \delta) \cdot K + (r_D - \tau) \cdot D$

(2.14) is one expression for debt accumulation which we have developed by the use of three market equilibrium conditions. The equilibrium condition of the fourth market, the market for public bonds, is given by (2.10). Employing the private bond market equilibrium condition (2.13), the public bond market equilibrium has the form:

(2.15) $\dot{D} = (z \cdot \alpha_K - \tau) \cdot K + (r_D - \tau) \cdot D$

The above statement of Walras' Law implies that (2.14) and (2.15) have to be equal. This equality implies:

(2.16) $r_D = \alpha_K - \delta$

In equilibrium, the short-term interest rate equals the marginal product of capital minus the depreciation rate. The prices can now be determined explicitly via integration of (2.2a-c).

Asset prices in this model version follow the same time path, i.e. they are perfectly correlated. This is clearly an unrealistic finding. Moreover, assuming that private bonds pay out 1 unit of the output good when due delivers a yield-to-return relationship that equals the short-term interest rate $\alpha_K - \delta$. Thus, the term structure is flat for all time. No asset price depends on fiscal policy or household characteristics. They are only affected by the technology parameters, rise with higher marginal product of capital α_K and sink for a higher depreciation rate δ. The model outcome resembles usual real models of small open economies where the interest rate is exogenously given from the rest of the world.

The time path of private consumption resulting from the Keynes-Ramsey-Rule (2.6) can now be written as:

$$(2.17) \qquad C = C_0 \cdot \exp\left(\frac{\alpha_K - \delta - \tau - \rho}{\gamma} \cdot t\right)$$

C_0 denotes the initial consumption and pins down the whole equilibrium consumption trajectory. It has to be determined such that the transversality condition is met. Looking at the growth rate, one can see that it depends positively on the marginal product of capital which stimulates wealth accumulation and hence output production in the future. An increase in the depreciation rate has the exact opposite effect since now more investment is needed to sustain the capital stock. Likewise, the tax rate and the rate of time preference diminish the growth rate of consumption.

Before we determine initial consumption C_0 by the transversality condition, we need to compute the time path for private wealth W since it appears in the transversality condition. We take the household budget constraint (2.3d) and use the optimality conditions (2.5b-c) together with equilibrium condition (2.16) and consumption equation (2.17). This delivers the following differential equation for private wealth:

$$(2.18) \qquad \dot{W} = (\alpha_K - \delta - \tau) \cdot W - C_0 \cdot \exp\left(\frac{\alpha_K - \delta - \tau - \rho}{\gamma} \cdot t\right)$$

The solution to (2.18) is derived in detail in Appendix 2.1. It yields the following result:

$$(2.19) \qquad W = \frac{\gamma \cdot C_0}{(\gamma - 1) \cdot (\alpha_K - \delta - \tau) + \rho} \cdot \left(e^{\frac{(\alpha_K - \delta - \tau - \rho)}{\gamma} \cdot t} - e^{(\alpha_K - \delta - \tau) \cdot t}\right) + W_0 \cdot e^{(\alpha_K - \delta - \tau) \cdot t}$$

In Appendix 2.2, we evaluate the transversality condition explicitly. Doing so, leads to the tax rate constraint (2.20) and initial consumption (2.21):

$$(2.20) \qquad \tau < \alpha_K - \delta + \frac{\rho}{\gamma - 1}$$

$$(2.21) \qquad C_0 = \frac{(\gamma - 1) \cdot (\alpha_K - \delta - \tau) + \rho}{\gamma} \cdot W_0$$

Condition (2.20) constrains governmental tax policy. The tax rate has to be smaller than the rate of return on capital plus a term reflecting the private sector's preferences regarding present and future consumption. If tax policy violates this constraint, then the private sector is unable to achieve an intertemporal optimum. The governmental leeway in setting the tax rate is smaller the bigger γ or the smaller ρ is. This is because a higher elasticity of substitution γ or a lower rate of time preferences ρ leads to lower discounted marginal utility. Since the marginal utility always equals the shadow price of wealth due to first-order condition (2.5a), this shadow price has to shrink. Since the lower tax rates lead to lower shadow price (see (2.5d)), the tax rate has to adjust downwards in order to decrease the shadow price. As a consequence, the leeway with regard to setting the tax rate becomes smaller. If the tax constraint became binding after an increase in γ, then the tax rate would have to fall in order to fulfill the constraint (2.20). If the rate of return on capital or, respectively, the identical short-term interest rate rises, then tax rates can also increase by the same amount without violating (2.20). The reason for this effect is clear: rising productivity of existing capital enhances future resources and gives the government higher taxation opportunities.

Initial consumption given by (2.21) equals a fixed percentage of initial wealth. As already remarked at the end of Appendix 2.2, the tax rate constraint (2.20) guarantees that this fixed percentage and thus initial consumption is positive. The signs of the consumption's derivatives with regard to the different parameters are as expected: higher γ, ρ and α_K increase initial consumption, higher δ and τ decrease initial consumption for obvious reasons. Using (2.21), we can finally calculate the complete time paths for consumption and wealth:

$$(2.22) \qquad C = \frac{(\gamma-1)\cdot(\alpha_K-\delta-\tau)+\rho}{\gamma}\cdot W_0\cdot e^{\frac{\alpha_K-\delta-\tau-\rho}{\gamma}\cdot t}$$

$$(2.23) \qquad W = W_0\cdot e^{\frac{\alpha_K-\delta-\tau-\rho}{\gamma}\cdot t}$$

Consumption and wealth remain positive for all time and share the same growth rate. The growth rate is positive for $\tau < \alpha_K - \delta - \rho$ and vice versa. Thus, the tax rate constraint (2.20) is not sufficient to guarantee positive growth rates.

2.6 Capital accumulation, viability and economic growth

Recalling production function (2.1), we can derive the growth rate g_Y:

$$(2.24) \qquad g_Y \equiv \frac{\dot{Y}}{Y} = \frac{\dot{K}}{K}$$

The growth rate of output equals the growth rate of the capital stock. To determine this growth rate, we have to solve for the time path of capital. This is done in Appendix 2.3 in greater detail. Depending on the parameter constellation, the following capital accumulation dynamics (2.25a-c) may result:

(2.25a)
$$K = \left(\frac{\gamma \cdot (z \cdot \alpha_K - \tau) \cdot (K_0 + D_0)}{\alpha_K - \delta - \tau - \rho - \gamma \cdot \left((1-z) \cdot \alpha_K - \delta \right)} - D_0 \right) \cdot e^{\left((1-z) \cdot \alpha_K - \delta \right) \cdot t}$$
$$+ \frac{\left((1-\gamma) \cdot (\alpha_K - \delta - \tau) - \rho \right) \cdot (K_0 + D_0)}{\alpha_K - \delta - \tau - \rho - \gamma \cdot \left((1-z) \cdot \alpha_K - \delta \right)} \cdot e^{\frac{\alpha_K - \delta - \tau - \rho}{\gamma} \cdot t}$$

given that either: $\dfrac{\alpha_K - \delta - \tau - \rho}{\gamma} > (1-z) \cdot \alpha_K - \delta \quad \wedge \quad z \cdot \alpha_K > \tau$

or: $\dfrac{\alpha_K - \delta - \tau - \rho}{\gamma} < (1-z) \cdot \alpha_K - \delta \quad \wedge \quad z \cdot \alpha_K > \tau \quad \vee \quad z \cdot \alpha_K < \tau$ *hold.*

(2.25b) $\quad K = (K_0 + D_0) \cdot e^{\frac{\alpha_K - \delta - \tau - \rho}{\gamma} \cdot t} - D_0 \cdot e^{(\alpha_K - \delta - \tau) \cdot t}$

given that: $\dfrac{\alpha_K - \delta - \tau - \rho}{\gamma} < (1-z) \cdot \alpha_K - \delta \quad \wedge \quad z \cdot \alpha_K = \tau$ *holds.*

(2.25c) $\quad K = \left[K_0 - (K_0 + D_0) \cdot (z \cdot \alpha_K - \tau) \cdot t \right] \cdot e^{\left((1-z) \cdot \alpha_K - \delta \right) \cdot t}$

given that: $\dfrac{\alpha_K - \delta - \tau - \rho}{\gamma} = (1-z) \cdot \alpha_K - \delta \quad \wedge \quad z \cdot \alpha_K > \tau$ *holds.*

The problem with (2.25a-c) is that we cannot be sure that the time paths of the different capital stock solutions will never reach zero. A zero capital stock, however, would imply that no income is generated and therefore nothing can be consumed. In a closed economy, new capital cannot be imported. The consequence would be that the economy remains in such a pathological state forever and 'dies out'. Intuitively, such a situation is the more likely to happen the higher the public expenditure ratio z. A higher expenditure ratio indicates that less resources will be left for the private sector to maintain capital accumulation. In order to guarantee viability of our economy, we obviously need a constraint with regard to z. We obtain it by examining the date at which capital could, at least theoretically, attain a zero value. This date will be called $t_{critical}$. If $t_{critical}$ is positive and bounded, then the economy will only be viable for a finite time. We require that fiscal policy parameters are such that long-lasting viability is guaranteed in our model. Doing so eliminates two of the three solution possibilities of the capital stock (2.25a-c). Let us first define precisely what we mean by viability:

Definition 2.1:

The economy is viable in the long-run if and only if $t_{critical} \notin (0, \infty)$.

The question is now: under which parameter constellation associated with (2.25a-c) does a positive critical time not appear hence guaranteeing viability? We claim that the following conditions are necessary to guarantee viability:

$$(2.26a) \qquad z = \frac{\tau}{\alpha_K}$$

$$(2.26b) \qquad D_0 \leq 0$$

The proof is given in Appendix 2.4.

The conditions (2.26a-b) seem surprising, at least at first sight. Ex ante, one might have expected that the public expenditure ratio z would have to be constrained from above but (2.26a) does not immediately reveal such an upper boundary on z. When we invoke tax rate constraint (2.20), however, and use (2.26a) to eliminate the tax rate in (2.20), then we get:

$$(2.27) \qquad z < 1 - \frac{\delta}{\alpha_K} + \frac{\rho}{\alpha_K \cdot (\gamma - 1)}$$

(2.27) shows that (2.20) and (2.26a) implicitly generate an upper boundary for public expenditure ratio. The higher the depreciation rate or the elasticity of substitution and the lower the time preference rate, the stricter becomes this constraint.

46

A higher depreciation rate results in lower net investment. If, as a result, constraint (2.27) became binding, the government expenditure ratio had to sink. Otherwise, resources would not be sufficient to maintain investment.

Higher elasticity of substitution implies less utility gains associated with higher consumption. Thus, the utility path shows a flatter pattern. The consequence is that households are not willing to shift consumption to the future but want to have a more symmetrical consumption level at all times, starting with higher initial consumption. The ceiling for public expenditure ratio adjusts downwards. Otherwise, there is the danger that too few resources are available to sustain capital accumulation.

A lower rate of time preference indicates that households discount future utility less strong. Future consumption gains importance. A too high expenditure ratio would hamper future capital accumulation and thus consumption opportunities so that the upper boundary on z has to fall.

Increasing α_K raises the ceiling for z if $\delta > \rho/(\gamma-1)$ and vice versa. An increase in α_K is per se wealth increasing and stimulates capital accumulation. Simultaneously, it increases the whole time path of consumption which in itself decreases capital accumulation. The overall effect on investment is hence ambiguous.

Even more striking is another fact: fiscal policy, though being characterized by two parameters, has just one degree of freedom to ensure viability of the model. Once the public expenditure ratio has been set subject to (2.27), the tax rate is automatically fixed via (2.26a). Accordingly, once the tax rate has been chosen subject to (2.20) then z is determined by (2.26a). We attribute this interesting outcome to the fact that the private sector does not take capital accumulation into account when setting up its decision problem. Simultaneously, equilibrium asset prices and rates of return are constant and identical among all assets. The price of capital hence does not reflect scarcity of capital in a way that automatically 'forces' the household to restrict its own consumption so as to avoid appearance of zero capital stocks [8]. As a consequence, fiscal policy bears a very special responsibility for maintaining positive capital stocks and long-run viability of the economy. There is only very restricted leeway for discretionary policy design and, as (2.26a) shows, the degree of freedom regarding fiscal policy instruments shrinks to 1.

Condition (2.26a) alone is not sufficient to guarantee long-run viability. (2.26b) has to hold, too. It implies that the initial stock of debt has to be zero or negative which means that the private sector has either to be a debtor of its own government or there is no public debt at all right at the beginning. At first sight, this condition seems a bit strange but the reasoning becomes clear when we look at the law of motion for capital (2.12b) and insert the consumption function (2.22):

$$(2.12c) \ \dot{K} = \left((1-z)\cdot\alpha_K - \delta\right)\cdot K - \frac{(\gamma-1)\cdot(\alpha_K - \delta - \tau) + \rho}{\gamma}\cdot W_0 \cdot e^{\frac{\alpha_K - \delta - \tau - \rho}{\gamma}\cdot t}$$

Supporting high investment through a sufficiently low choice of z may not be enough to maintain capital growth since too high private consumption could lead to disinvestment as the only way to finance consumption. Since the whole time path of private consumption depends on initial wealth W_0, which is the sum of initial capital K_0 and initial public debt D_0, there are initial values of public debt so that the time pattern of private consumption never threatens the stock of capital to become zero. And (2.26b) shows that this reasoning holds for zero or negative initial stocks of public debt.

Since Proposition 2.2 showed that (2.25b) is the relevant solution of capital, we will use it to calculate the growth rate g_Y using (2.24):

---

[8] Of course, one could ask why we did not include capital accumulation as another dynamic constraint into the decision problem of the representative household since this would probably have led to a consumption/saving behavior of the private sector that does not include the danger of zero capital stocks. The reason is simple: it seems unreasonable that private households take into consideration the aggregate capital accumulation of the economy. If they did, the assumption of price taking behavior would become logically unsustainable.

(2.28)

$$g_Y = \frac{\dfrac{(\alpha_K - \delta - \tau - \rho)}{\gamma} \cdot (D_0 + K_0) \cdot e^{\left(\frac{\alpha_K - \delta - \tau - \rho}{\gamma} - \alpha_K + \delta + \tau\right) \cdot t} - (\alpha_K - \delta - \tau) \cdot D_0}{(D_0 + K_0) \cdot e^{\left(\frac{\alpha_K - \delta - \tau - \rho}{\gamma} - \alpha_K + \delta + \tau\right) \cdot t} - D_0}$$

The most salient feature of the growth rate is that it is time dependent. It is not surprising that we face continuous growth since our production function choice lends itself easily to endogenous growth. The reason is that there is no declining marginal productivity of capital over time. But in standard A-K models the growth rate is a positive constant and not time dependent. The fact that we face ongoing, time-dependent growth here is due to the way we introduced fiscal policy. We will come back to the influence of fiscal policy on growth later on. The growth rate in the short- as well as in the long-run is calculated in (2.29a-b):

$$(2.29a) \quad \lim_{t \to 0}(g_Y) = \frac{(\alpha_K - \delta - \tau - \rho) \cdot K_0 - \left((\gamma - 1) \cdot (\alpha_K - \delta - \tau) + \rho\right) \cdot D_0}{\gamma \cdot K_0}$$

$$(2.29b) \quad \lim_{t \to \infty}(g_Y) = \alpha_K - \delta - \tau$$

Computation of the derivative of g_Y with respect to time denoting the time change in growth yields:

(2.29c)

$$\dot{g}_Y = \frac{-D_0 \cdot \left(\dfrac{\alpha_K - \delta - \tau - \rho}{\gamma} - \alpha_K + \delta + \tau\right)^2 \cdot (D_0 + K_0) \cdot e^{\left(\frac{\alpha_K - \delta - \tau - \rho}{\gamma} - \alpha_K + \delta + \tau\right) \cdot t}}{\left((D_0 + K_0) \cdot e^{\left(\frac{\alpha_K - \delta - \tau - \rho}{\gamma} - \alpha_K + \delta + \tau\right) \cdot t} - D_0\right)^2} \geq 0$$

(2.29c) shows that the time derivative of the growth rate is strictly positive if we exclude the extreme cases $t \to \infty$ or $D_0 = 0$ for which the derivative becomes zero. The growth rate is thus strictly increasing in time. From this important result, we can deduce that the asymptotic (i.e. long-run) value of g_Y given by (2.29b) represents the maximum growth rate whereas the short-run growth rate given by (2.29a) corresponds to the minimal growth rate. These results are interesting because they contradict the usual opinion that economic growth will slow down finally. The reason for this rather surprising finding is that only increasing economic growth rates are compatible with the requirement that a zero capital stock must not be attained.

Of special interest is the long-run growth rate (2.29b): it can be either positive, zero or negative depending on the choice of the tax rate. In order to guarantee positive asymptotic growth rates, it is necessary and sufficient that the tax rate does not exceed the return on capital given by the marginal product on capital minus the depreciation rate. This is self-explaining: taxing away more than the return on capital does not leave back enough resources to foster capital accumulation and hence economic growth. Note, however, that positive long-run growth does not imply that growth is always positive. If, for example, the tax rate lies within the interval $(\alpha_K - \delta - \rho, \alpha_K - \delta)$ then a sufficiently high initial capital stock implies an initial negative growth rate [9]. Hence, the sign of the growth rate can change from negative to positive during the transition to the steady state characterized by the long-run growth rate. The reason for this effect can be understood when we recall that a high initial stock of capital positively affects initial wealth, both as tax base and as starting point for consumption. Since both consumption and taxation shrink available resources for investment, this effect becomes clear.

Having gained some insights regarding the time dependency structure of the growth rate, we now want to examine the influence of the initial capital as well as debt stock values on the growth rate. Differentiating the growth rate with respect to K_0 and D_0, we obtain:

---

[9] Simultaneously, we can also see that it is sufficient in order to get always positive growth rates when $\tau \leq \alpha_K - \delta - \rho$ holds.

$$(2.30) \quad \frac{dg_Y}{dK_0} = \frac{-D_0 \cdot \left(\dfrac{\alpha_K - \delta - \tau - \rho}{\gamma} - \alpha_K + \delta + \tau \right) \cdot e^{\left(\frac{\alpha_K - \delta - \tau - \rho}{\gamma} - \alpha_K + \delta + \tau \right) \cdot t}}{\left((D_0 + K_0) \cdot e^{\left(\frac{\alpha_K - \delta - \tau - \rho}{\gamma} - \alpha_K + \delta + \tau \right) \cdot t} - D_0 \right)^2} \leq 0$$

$$(2.31) \quad \frac{dg_Y}{dD_0} = \frac{K_0 \cdot \left(\dfrac{\alpha_K - \delta - \tau - \rho}{\gamma} - \alpha_K + \delta + \tau \right) \cdot e^{\left(\frac{\alpha_K - \delta - \tau - \rho}{\gamma} - \alpha_K + \delta + \tau \right) \cdot t}}{\left((D_0 + K_0) \cdot e^{\left(\frac{\alpha_K - \delta - \tau - \rho}{\gamma} - \alpha_K + \delta + \tau \right) \cdot t} - D_0 \right)^2} < 0$$

Assuming $D_0 < 0$ (i.e. the stronger form of (2.26b)), we note that the effects of an increase in initial capital or debt on the growth rate are both strictly negative. It is interesting to note that our model hence confirms a concept frequently uttered in empirical work: the notion of β-convergence [10]. Result (2.30) suggests that the growth rate is higher for an economy with initially less capital. But less initial capital means also less initial output and income. The conclusion is that the poorer the economy is initially, the higher becomes its growth rate. The same holds for the initial stock of debt: the smaller D_0, the higher economic growth will be. Since D_0 has to be smaller or equal to zero in order to guarantee long-run viability of the economy, a small amount of negative initial debt is sufficient to guarantee viability and growth.

Even more important than the influences of initial conditions on economic growth is the question, how fiscal policy impacts on growth. For this purpose, we have to calculate the derivative of g_Y with respect to τ. Since this yields a rather lengthy expression, we will just state the outcome in Proposition 2.1 and leave the detailed calculations to Appendix 2.5:

---

[10] This means that „...a poor economy tends to grow faster than a rich one, so that the poor country tends to catch up with the rich one..." (Barro/Sala-i-Martin (1995, p. 383)).

Proposition 2.1:

The derivative of the growth rate g_Y with respect to the tax rate τ is negative.

Proof: see Appendix 2.5

The result is in accordance with usual economic insight. An increase in the tax rate leads to lower growth rates and vice versa. If the goal was to achieve the highest possible growth rates, a tax rate of zero would be desirable. This would also require zero government expenditure (see (2.26a)) if the economy shall be protected against a situation where no capital is left. Hence, existing government expenditure in our model requires corresponding taxation. Pure deficit financing leads to the economy's collapse and would violate the transversality and hence the no Ponzi-game condition. In a model where (at least part of) public spending contributed to the economy's production as an input factor raising the productivity of private capital, it would be conceivable that parts of public spending may be deficit-financed and paid back later on when the induced growth effect has increased income and hence the tax base.

As already emphasized in the introductory chapter, our main interest in this whole work is to examine the dynamic interactions between fiscal policy and financial markets in a stochastic setting. In order to achieve this purpose, we have to sacrifice a more realistic view regarding the channels of public spending. Our model simply implies that fiscal policy really matters with regard to economic growth. This influence is not transmitted via equilibrium prices, but via the direct influence of taxation on wealth accumulation.

The last point of interest concerns the dependence of the growth rate on the short-term interest rate r_D. Since r_D equals $\alpha_K-\delta$ in equilibrium, we have to take derivatives of g_Y with respect to $\alpha_K-\delta$. The derivative is equal to the one already calculated in Appendix 2.5, except for the sign. The sign is positive. Thus, an increase in the short-term interest rate brought about by an increase in $\alpha_K-\delta$ raises the growth rate. This effect is not so clear at first sight: of course, a higher short-term interest rate implies a higher return on capital due to the strict equality of returns on all assets in this model. This makes capital accumulation more attractive, other things being equal. But at the same time, consumption is also rising at the detriment of investment. This negative effect is, however, more than compensated by the positive effect on capital accumulation. Rising rates of returns on asset markets are always positive for economic growth in this model.

2.7 Public debt and deficit dynamics

The final theoretical question in this chapter concerns the evolution of public deficits and debt. Recalling the solution for the evolution of public debt from Appendix 2.3, (A2.3.12), as well as the deficit equation (2.9), we get the following solutions for the respective time paths:

(2.32) $\quad D = D_0 \cdot e^{(\alpha_K - \delta - \tau) \cdot t}$

(2.33) $\quad \text{Def} = (\alpha_K - \delta - \tau) \cdot D_0 \cdot e^{(\alpha_K - \delta - \tau) \cdot t}$

We have already seen in (2.26b) that public debt is always negative, assuming that D_0 does not equal zero. (2.33) indicates that deficits are always positive, but only if the tax rate exceeds the return on capital. As (2.29b) shows, however, we would then never face positive growth rates. Positive growth rates hence go hand in hand with public surpluses. This does not necessarily imply primary surpluses. Primary surpluses can be obtained by subtracting interest payments from (2.33) where 'PrimDef' stands for primary deficit:

(2.34) $\quad \text{PrimDef} = -\tau \cdot D_0 \cdot e^{(\alpha_K - \delta - \tau) \cdot t} > 0$

As we can see, the government runs primary deficits all the time but the interest rate revenues overcompensate these primary deficits. Overall, surpluses are generated as long as $\alpha_K - \delta > \tau$. In such a situation, the creditor position of the government towards the private sector grows for all times. Nevertheless, the government's intertemporal solvency constraint is not violated as the following calculation shows:

$$(2.35) \quad \lim_{t\to\infty}\left(D\cdot e^{-r_D\cdot t}\right)=\lim_{t\to\infty}\left(D_0\cdot e^{(\alpha_K-\delta-\tau)\cdot t}\cdot e^{-(\alpha_K-\delta)\cdot t}\right)=\lim_{t\to\infty}\left(D_0\cdot e^{-\tau\cdot t}\right)=0$$

Thus, there is no Ponzi-game dynamics at work concerning public debt. This is implied by the holding of thetransversality condition[11].

More interesting than the absolute figures of public deficits and debt are their respective ratios with regard to output. We concentrate on the debt ratio only since the dynamics of deficit per output is pretty much the same. Dividing (2.32) by (2.1) using (2.25b), we obtain:

$$(2.36) \quad \frac{D}{Y}=\frac{D_0}{\alpha_K\cdot\left((D_0+K_0)\cdot e^{\left(\frac{\alpha_K-\delta-\tau-\rho}{\gamma}-\alpha_K+\delta+\tau\right)\cdot t}-D_0\right)}$$

This yields the following short-run (i.e. initial) and long-run (i.e. asymptotic) debt ratios:

$$(2.37a) \qquad \lim_{t\to 0}\left(\frac{D}{Y}\right)=\frac{D_0}{\alpha_K\cdot K_0}$$

$$(2.37b) \qquad \lim_{t\to\infty}\left(\frac{D}{Y}\right)=-\frac{1}{\alpha_K}$$

It is interesting to note that neither the fiscal policy nor the household parameters have any influence on the initial and terminal values of the debt ratio. It is also not important whether the economy faces positive or negative growth rates: debt per output always converges to a value equal to the negative inverse of the marginal rate of capital. The higher the capital productivity in the economy, the larger the government's creditor position in

---

[11] As Obstfeld/Rogoff (1996, Supplements to Chapter 2) argue for the case of infinite-horizon representative agent models, the government's intertemporal solvency or no Ponzi-game constraint is always fulfilled when the transversality condition holds.

terms of output towards the private sector. The reason for this effect is that higher values for α_K enhance economic growth as well as growth of the government's creditor position, but the latter to a bigger extent.

The next question is how the debt ratio evolves over time. To settle this question, we compute the derivative of D/Y with respect to time:

(2.38)

$$\frac{d}{dt}\left(\frac{D}{Y}\right) = \frac{-D_0 \cdot (D_0 + K_0) \cdot \left(\dfrac{\alpha_K - \delta - \tau - \rho}{\gamma} - \alpha_K + \delta + \tau\right) \cdot e^{\left(\frac{\alpha_K - \delta - \tau - \rho}{\gamma} - \alpha_K + \delta + \tau\right) \cdot t}}{\alpha_K \cdot \left((D_0 + K_0) \cdot e^{\left(\frac{\alpha_K - \delta - \tau - \rho}{\gamma} - \alpha_K + \delta + \tau\right) \cdot t} - D_0\right)^2}$$

Due to all the parameter constraints, this derivative is negative. The debt ratio becomes smaller over time. In a growing economy, this means that the government's creditor position increases faster than capital accumulation. In a stagnating economy, it sinks more slowly than output and private income.

Although we have already learned that fiscal policy does not impact on initial and terminal debt ratio values, (2.36) shows that the debt ratio depends on the tax rate while being the equilibrium transition path. The calculation of the respective derivative yields:

(2.39)

$$\frac{d}{d\tau}\left(\frac{D}{Y}\right) = \frac{-D_0 \cdot (D_0 + K_0) \cdot (\gamma - 1) \cdot t \cdot e^{\left(\frac{\alpha_K - \delta - \tau - \rho}{\gamma} - \alpha_K + \delta + \tau\right) \cdot t}}{\alpha_K \cdot \gamma \cdot \left((D_0 + K_0) \cdot e^{\left(\frac{\alpha_K - \delta - \tau - \rho}{\gamma} - \alpha_K + \delta + \tau\right) \cdot t} - D_0\right)^2} > 0$$

Increasing the tax rate raises the debt ratio. This implies that debt grows less strongly than output. The time path for the debt ratio becomes more 'bended' over time but finally reaches the tax rate-independent terminal state given by (2.37b). This bending behavior can be understood by looking at the primary deficit (2.34): an increase in τ immediately increases the primary deficit, thereby 'steepening' its curvature. It also leads to a decrease in the growth rate of primary deficits and hence to a flatter course in its time path. This effect transmits completely into the time path of deficit and hence debt. Simultaneously, capital and thus output is decreased by growing tax rates so that we obtain the overall effect calculated in (2.39).

The last issue to be discussed here is the dependency of the debt ratio on α_K, δ and thus the short-term interest rate r_D. The respective derivatives are:

(2.40)
$$\frac{d}{d\delta}\left(\frac{D}{Y}\right) = \frac{-D_0 \cdot (D_0 + K_0) \cdot \dfrac{\gamma-1}{\gamma} \cdot t \cdot e^{\left(\frac{\alpha_K - \delta - \tau - \rho}{\gamma} - \alpha_K + \delta + \tau\right) \cdot t}}{\alpha_K \cdot \left((D_0 + K_0) \cdot e^{\left(\frac{\alpha_K - \delta - \tau - \rho}{\gamma} - \alpha_K + \delta + \tau\right) \cdot t} - D_0\right)^2} < 0$$

(2.41)

$$\frac{d}{d\alpha_K}\left(\frac{D}{Y}\right) = \frac{D_0^2 + \left(\dfrac{\gamma-1}{\gamma} \cdot \alpha_K \cdot t - 1\right) \cdot D_0 \cdot (D_0 + K_0) \cdot e^{\left(\frac{\alpha_K - \delta - \tau - \rho}{\gamma} - \alpha_K + \delta + \tau\right) \cdot t}}{\alpha_K^2 \cdot \left((D_0 + K_0) \cdot e^{\left(\frac{\alpha_K - \delta - \tau - \rho}{\gamma} - \alpha_K + \delta + \tau\right) \cdot t} - D_0\right)^2}$$

(2.40) says that higher depreciation rates lead to lower debt ratios. The reason for this effect is that a higher depreciation rate causes a lower short-term interest rate which, in turn, decreases debt for obvious reasons. Simultaneously, higher depreciation rates have a negative impact on the direct capital accumulation effect (i.e. on the first term on the right-hand side in (2.12)) and a negative effect on consumption. This effect on consumption affects capital accumulation positively and may hence partly or even completely compensate for the negative direct effect. In any case, capital and thus output is less strongly impaired by rising δ than debt so that the debt ratio sinks.

(2.41) is much more complex. The denominator is positive but the numerator may change its sign during time. For $t = 0$, the numerator attains a value of $-D_0 K_0 > 0$. For t tending to infinity, the asymptotic value of the numerator is $D_0^2 > 0$. Between these two points in time, there is a minimum of the numerator. Calculating the time derivative of the numerator in (2.41), one can show that this minimum happens at t_{min}:

$$(2.42) \qquad t_{min} = \frac{\gamma}{(\gamma - 1) \cdot \alpha_K} - \frac{\gamma}{\alpha_K - \delta - \tau - \rho - \gamma \cdot (\alpha_K + \delta + \tau)} > 0$$

t_{min} is strictly positive. The value of the numerator at t_{min} is:

$$(2.43) \qquad D_0^2 + \frac{-(\gamma - 1) \cdot \alpha_K \cdot D_0 \cdot (D_0 + K_0)}{\alpha_K - \delta - \tau - \rho - \gamma \cdot (\alpha_K + \delta + \tau)} \cdot e^{\left(\frac{\alpha_K - \delta - \tau - \rho}{\gamma} - \alpha_K + \delta + \tau \right) \cdot t_{min}}$$

The sign of the expression (2.43) is ambiguous. However, a necessary and sufficient condition for the sign of the derivative (2.41) to be positive is that (2.43) is positive. This guarantees that the numerator in (2.41) is positive all the time. In this case, an increase in the marginal product of capital raises the debt ratio through an increase in the short-term interest rate. But if (2.43) is negative, then there will be a time range enclosed by the two roots of the numerator in (2.41) where the effect of an increase in α_K on the debt ratio will turn: a rising marginal product of capital then leads to sinking debt ratios although the short-term interest rate rises. At first sight, this is astonishing but it can be explained as follows: rising α_K will certainly increase public debt. But taking in mind the explanation for the effect (2.40), we recognize that the effect of rising α_K on capital and thus output may be ambiguous. There is a capital enhancing investment effect and a capital decreasing consumption effect visible in (2.12). If the investment effect triggered by increasing α_K is relatively more important than the consumption effect, then capital and especially output may rise faster than debt. As a consequence, the debt ratio decreases. If the investment effect is less important than the consumption effect, then the debt ratio will increase.

2.8 Short summary

Summarizing this chapter, we have seen that in equilibrium, prices do not react to fiscal policy in our model. Since equilibrium rates of return are even constant, the possible scarcity of capital near zero values is not taken into account by the private sector. Thus, fiscal policy bears significant responsibility. Without a public sector, of course, the danger of running into a situation of zero capital stocks would not even be present. Given the exogenous need for public spending for what reason ever, fiscal policy, though consisting of two instruments, has just a degree of freedom of 1 when it focuses on viability of the economy. Setting either the tax rate or the public expenditure ratio automatically fixes the other policy instrument if fiscal policy wants to prevents the economy from attaining a zero capital stock. This, however, is only one necessary condition for the capital stock not to reach zero. Another condition is a non-positive initial stock of public debt. Hence, the government has to start as a creditor with regard to its private sector. Otherwise, the private sector would choose a too high consumption path that finally jeopardizes capital accumulation. Sticking to such a fiscal policy is not sufficient in itself for economic growth. The tax rate has to be sufficiently smaller than the return on capital in order to guarantee ongoing growth.

In a situation with positive economic growth rates, we found out that the government's creditor position improves more and more. This happened despite the primary deficits the government keeps running. It is due to the fact that the interest payments the government gets from the households generate budget surpluses. As a consequence, the debt ratio decreases steadily and reaches a terminal value independent of all model parameters except for the marginal product of capital.

We learn from this model setting that if the government extracts resources for own unproductive use, then it has not only to set its fiscal policy according to quite strict rules. Through these rules, it is also assured that the government runs budget surpluses despite primary deficits so that it remains a creditor to the own private sector forever. Otherwise, private wealth accumulation and thus consumption (since wealth is the base for private consumption) would happen 'too fast' to maintain capital accumulation sufficiently[12].

Having introduced the basic model of a deterministic economy as a quasi benchmark, we will expand this model into a stochastic setting of financial markets in the next chapter. Doing so will prepare the ground for the then following investigations of important economic topics in Chapters 4 to 6.

Appendix 2.1: Solution of the inhomogeneous first-order differential equation of private wealth

We will derive here the solution of (2.18). The first step is to solve the corresponding homogeneous first-order differential equation by integration with integration constant c_0:

$$(A2.1.1) \qquad \dot{W} = (\alpha_K - \delta - \tau) \cdot W \Rightarrow W = c_0 \cdot e^{(\alpha_K - \delta - \tau) \cdot t}$$

The next step consists of using the so-called 'method of variation of constants' which means that the integration constant c_0 is treated as if it were a function of the independent variable time t:

$$(A2.1.2) \qquad \begin{aligned} W &= c_0 \cdot e^{(\alpha_K - \delta - \tau) \cdot t} \\ \Rightarrow \dot{W} &= \left(\dot{c}_0 + c_0 \cdot (\alpha_K - \delta - \tau) \right) \cdot e^{(\alpha_K - \delta - \tau) \cdot t} \end{aligned}$$

Plugging these results into (A2.1.1) yields:

$$(A2.1.3) \qquad \begin{aligned} &\dot{c}_0 \cdot e^{(\alpha_K - \delta - \tau) \cdot t} + (\alpha_K - \delta - \tau) \cdot c_0 \cdot e^{(\alpha_K - \delta - \tau) \cdot t} = \\ &(\alpha_K - \delta - \tau) \cdot c_0 \cdot e^{(\alpha_K - \delta - \tau) \cdot t} - C_0 \cdot e^{\frac{\alpha_K - \delta - \tau - \rho}{\gamma} \cdot t} \end{aligned}$$

We note that the second term on the left side of (A2.1.3) cancels against the first term of the right side. Dividing through by the exponential term of the left side delivers:

---

[12] We are well aware of the fact that this interpretation has a kind of Malthusian-flavored character which many economists do not like and share.

(A2.1.4) $\dot{c}_0 = -C_0 \cdot e^{\frac{(1-\gamma)\cdot(\alpha_K-\delta-\tau)-\rho}{\gamma}\cdot t}$

This equation can easily be integrated with c_1 being another integration constant:

(A2.1.5) $c_0 = \dfrac{C_0 \cdot \gamma}{(\gamma-1)\cdot(\alpha_K-\delta-\tau)+\rho} \cdot e^{-\frac{(\gamma-1)\cdot(\alpha_K-\delta-\tau)+\rho}{\gamma}\cdot t} + c_1$

Of course, we have to assume that the denominator of the fraction in (A2.1.5) is not zero. Having calculated the transversality condition later on, we will see that this denominator is always positive. Using (A2.1.5), we eliminate c_0 from (A2.1.2) and get:

(A2.1.6) $W = \dfrac{C_0 \cdot \gamma}{(\gamma-1)\cdot(\alpha_K-\delta-\tau)+\rho} \cdot e^{\frac{\alpha_K-\delta-\tau-\rho}{\gamma}\cdot t} + c_1 \cdot e^{(\alpha_K-\delta-\tau)t}$

Setting $t = 0$ in (A2.1.6), we obtain W_0, the historically given initial wealth as the sum of historically given capital K_0 and debt D_0, on the left side and calculate c_1 as follows:

(A2.1.7) $c_1 = W_0 - \dfrac{C_0 \cdot \gamma}{(\gamma-1)\cdot(\alpha_K-\delta-\tau)+\rho}$

Plugging c_1 into (A2.1.6) delivers the final result:

(A2.1.8)

$$W = \dfrac{C_0 \cdot \gamma}{(\gamma-1)\cdot(\alpha_K-\delta-\tau)+\rho} \cdot e^{\frac{\alpha_K-\delta-\tau-\rho}{\gamma}\cdot t}$$

$$+ \left(W_0 - \dfrac{C_0 \cdot \gamma}{(\gamma-1)\cdot(\alpha_K-\delta-\tau)+\rho}\right) \cdot e^{(\alpha_K-\delta-\tau)t}$$

Equation (A2.1.8) is equation (2.19) in the main text.

Appendix 2.2: Evaluation of the transversality condition

The transversality condition (2.5e) is given as:

(A2.2.1) $\lim_{t \to \infty}(\lambda \cdot W) = 0$

Using first-order condition (2.3a) in order to eliminate λ from (A2.2.1), we obtain:

(A2.2.2) $\lim_{t \to \infty}\left(e^{-\rho \cdot t} \cdot C^{-\gamma} \cdot W\right) = 0$

Making use of the results (2.17) and (2.19) in (A2.2.2), we can write the transversality condition:

(A2.2.3)

$$\lim_{t \to \infty}\left(\begin{array}{l} e^{-\rho \cdot t} \cdot C_0^{-\gamma} \cdot e^{(\rho - \alpha_K + \delta + \tau) \cdot t} \cdot \left(W_0 - \dfrac{\gamma \cdot C_0}{(\gamma - 1) \cdot (\alpha_K - \delta - \tau) + \rho} \right) \cdot e^{(\alpha_K - \delta - \tau) \cdot t} \\ + e^{-\rho \cdot t} \cdot C_0^{-\gamma} \cdot e^{(\rho - \alpha_K + \delta + \tau) \cdot t} \cdot \dfrac{\gamma \cdot C_0}{(\gamma - 1) \cdot (\alpha_K - \delta - \tau) + \rho} \cdot e^{\frac{(\alpha_K - \delta - \tau - \rho)}{\gamma} \cdot t} \end{array} \right) = 0$$

After some algebraic simplifications, we get:

(A2.2.4)

$$\lim_{t \to \infty}\left(\frac{W_0}{C_0^{\gamma}} - \frac{\gamma \cdot C_0^{1-\gamma}}{(\gamma - 1) \cdot (\alpha_K - \delta - \tau) + \rho} + \frac{\gamma \cdot C_0^{1-\gamma} \cdot e^{\frac{-(\gamma-1)\cdot(\alpha_K - \delta - \tau) - \rho}{\gamma} \cdot t}}{(\gamma - 1) \cdot (\alpha_K - \delta - \tau) + \rho} \right) = 0$$

(A2.2.4) shows that the limit depends critically on the sign of $\frac{-(\gamma-1)\cdot(\alpha_K - \delta - \tau) - \rho}{\gamma}$, which is the argument of the exponential function in the third term of the bracket. We have to rule out a positive sign of this argument. Otherwise, the third term within (A2.2.4) would explode in the limit and the transversality condition would be violated. The second possibility is that this argument equals zero. In this case, the third term within the bracket of (A2.2.4) tends in the limit to the second term but with a different sign. Hence, these two terms cancel out. The remaining first term, W_0/C_0^{γ}, can only equal zero for infinitely high initial consumption. This cannot hold, too, so that $\frac{-(\gamma-1)\cdot(\alpha_K-\delta-\tau)-\rho}{\gamma}$ can only have a negative sign. This implies the following condition:

$$(A2.2.5) \qquad \frac{-(\gamma-1)\cdot(\alpha_K-\delta-\tau)-\rho}{\gamma} < 0 \Leftrightarrow \tau < \alpha_K - \delta + \frac{\rho}{\gamma-1}$$

Note that (A2.2.5) is the desired condition (2.20). It is a restriction for the tax rate and thus for fiscal policy and also guarantees the validity of the derivation of the solution for the wealth equation in the Appendix 2.1. Assuming that (A2.2.5) holds, the transversality condition implies:

$$(A2.2.6) \qquad \frac{W_0}{C_0^{\gamma}} - \frac{\gamma\cdot C_0^{1-\gamma}}{(\gamma-1)\cdot(\alpha_K-\delta-\tau)+\rho} = 0$$

This equation can be solved for initial consumption C_0 and we finally obtain:

$$(A2.2.7) \qquad C_0 = \frac{(\gamma-1)\cdot(\alpha_K-\delta-\tau)+\rho}{\gamma}\cdot W_0$$

(A2.2.7) is equation (2.21) in the chapter. Due to condition (A2.2.5), initial consumption is guaranteed to be positive for positive initial wealth.

Appendix 2.3: Solution of the debt and capital accumulation equation

In order to calculate the time paths of capital and debt, we recall the respective equations (2.12b) and (2.15):

$$(2.12) \qquad \dot{K} = \left((1-z)\cdot\alpha_K-\delta\right)\cdot K - C$$

$$(2.15) \qquad \dot{D} = (z\cdot\alpha_K-\tau)\cdot K + (\alpha_K-\delta-\tau)\cdot D$$

Eliminating consumption C from (2.12) by (2.22) and (2.23) together with the wealth identity W = K + D yields:

(A2.3.1)

$$\dot{K} = \left((1-z)\cdot\alpha_K - \delta + \frac{(1-\gamma)\cdot(\alpha_K - \delta - \tau) - \rho}{\gamma} \right)\cdot K + \frac{(1-\gamma)\cdot(\alpha_K - \delta - \tau) - \rho}{\gamma}\cdot D$$

We can write the evolution of capital and debt as a two-dimensional homogeneous system of differential equations:

(A2.3.2)

$$\begin{pmatrix} \dot{K} \\ \dot{D} \end{pmatrix} = \underbrace{\begin{pmatrix} \tau - z\cdot\alpha_K + \dfrac{\alpha_K - \delta - \tau - \rho}{\gamma} & -\alpha_K + \delta + \tau + \dfrac{\alpha_K - \delta - \tau - \rho}{\gamma} \\ z\cdot\alpha_K - \tau & \alpha_K - \delta - \tau \end{pmatrix}}_{A}\cdot\begin{pmatrix} K \\ D \end{pmatrix}$$

To solve this system, we have to proceed as follows [13]: first, we calculate the eigenvalues of matrix A. Second, we solve for the corresponding eigenvectors and write down the fundamental solution. Finally, we determine the integration constants using the initial conditions which state that capital and debt equal their historically given initial values K_0 and D_0 when time t equals zero.

The eigenvalues of a 2x2 matrix are given as the solution to the following, so-called characteristic equation where 'tr A' denotes the trace and 'det A' the determinant of matrix A:

(A2.3.3) $\qquad \lambda_{1/2} = \dfrac{1}{2}\cdot\left(\text{tr}A \pm \sqrt{(\text{tr}A)^2 - 4\cdot\det A} \right)$

Using the characteristics of A, we obtain the eigenvalues:

---

[13] For a general exposition of how to solve systems of first-order differential equations, see Boyce/DiPrima (1997, Chapter 7).

$$\lambda_1 = (1-z)\cdot\alpha_K - \delta$$

(A2.3.4)
$$\lambda_2 = \frac{\alpha_K - \delta - \tau - \rho}{\gamma}$$

The sign of the eigenvalues cannot be determined so far. If the eigenvalues are distinct, then the fundamental solution is:

(A2.3.5)
$$\begin{pmatrix} K \\ D \end{pmatrix} = c_1 \cdot \begin{pmatrix} a_{11} \\ a_{12} \end{pmatrix} \cdot e^{((1-z)\cdot\alpha_K - \delta)\cdot t} + c_2 \cdot \begin{pmatrix} a_{21} \\ a_{22} \end{pmatrix} \cdot e^{\frac{\alpha_K - \delta - \tau - \rho}{\gamma}\cdot t}$$

where c_1, c_2 are integration constants and a_{ii} (for i = 1, 2) are the coefficients of the eigenvectors associated with the eigenvalues.

A special case occurs when both eigenvalues are identical. The fundamental solution is then given as[14]:

(A2.3.6)
$$\begin{pmatrix} K \\ D \end{pmatrix} = c_1 \cdot \begin{pmatrix} a_{11} \\ a_{12} \end{pmatrix} \cdot e^{((1-z)\cdot\alpha_K - \delta)\cdot t} + c_2 \cdot \left(\begin{pmatrix} a_{11} \\ a_{12} \end{pmatrix} \cdot t + \begin{pmatrix} a_{21} \\ a_{22} \end{pmatrix} \right) \cdot e^{((1-z)\cdot\alpha_K - \delta)\cdot t}$$

We first concentrate on the situation of distinct eigenvalues and calculate the corresponding eigenvectors. This is accomplished as follows: subtract the eigenvalues from the coefficients on the main diagonal of A and multiply the resulting matrix by the eigenvector which coefficients are not yet determined. The resulting two linear equations must both equal zero. The solution determines the components of the eigenvector. For the first eigenvalue λ_1, we obtain the following eigenvector:

(A2.3.7)
$$\begin{pmatrix} \delta + \tau - \alpha_K + \dfrac{\alpha_K - \delta - \tau - \rho}{\gamma} & \delta + \tau - \alpha_K + \dfrac{\alpha_K - \delta - \tau - \rho}{\gamma} \\ z \cdot \alpha_K - \tau & z \cdot \alpha_K - \tau \end{pmatrix} \cdot \begin{pmatrix} a_{11} \\ a_{12} \end{pmatrix} = \begin{pmatrix} 0 \\ 0 \end{pmatrix}$$

---

[14] Compare Boyce/DiPrima (1997, Chapter 7.7).

$$\text{(A2.3.7)} \qquad \Rightarrow \begin{pmatrix} a_{11} \\ a_{12} \end{pmatrix} = \begin{pmatrix} -1 \\ 1 \end{pmatrix}$$

For eigenvalue λ_2 we get, assuming $z \cdot \alpha_K \neq \tau$, the eigenvector:

(A2.3.8)

$$\left(\begin{matrix} -(z \cdot \alpha_K - \tau) & -\left(\alpha_K - \delta - \tau - \dfrac{\alpha_K - \delta - \tau - \rho}{\gamma}\right) \\[2ex] z \cdot \alpha_K - \tau & \alpha_K - \delta - \tau - \dfrac{\alpha_K - \delta - \tau - \rho}{\gamma} \end{matrix} \right) \cdot \begin{pmatrix} a_{21} \\ a_{22} \end{pmatrix} = \begin{pmatrix} 0 \\ 0 \end{pmatrix}$$

$$\Rightarrow \begin{pmatrix} a_{21} \\ a_{22} \end{pmatrix} = \begin{pmatrix} \dfrac{(1-\gamma) \cdot (\alpha_K - \delta - \tau) - \rho}{\gamma \cdot (z \cdot \alpha_K - \tau)} \\[2ex] 1 \end{pmatrix}$$

and for $z \cdot \alpha_K = \tau$, the resulting eigenvector becomes:

$$\left(\begin{matrix} 0 & -\left(\alpha_K - \delta - \tau - \dfrac{\alpha_K - \delta - \tau - \rho}{\gamma}\right) \\[2ex] 0 & \alpha_K - \delta - \tau - \dfrac{\alpha_K - \delta - \tau - \rho}{\gamma} \end{matrix} \right) \cdot \begin{pmatrix} a_{21} \\ a_{22} \end{pmatrix} = \begin{pmatrix} 0 \\ 0 \end{pmatrix}$$

(A2.3.9)

$$\Rightarrow \begin{pmatrix} a_{21} \\ a_{22} \end{pmatrix} = \begin{pmatrix} 1 \\ 0 \end{pmatrix}$$

Before we put the results (A2.3.4), (A2.3.5), (A2.3.7) - (A2.3.9) together, we need to think about a further crucial point: the fact whether $z \cdot \alpha_K$ equals τ or not may not be compatible with any ranking of the two eigenvalues λ_1 and λ_2. Assume, for example, the parameter constellation $z \cdot \alpha_K = \tau$. This constellation is only compatible with $\lambda_1 > \lambda_2$ since otherwise the tax rate constraint (2.20) is violated.

Depending upon the feasible parameter constellations, we get the following fundamental solutions:

Case 1): $\qquad \dfrac{\alpha_K - \delta - \tau - \rho}{\gamma} > (1 - z) \cdot \alpha_K - \delta \ \land \ z \cdot \alpha_K > \tau$

$$\begin{pmatrix} K \\ D \end{pmatrix} = c_2 \cdot \begin{pmatrix} \dfrac{(1-\gamma)\cdot(\alpha_K - \delta - \tau) - \rho}{\gamma \cdot (z \cdot \alpha_K - \tau)} \\ 1 \end{pmatrix} \cdot e^{\frac{\alpha_K - \delta - \tau - \rho}{\gamma} \cdot t}$$

(A2.3.10)

$$+ c_1 \cdot \begin{pmatrix} -1 \\ 1 \end{pmatrix} \cdot e^{((1-z)\cdot\alpha_K - \delta)t}$$

Case 2): $\quad \dfrac{\alpha_K - \delta - \tau - \rho}{\gamma} < (1-z)\cdot\alpha_K - \delta \wedge z\cdot\alpha_K > \tau \vee z\cdot\alpha_K < \tau$

$$\begin{pmatrix} K \\ D \end{pmatrix} = c_2 \cdot \begin{pmatrix} \dfrac{(1-\gamma)\cdot(\alpha_K - \delta - \tau) - \rho}{\gamma \cdot (z \cdot \alpha_K - \tau)} \\ 1 \end{pmatrix} \cdot e^{\frac{\alpha_K - \delta - \tau - \rho}{\gamma} \cdot t}$$

(A2.3.11)

$$+ c_1 \cdot \begin{pmatrix} -1 \\ 1 \end{pmatrix} \cdot e^{((1-z)\cdot\alpha_K - \delta)t}$$

Case 3): $\quad \dfrac{\alpha_K - \delta - \tau - \rho}{\gamma} < (1-z)\cdot\alpha_K - \delta \quad \wedge \quad z\cdot\alpha_K = \tau$

(A2.3.12) $\quad \begin{pmatrix} K \\ D \end{pmatrix} = c_1 \cdot \begin{pmatrix} -1 \\ 1 \end{pmatrix} \cdot e^{((1-z)\cdot\alpha_K - \delta)\cdot t} + c_2 \cdot \begin{pmatrix} 1 \\ 0 \end{pmatrix} \cdot e^{\frac{\alpha_K - \delta - \tau - \rho}{\gamma} \cdot t}$

We note that case 1) and 2) 'produce' the same structure of the fundamental solution. We will hence consider both as one common case further.

Setting $t = 0$ and using the initial conditions, we get as integration constants for case 1) and 2) (note that the denominators in both integration constants are different from zero):

$$c_1 = D_0 - \frac{\gamma \cdot (z \cdot \alpha_K - \tau) \cdot (K_0 + D_0)}{\alpha_K - \delta - \tau - \rho - \gamma \cdot ((1-z)\cdot\alpha_K - \delta)}$$

(A2.3.13)

$$c_2 = \frac{\gamma \cdot (z \cdot \alpha_K - \tau) \cdot (K_0 + D_0)}{\alpha_K - \delta - \tau - \rho - \gamma \cdot ((1-z)\cdot\alpha_K - \delta)}$$

Case 3) delivers the integration constants:

(A2.3.14)
$$c_1 = D_0$$
$$c_2 = K_0 + D_0$$

Now consider the situation where the two eigenvalues are identical. The fundamental solution consists now of a linear combination of the following two solutions [15]:

(A2.3.15a)
$$\begin{pmatrix} K \\ D \end{pmatrix} = \begin{pmatrix} a_{11} \\ a_{12} \end{pmatrix} \cdot e^{((1-z)\cdot \alpha_K - \delta)\cdot t}$$

(A2.3.15b)
$$\begin{pmatrix} K \\ D \end{pmatrix} = \left(\begin{pmatrix} a_{11} \\ a_{12} \end{pmatrix} \cdot t + \begin{pmatrix} a_{21} \\ a_{22} \end{pmatrix} \right) \cdot e^{((1-z)\cdot \alpha_K - \delta)\cdot t}$$

Identical eigenvalues imply here that only $z \cdot \alpha_K > \tau$ is compatible with the tax rate constraint (2.20). The eigenvector $\begin{pmatrix} a_{11} \\ a_{12} \end{pmatrix}$ is given by (A2.3.7). Accordingly, the fundamental solution is given as:

(A2.3.16)
$$\begin{pmatrix} K \\ D \end{pmatrix} = c_1 \cdot \begin{pmatrix} -1 \\ 1 \end{pmatrix} \cdot e^{((1-z)\cdot \alpha_K - \delta)\cdot t} + c_2 \cdot \left(\begin{pmatrix} -1 \\ 1 \end{pmatrix} \cdot t + \begin{pmatrix} a_{21} \\ a_{22} \end{pmatrix} \right) \cdot e^{((1-z)\cdot \alpha_K - \delta)\cdot t}$$

The eigenvector $\begin{pmatrix} a_{21} \\ a_{22} \end{pmatrix}$ is determined by plugging (A2.3.15b) into (A2.3.2) and solving the resulting system of linear equations. Doing so yields:

(A2.3.17)
$$\begin{pmatrix} a_{21} \\ a_{22} \end{pmatrix} = \begin{pmatrix} \dfrac{1}{z \cdot \alpha_K - \tau} \\ 0 \end{pmatrix}$$

Together with the initial conditions, the final solution is:

---

[15] We decided to put the first eigenvalue into the fundamental solution instead of the second. The other way round is, of course, also possible since we consider the case were both eigenvalues are identical.

$$(A2.3.18) \quad \begin{pmatrix} K \\ D \end{pmatrix} = \left(\begin{pmatrix} K_0 \\ D_0 \end{pmatrix} + \begin{pmatrix} -K_0 - D_0 \\ K_0 + D_0 \end{pmatrix} \cdot (z \cdot \alpha_K - \tau) \cdot t \right) \cdot e^{((1-z) \cdot \alpha_K - \delta) \cdot t}$$

Summarizing, we have calculated the following solutions for the time path of capital given the respective parameter constellations:

$$(A2.3.19a) \quad K = \left(\frac{\gamma \cdot (z \cdot \alpha_K - \tau) \cdot (K_0 + D_0)}{\alpha_K - \delta - \tau - \rho - \gamma \cdot ((1-z) \cdot \alpha_K - \delta)} - D_0 \right) \cdot e^{((1-z) \cdot \alpha_K - \delta) \cdot t}$$
$$+ \frac{((1-\gamma) \cdot (\alpha_K - \delta - \tau) - \rho) \cdot (K_0 + D_0)}{\alpha_K - \delta - \tau - \rho - \gamma \cdot ((1-z) \cdot \alpha_K - \delta)} \cdot e^{\frac{\alpha_K - \delta - \tau - \rho}{\gamma} \cdot t}$$

given that either: $\dfrac{\alpha_K - \delta - \tau - \rho}{\gamma} > (1-z) \cdot \alpha_K - \delta \quad \wedge \quad z \cdot \alpha_K > \tau$

or: $\dfrac{\alpha_K - \delta - \tau - \rho}{\gamma} < (1-z) \cdot \alpha_K - \delta \quad \wedge \quad z \cdot \alpha_K > \tau \quad \vee \quad z \cdot \alpha_K < \tau$ hold.

$$(A2.3.19b) \quad K = (K_0 + D_0) \cdot e^{\frac{\alpha_K - \delta - \tau - \rho}{\gamma} \cdot t} - D_0 \cdot e^{(\alpha_K - \delta - \tau) \cdot t}$$

given that: $\dfrac{\alpha_K - \delta - \tau - \rho}{\gamma} < (1-z) \cdot \alpha_K - \delta \quad \wedge \quad z \cdot \alpha_K = \tau$ holds.

$$(A2.3.19c) \quad K = \left[K_0 - (K_0 + D_0) \cdot (z \cdot \alpha_K - \tau) \cdot t \right] \cdot e^{((1-z) \cdot \alpha_K - \delta) \cdot t}$$

given that: $\dfrac{\alpha_K - \delta - \tau - \rho}{\gamma} = (1-z) \cdot \alpha_K - \delta \quad \wedge \quad z \cdot \alpha_K > \tau$ holds.

The further analysis will show that only one of these 'candidate' capital dynamics (A2.3.19a-c) will remain.

68

Appendix 2.4: Proof that (2.26a-b) imply viability

In this appendix, we calculate the critical time when the capital stock reaches zero for all candidate dynamics (2.25a-c). We first consider (2.25a):

(2.25a)
$$K = \left(\frac{\gamma \cdot (z \cdot \alpha_K - \tau) \cdot (K_0 + D_0)}{\alpha_K - \delta - \tau - \rho - \gamma \cdot ((1-z) \cdot \alpha_K - \delta)} - D_0 \right) \cdot e^{((1-z) \cdot \alpha_K - \delta) \cdot t}$$
$$+ \frac{((1-\gamma) \cdot (\alpha_K - \delta - \tau) - \rho) \cdot (K_0 + D_0)}{\alpha_K - \delta - \tau - \rho - \gamma \cdot ((1-z) \cdot \alpha_K - \delta)} \cdot e^{\frac{\alpha_K - \delta - \tau - \rho}{\gamma} \cdot t}$$

given that either: $\dfrac{\alpha_K - \delta - \tau - \rho}{\gamma} > (1-z) \cdot \alpha_K - \delta \;\wedge\; z \cdot \alpha_K > \tau$

or: $\dfrac{\alpha_K - \delta - \tau - \rho}{\gamma} < (1-z) \cdot \alpha_K - \delta \;\wedge\; z \cdot \alpha_K > \tau \;\vee\; z \cdot \alpha_K < \tau$ hold.

Setting $K = 0$, we get $t_{critical}$:

(A2.4.1)
$$t_{critical} = \frac{\log \left[\frac{D_0 \cdot \left(\frac{\alpha_K - \delta - \tau - \rho -}{\gamma \cdot ((1-z) \cdot \alpha_K - \delta)} \right) - \gamma \cdot (z \cdot \alpha_K - \tau) \cdot (K_0 + D_0)}{((1-\gamma) \cdot (\alpha_K - \delta - \tau) - \rho) \cdot (K_0 + D_0)} \right]}{\frac{\alpha_K - \delta - \tau - \rho}{\gamma} - ((1-z) \cdot \alpha_K - \delta)}$$

The way to proceed now is to assume that $t_{critical}$ does not exist and then to show that this yields a contradiction to the assumption of a positive initial capital stock.

The first parameter constellation from above implies that the denominator of $t_{critical}$ is positive. For $t_{critical}$ not to exist, the numerator must be negative which requires the argument of the log function to be smaller than 1:

(A2.4.2)

$$\frac{D_0 \cdot \left(\alpha_K - \delta - \tau - \rho - \gamma \cdot ((1-z) \cdot \alpha_K - \delta)\right) - \gamma \cdot (z \cdot \alpha_K - \tau) \cdot (K_0 + D_0)}{\left((1-\gamma) \cdot (\alpha_K - \delta - \tau) - \rho\right) \cdot (K_0 + D_0)} < 1$$

Multiplying (A2.4.2) through by the denominator, which is negative due to tax rate constraint (2.20) so that the '<' sign turns to '>', adding $\gamma \cdot (z \cdot \alpha_K - \tau) \cdot (K_0 + D_0)$ on both sides and dividing by $\alpha_K - \delta - \tau - \rho - \gamma \cdot ((1-z) \cdot \alpha_K - \delta)$, we get:

(A2.4.3) $D_0 > K_0 + D_0 \Rightarrow 0 > K_0$

This is a contradiction since the initial capital stock must be nonnegative. Moreover, one can show that for the second valid parameter constellation of (2.25a) the same contradiction occurs. As a consequence, we have to give up the assumption that $t_{critical}$ does not exist for the time path (2.25a). Therefore, the capital stock becomes 0 at $t_{critical}$ and the economy is hence not viable in the long-run.

Consider now (2.25c):

(2.25c) $K = \left[K_0 - (K_0 + D_0) \cdot (z \cdot \alpha_K - \tau) \cdot t\right] \cdot e^{((1-z) \cdot \alpha_K - \delta) \cdot t}$

given that: $\dfrac{\alpha_K - \delta - \tau - \rho}{\gamma} = (1-z) \cdot \alpha_K - \delta \;\wedge\; z \cdot \alpha_K > \tau$ holds.

Critical time is:

(A2.4.4) $t_{critical} = \dfrac{K_0}{(K_0 + D_0) \cdot (z \cdot \alpha_K - \tau)}$

Due to the parameter constraint $z \cdot \alpha_K > \tau$ associated with (2.25c), we recognize that $t_{critical}$ is positive and finite. Thus, the economy is also not viable in the long-run.

The last time path of capital that remains is (2.25b):

$$(2.25b) \qquad K = (K_0 + D_0) \cdot e^{\frac{\alpha_K - \delta - \tau - \rho}{\gamma} \cdot t} - D_0 \cdot e^{((1-z) \cdot \alpha_K - \delta) \cdot t}$$

given that: $\dfrac{\alpha_K - \delta - \tau - \rho}{\gamma} < (1-z) \cdot \alpha_K - \delta \quad \wedge \quad z \cdot \alpha_K = \tau$ holds.

Critical time can be calculated as follows:

$$(A2.4.5) \qquad t_{critical} = \frac{\log\left(\dfrac{K_0}{D_0} + 1\right)}{(1-z) \cdot \alpha_K - \delta - \dfrac{\alpha_K - \delta - \tau - \rho}{\gamma}}$$

The denominator is positive owing to the parameter constellation associated with (2.25b). Furthermore, the numerator is positive for any positive initial stock of debt. The critical time is positive and finite. In contrast, for zero or negative-valued initial debt, critical time does not exist. Consequently, $z \cdot \alpha_K = \tau$ together with $D_0 \leq 0$ guarantee viability in the long-run.

Appendix 2.5: Proof of Proposition 2.1

First, we state the economic growth rate g_Y again in somewhat different form, however:

$$(A2.5.1) \qquad g_Y = \frac{\dfrac{b - \rho}{\gamma} \cdot (D_0 + K_0) \cdot e^{\left(\frac{b-\rho}{\gamma} - b\right) \cdot t} - b \cdot D_0}{(D_0 + K_0) \cdot e^{\left(\frac{b-\rho}{\gamma} - b\right) \cdot t} - D_0}$$

with: $\qquad b \equiv \alpha_K - \delta - \tau$

The derivative of g_Y with respect to τ is:

$$(A2.5.2) \qquad \frac{dg_Y}{d\tau} = \frac{dg_Y}{db} \cdot \frac{db}{d\tau} = -\frac{dg_Y}{db}$$

Taking derivatives of g_Y with respect to b using (A2.5.1) yields:

(A2.5.3)

$$\frac{dg_Y}{db} = \frac{-\left(\gamma \cdot (\gamma + 1) + t \cdot (\gamma - 1) \cdot (b \cdot (\gamma - 1) + \rho)\right) \cdot D_0 \cdot \left(D_0 + K_0\right) \cdot e^{\left(\frac{b-\rho}{\gamma} - b\right) \cdot t}}{\gamma^2 \cdot \left((D_0 + K_0) \cdot e^{\left(\frac{b-\rho}{\gamma} - b\right) \cdot t} - D_0\right)^2}$$

$$+ \frac{\gamma^2 \cdot D_0^2 + \gamma \cdot \left(D_0 + K_0\right)^2 \cdot e^{2\left(\frac{b-\rho}{\gamma} - b\right) \cdot t}}{\gamma^2 \cdot \left((D_0 + K_0) \cdot e^{\left(\frac{b-\rho}{\gamma} - b\right) \cdot t} - D_0\right)^2} > 0$$

To see the validity of the claimed sign, we will argue as follows: the derivative consists of two fractions having both positive denominators. Consider the second fraction first: its numerator contains a sum of two obvious positive terms. This fraction is hence positive. The first fraction's sign is not so obvious: since $-D_0$ is positive due to (2.26b), the numerator's sign depends only on the first term which is in parenthesis. The first term in parenthesis is also positive, $t \cdot (\gamma - 1)$ is positive, too, but what about $b \cdot (\gamma - 1) + \rho$? Inserting $b \equiv \alpha_K - \delta - \tau$ and recalling the tax rate constraint (2.20), we recognize that $b \cdot (\gamma - 1) + \rho$ is nothing but (2.20) and is hence positive. Thus, the whole numerator of the first fraction in (A2.5.3) is positive and so is the derivative of g_Y with respect to b. As a consequence of (A2.5.2), the derivative of growth rate g_Y with respect to τ is negative.

3 The basic stochastic macroeconomic model and the short-term interest rate dynamics

3.1 Introduction

In this chapter, we will develop a stochastic analogue to the dynamic macroeconomic model already discussed in the last chapter. This is accomplished by modeling the economy's technology not as a fixed parameter, but as a certain continuous-time stochastic process. As a consequence, holding capital involves the bearing of risk. The intertemporal consumption/asset allocation problem of the private households becomes risky. This risky decision-making reflects the reality of how financial markets form their behavioral rules much better than the deterministic model in the previous chapter. Hence, we can expect our model to 'produce' prices for assets traded on the financial market that will generally not be constant but change dynamically as it happens in reality. Specifically, interest rates will no longer be equal to the net return on capital but rather react on changes in the economy, especially on fiscal policy changes. The link between fiscal policy and the term structure of interest rates is a new aspect of this model. In equilibrium, the model in this chapter will produce nonlinear, stochastic dynamics describing the evolution of output, capital, private wealth and public debt. For this reason, this chapter lays the basis for the analysis of all interesting economic aspects to be discussed in subsequent chapters: the relationship between fiscal policy and the term structure of interest rates, the question how economic growth is affected by the financial market, and the dynamics of public debt in the light of stochastically varying interest rates.

The further course of this chapter is as follows: in Section 2, the basic structure of the economy - especially the production technology and the financial market - is outlined. Section 3 derives and solves the intertemporal decision problem of the representative household yielding its optimal consumption and asset demands. Fiscal policy, i.e. the behavioral equations characterizing governmental expenditure, taxation and financing of the accruing deficit via debt emission, is introduced and explained in Section 4.

Subsequently, Section 5 is devoted to the determination and interpretation of the stochastic general equilibrium. Additionally, an algebraic condition on the tax rate for given parameter sets of both production technology and household behavior is derived. Given that the short-term interest rate evolves within a two-sided bounded interval, it is shown that this tax constraint is necessary to assure sufficiency of the optimal solution of the household problem, non-negativity of consumption and validity of the transversality condition. In Section 6, we derive and scrutinize the stochastic dynamics of the short-term interest rate process. We derive algebraic conditions constraining the public expenditure ratio ensuring fiscal policy does not drive the stock of capital to zero. These conditions assure that private wealth always remains strictly positive so that the household decision problem is always well-posed. In Section 7, we eventually study and interpret the short run and long run effects of fiscal policy on the short-term interest rate dynamics. The chapter closes with a short summary in Section 8.

3.2 Basic structure of the economy and the financial market

In contrast to the production function (2.1) in Chapter 2, we introduce risk into the production function by assuming productivity to be a stochastic process. The new production function can be presented in form of a stochastic differential equation (SDE)[1]:

$$(3.1) \qquad dY = \alpha_K \cdot K \cdot dt + \beta_K \cdot K \cdot dB$$

α_K is the instantaneously expected mean and β_K the instantaneous variance of the Hicks-neutral technological progress [2]. Both parameters are exogenous constants. B is a so-called Wiener process (or Brownian motion) whose increments over non-overlapping time intervals are independent and normally

---

[1] Turnovsky (1995, Chapter 14) points out that this specification of a production function is the stochastic analog to the deterministic linear A-K production technology as was already used in Eaton (1981).

[2] They can also be interpreted as the instantaneously expected marginal product of capital and instantaneous variance of the marginal product of capital.

distributed with zero mean and linearly growing variance in time [3,4]. Since this Wiener process is the only source for the generation of risk in this model, the technological progress and thus output become stochastic processes in continuous time, namely diffusion processes [5].

The financial market setting is essentially the same as in Chapter 2. It is well known that in such a setting with risk being driven by Brownian motion the price processes are characterized by diffusion processes written as SDEs (see Huang (1985), Turnovsky/Grinols (1993)). The price process, P_K, and thus the rate of return process on capital, r_K, is characterized by the following SDE:

$$(3.2a) \qquad \frac{dP_K}{P_K} \equiv dr_K = \mu_K \cdot dt + \sigma_K \cdot dB$$

μ_K and σ_K (and later also r_D, μ_F and σ_F) are not parameters but functions of the model parameters as well as the model state variables. They will be determined later on in stochastic equilibrium.

Since government bonds are assumed to be short-term bonds, they are paid back with interest at every moment in time. Assuming that government bonds are 'locally riskless' enables us to write the price process, P_B, and thus the process of the rate of return, r_B, as a quasi diffusion process. This means that the drift term remains but the diffusion term vanishes [6]. Hence, the financial market is dynamically complete in the sense of Harrison/Kreps (1979) which guarantees a unique equilibrium price process[7]. We obtain:

---

[3] Note that we have omitted time subscripts for the Brownian motion B, output Y and capital stock K and that we will continue to do so for all the other variables in the further course of the model, mainly for notational convenience. However, it should be clear from the formulation that these variables are time-dependent.

[4] For a more detailed discussion of Brownian motion, see General Appendix 1.

[5] A diffusion process is a Markov process with almost surely (i.e. probability one) continuous sample paths. For a brief discussion of diffusion processes, see General Appendix 2.

[6] For a brief discussion of the notions 'drift term' and 'diffusion term', see General Appendix 2.

[7] If we had not assumed that the price process (and thus the rate of return process, too) of government bonds has a vanishing diffusion term (i.e. that government bonds are not

(3.2b) $$\frac{dP_B}{P_B} \equiv dr_B = r_D \cdot dt$$

We will call r_D the 'short-term interest rate' which will be determined in stochastic equilibrium.

The price P_F of private bonds, which pay back 1 unit of the good when due per definition, is assumed to depend on the short-term interest rate r_D and on time t only. Applying Ito's Lemma in order to calculate the diffusion process of this price yields thus[8]:

$$dP_F = \frac{\partial P_F}{\partial t} \cdot dt + \frac{\partial P_F}{\partial r_D} \cdot dr_D + \frac{1}{2} \cdot \frac{\partial^2 P_F}{\partial r_D^2} \cdot d\langle r_D \rangle$$

(3.2c) $$\Rightarrow \frac{dP_F}{P_F} \equiv dr_F = \frac{\dfrac{\partial P_F}{\partial t} \cdot dt + \dfrac{\partial P_F}{\partial r_D} \cdot dr_D + \dfrac{1}{2} \cdot \dfrac{\partial^2 P_F}{\partial r_D^2} \cdot d\langle r_D \rangle}{P_F}$$

$$\equiv \mu_F \cdot dt + \sigma_F \cdot dB$$

The last equality in (3.2c) will lead to the valuation equation for private bonds in form of a partial differential equation after a relationship between μ_F and σ_F has been calculated in stochastic equilibrium on the private bond market. It is noteworthy that μ_F and σ_F are functions of the private bond price, its derivatives and the short-term interest rate according to the last equality in the second line of (3.2c).

3.3 Decision problem of the representative household

As in Chapter 2, private wealth W of the representative household consists of capital K, government debt D and private debt F. Introducing n_K, n_B and n_F

'locally riskless') then we would have ended up with infinitely many equilibrium price processes. The reason for this outcome is the fact that then the financial market would have been incomplete which usually prevents equilibrium price processes to be unique.

[8] Note that the symbol „<>" denotes the so-called 'quadratic variation' of a diffusion process. For a detailed explanation of it as well as an introduction to stochastic integration and Ito's Lemma, see Durrett (1996). For a short discussion, see General Appendix 2.

as the number of shares held in the respective asset, the static wealth equation looks:

$$W = K + D + F$$

(3.3a)

$$= n_K \cdot P_K + n_B \cdot P_B + n_F \cdot P_F$$

We now obtain the dynamic budget constraint by the following considerations [9]: since the asset holdings n_i ($i = K, D, F$) and the prices P_i ($i = K, D, F$) are diffusion processes, we apply Ito's Lemma to calculate the change in private wealth as follows:

$$dW = \underbrace{dn_K \cdot P_K + dn_B \cdot P_B + dn_F \cdot P_F + d\langle n_K, P_K \rangle + d\langle n_B, P_B \rangle + d\langle n_F, P_F \rangle}_{\text{voluntary wealth change}}$$

$$+ \underbrace{n_K \cdot dP_K + n_B \cdot dP_B + n_F \cdot dP_F}_{\text{involuntary wealth change}}$$

As in Chapter 2, the voluntary wealth change together with the outlays for taxation and consumption have to equal zero. Taxation is hereby again supposed to result from a proportional tax on wealth:

$$\underbrace{dn_K \cdot P_K + dn_B \cdot P_B + dn_F \cdot P_F + d\langle n_K, P_K \rangle + d\langle n_B, P_B \rangle + d\langle n_F, P_F \rangle}_{\text{voluntary wealth change}} = -\tau \cdot W \cdot dt - C \cdot dt$$

Plugging the financing condition into the equation for the wealth change yields:

$$dW = n_K \cdot P_K \cdot \frac{dP_K}{P_K} + n_B \cdot P_B \cdot \frac{dP_B}{P_B} + n_F \cdot P_F \cdot \frac{dP_F}{P_F} - \tau \cdot W \cdot dt - C \cdot dt$$

The final equation for the dynamic budget constraint of the representative household is now obtained by making use of the wealth identity (3.3a) together with the price equations (3.2a-c):

---

[9] For a lucid exposition of these considerations, see Merton (1971).

$$\text{(3.3b)} \quad dW = \left(K \cdot (\mu_K - r_D) + F \cdot (\mu_F - r_D) + W \cdot (r_D - \tau) - C\right) \cdot dt$$
$$+ \left(K \cdot \sigma_K + F \cdot \sigma_F\right) \cdot dB$$

The household decision how much of the different assets to hold is risky. The household only knows the a priori probability distribution for the asset prices but not its future realizations. Taking the drift and diffusion terms of the price processes as parametrically given, the representative household chooses consumption stream C, capital holdings K and private bond holdings F, thereby determining holdings of government bonds via (3.3a). Beginning with an initial endowment of private wealth W_0, (3.3b) denotes the evolution of future private wealth.

The objective of the representative household is the maximization of expected, intertemporally discounted consumption utility:

$$\text{(3.4)} \quad V(W_{t_0}, t_0) = \max_{C,K,F} E\left[\int_{t_0}^{\infty} e^{-\rho \cdot t} \cdot \frac{C^{1-\gamma} - 1}{1-\gamma} \cdot dt | \Im_{t_0}\right]$$

subject to:
$$dW = \left(K \cdot (\mu_K - r_D) + F \cdot (\mu_F - r_D) + W \cdot (r_D - \tau) - C\right) \cdot dt$$
$$+ \left(K \cdot \sigma_K + F \cdot \sigma_F\right) \cdot dB$$

$$W(t_0) = W_0, W(t) > 0 \text{ for } t \in [t_0, \infty)$$

with $\Im_{t_0}$: information set at time t_0 and E: expectation operator.

The optimization problem (3.4) is similar to the almost classical problem of theoretical finance which was first solved by Merton (1969, 1971) using Bellman's method of dynamic programming [10]. Heuristically, the dynamic programming principle implies that the household is assumed to choose at every point in time t its optimal choices having observed the whole

---

[10] Detailed descriptions of this method as well as economic applications can be found, among others, in Malliaris/Brock (1982), Dixit/Pindyck (1994) and Turnovsky (1995). More rigorous mathematical treatments on dynamic control theory for Markovian processes can be found in Fleming/Rishel (1975) or Fleming/Soner (1993). A brief introduction of the idea can also be found in General Appendix 3.

realization of the stochastic process driving its private wealth W. The optimal choices are, technically spoken, adapted to the filtration (i.e. whole story) $\mathfrak{I}_t$ generated by the stochastic process driving W and are hence said to be non-anticipating. This intuitively means that optimal decisions are based on past and present information but not on future one. Hence, the optimal policies calculated by using Bellman's principle are feedback policies depending on the state variable W.

Carrying out the optimization problem yields the following first-order conditions (3.5a-c) and second-order condition (3.6) [11]:

$$(3.5a) \quad C = \left(\frac{\gamma - 1}{\gamma} \cdot (r_D - \tau) + \frac{\rho}{\gamma} + \frac{1}{2} \cdot \frac{(\mu_K - r_D)^2}{\sigma_K^2} \cdot \frac{\gamma - 1}{\gamma^2} \right) \cdot W$$

$$(3.5b) \quad K = \frac{\mu_K - r_D}{\sigma_K^2 \cdot \gamma} \cdot W - \frac{\sigma_F}{\sigma_K} \cdot F$$

$$(3.5c) \quad \frac{\mu_F - r_D}{\sigma_F} = \frac{\mu_K - r_D}{\sigma_K}$$

$$(3.6) \quad \frac{\gamma \cdot \left(\frac{\gamma - 1}{\gamma} \cdot (r_D - \tau) + \frac{\rho}{\gamma} + \frac{1}{2} \cdot \frac{(\mu_K - r_D)^2}{\sigma_K^2} \cdot \frac{\gamma - 1}{\gamma^2} \right) + \frac{(\mu_K - r_D)^2}{\gamma \cdot \sigma_K^2}}{\left(\frac{\gamma - 1}{\gamma} \cdot (r_D - \tau) + \frac{\rho}{\gamma} + \frac{1}{2} \cdot \frac{(\mu_K - r_D)^2}{\sigma_K^2} \cdot \frac{\gamma - 1}{\gamma^2} \right)^{\gamma} \cdot W^{\gamma - 1}} > 0$$

At first sight, optimal consumption (3.5a) seems to be a linear function of the private sector's state variable W. But as we will see later in stochastic equilibrium, r_D itself becomes a function of state variable W and the consumption-wealth relation ceases to be linear. An interesting special case would occur if we allowed the marginal rate of substitution γ to equal 1. Then, the consumption stream would become a fixed share ρ (the rate of time preferences) of wealth W and the representative household would be characterized by log-utility in consumption. This special case is known as the

---

[11] For a detailed derivation see Appendix 3.1.

case of a myopic household (see Ingersoll (1987, p. 257-258)) whose consumption decision is not affected by any risk.

The economic interpretation of equation (3.5b) is as follows: demand for capital is the sum of two parts, one depending on the level of private wealth and the other depending on the level of private bonds. The latter part will drop out in equilibrium for F has than to become zero since private bonds are in net-zero supply. Apart from the dependence on F, demanded capital is given as a variable share of private wealth. The share is determined by the excess instantaneous return of capital over the riskless rate of return, $\mu_K - r_D$, divided by the instantaneous volatility of return on capital, σ_K^2, times the marginal rate of substitution γ which can be interpreted as a measure of relative risk aversion. Other things being equal, a higher excess return drives up the demanded capital, while the higher the risk (reflected by σ_K^2) and the risk aversion (reflected by γ) drive it down.

Equation (3.5c) says that in the optimum the excess return on private bonds, $\mu_F - r_D$, per unit of risk (the instantaneous standard deviation of the private bond's rate of return σ_F) has to equal the excess return on capital, $\mu_K - r_D$, per unit of risk σ_K. This is a quite common condition in finance literature (compare Vasicek (1977)) [12].

Finally, we take a look on the second-order condition (3.6). If it holds in the stated form (3.6), then optimality of the household problem will be guaranteed. Given that private wealth remains always positive, it is sufficient for (3.6) to hold that its denominator is positive. In Proposition 3.1 to come later on, we will develop a parameter condition that always guarantees positive consumption and simultaneously assures the validity of the sufficient optimality condition (3.6).

---

[12] As we will see later on in Chapter 4, this condition finally yields, together with equation (3.2c) and the diffusion process describing the stochastic evolution of the equilibrium short-term real interest rate, a valuation equation for the pricing of private bonds in the form of a parabolic partial differential equation of second order. The solution of this equation will provide the base in Chapter 4 for the examination how fiscal policy influences the term structure of interest rates.

We close this section by remarking that we will use the optimal policies (3.5a-b) in Section 5 in order to find the equilibrium price processes and the stochastic accumulation equations for K, D and W.

3.4 Fiscal policy

Given the fiscal policy rules in Chapter 2, the stochastic version of public expenditure and tax revenue is as follows:

(3.7)
$$G = z \cdot Y$$
$$\Rightarrow dG = z \cdot \alpha_K \cdot K \cdot dt + z \cdot \beta_K \cdot K \cdot dB$$

(3.8)
$$T = \tau \cdot W \Rightarrow T \cdot dt = \tau \cdot W \cdot dt$$

A government expenditure specification like (3.7) can, for example be found in Eaton (1981), Turnovsky (1993) and Turnovsky/Grinols (1994).

Using (3.7) and (3.8), the change of the public deficit is now given by:

(3.9)
$$dDef = dG - dT + r_D \cdot D \cdot dt$$

We again assume that the financing of the public deficit is carried out by emitting new government bonds so that we get the stochastic evolution equation for public debt:

(3.10)
$$dD = \left(r_D \cdot D + z \cdot \alpha_K \cdot K - \tau \cdot W \right) \cdot dt + z \cdot \beta_K \cdot K \cdot dB$$

A further scrutinization of the debt equation (3.10) cannot be done before the short-term real interest rate has been determined which will happen in the next section. Chapter 6 will then focus on the examination of public debt dynamics.

3.5 Stochastic general equilibrium

As in Chapter 2, we will derive a debt accumulation equation using the equilibrium conditions on goods, capital and private bond market. Since

Walras' Law implies that equilibrium on these three markets induce equilibrium on the fourth market, the public bond market, we will compare the public bond market equilibrium condition resulting from (3.10) with the one just described. The rate of returns and hence asset prices will be chosen such that both debt dynamics equalize and general equilibrium is attained.

The goods market equilibrium is written in differential form:

(3.11) $\qquad dY = C \cdot dt + dG + dI$

The capital market equilibrium has the following differential form:

(3.12) $\qquad dK + \delta \cdot K \cdot dt = dI$

Replacing the differential of investment, dI, in (3.12) by (3.11), plugging in (3.1) for dY, (3.7) for dG, (3.5a) for C and using the private bond market condition ($F = 0 \Rightarrow W = K + D$), we obtain:

(3.13)
$$dK = \left(\begin{array}{l} ((1-z) \cdot \alpha_K - \delta) \cdot \dfrac{\mu_K - r_D}{\sigma_K^2 \cdot \gamma} - \dfrac{\gamma - 1}{\gamma} \cdot (r_D - \tau) \\[2mm] -\dfrac{\rho}{\gamma} - \dfrac{1}{2} \cdot \dfrac{(\mu_K - r_D)^2}{\sigma_K^2} \cdot \dfrac{\gamma - 1}{\gamma^2} \end{array} \right) \cdot W \cdot dt$$
$$+ (1-z) \cdot \beta_K \cdot \dfrac{\mu_K - r_D}{\sigma_K^2 \cdot \gamma} \cdot W \cdot dB$$

Finally, the private bond equilibrium condition yields:

(3.14) $\qquad F = 0 \Rightarrow W = K + D \Rightarrow dD = dW - dK$

We take the differential form of (3.14), replace dK by (3.13), dW by the household budget constraint (3.3b) - after we have already used the above equilibrium conditions to simplify (3.3b) - and end up with:

(3.15)
$$dD = \left((\mu_K - r_D - (1-z) \cdot \alpha_K + \delta) \cdot \dfrac{\mu_K - r_D}{\sigma_K^2 \cdot \gamma} + r_D - \tau \right) \cdot W \cdot dt$$
$$+ (\sigma_K - \beta_K + z \cdot \beta_K) \cdot \dfrac{\mu_K - r_D}{\sigma_K^2 \cdot \gamma} \cdot W \cdot dB$$

We turn to the debt accumulation equation (3.10). Replacing D by W - K according to (3.14) and eliminating K via (3.5b), we obtain the equilibrium debt accumulation equation for which the public bond market is cleared given the equilibrium price processes:

(3.16)
$$dD = \left((z \cdot \alpha_K - r_D) \cdot \frac{\mu_K - r_D}{\sigma_K^2 \cdot \gamma} + r_D - \tau \right) \cdot W \cdot dt$$
$$+ z \cdot \beta_K \cdot \frac{\mu_K - r_D}{\sigma_K^2 \cdot \gamma} \cdot W \cdot dB$$

In stochastic general equilibrium, (3.15) and (3.16) have to be equal. Comparing drift and diffusion terms of both equations, yields the following rate of returns:

(3.17a) $\mu_K = \alpha_K - \delta$

(3.17b) $\sigma_K = \beta_K$

In equilibrium, the instantaneously expected rate of return on capital equals the instantaneously expected marginal product of capital minus depreciation rate. The instantaneous volatility of the rate of return equals the instantaneous volatility of the marginal product of capital. With (3.17a-b), the price process P_K is determined via (3.2a).

We are now able to calculate the equilibrium short-term interest rate r_D and thus the price process of government bonds. Making use of (3.5b) and equilibrium condition F = 0, we get:

(3.18) $$r_D = \alpha_K - \delta - \beta_K^2 \cdot \gamma \cdot \frac{K}{W} = \alpha_K - \delta - \beta_K^2 \cdot \gamma \cdot \frac{K}{K+D}$$

The short-term interest rate r_D equals the net rate of return from holding capital minus a 'risk premium'. For our parameter assumption $\gamma \in (1; \infty)$, the representative household is said to be risk averse and the risk premium becomes positive. Risk-averse investors thus demand this premium for holding the risky asset 'capital' compared to the (locally) riskless asset

84

'private bonds'. The risk premium compensates them for holding the risk [13]. Another observation is that the higher the risk inherent in the asset 'capital' (i.e. the higher β_K) and the higher the risk aversion (i.e. the higher γ), the bigger must be the risk premium required to compensate the risk-averse household. Similarly, higher net rates of return on capital (either due to rising α_K or sinking δ) seem to lead to rising values of the short-term interest rate. However, all these interpretations could be misleading since they assume implicitly that changes in the model parameters leave the evolution of the capital wealth ratio K/W, which is also part of (3.18), unaffected.

Since we already saw above that K, D and thus W evolve stochastically, the short-term interest rate r_D also evolves stochastically. We will examine the short-term interest rate dynamics more explicitly later on. As a consequence, we have to postpone the comparative dynamics for the short-term interest rate r_D with regard to the model parameters until we have derived the stochastic dynamics of r_D.

(3.18) shows clearly that increasing wealth diminishes the risk premium and thus raises the short-term interest rate. Since growing public indebtedness means higher wealth, this implies that the interest rate, other things being equal, grows when public debt grows. This is an interesting feature of this stochastic model. In the deterministic model, the interest rate did not react at all when public indebtedness changed. It means that risk averse financial markets do not allow the government to raise debts without charging higher interest rates.

The next step is to derive the equilibrium stochastic dynamics of W, K and D. Eliminating r_D by the use of (3.18), we obtain the following dynamics:

---

[13] The risk premium term would become positive only if $\gamma < 0$ held, i.e. when the representative household is risk loving. The household would then require higher returns on safe bonds than on risky capital. Besides, the risk premium can get zero when γ equals zero. In this case, the household is said to be risk neutral and appreciates capital as much as safe bonds. This case leads to the same rates of return as in Chapter 2. Both cases are excluded for we assumed $\gamma > 1$.

$$(3.19) \quad dK = \begin{pmatrix} (1-z)\cdot\alpha_K - \delta + (\gamma-1)\cdot\beta_K^2 - \dfrac{(\gamma-1)\cdot\beta_K^2}{2}\cdot\dfrac{K}{W} \\[2mm] -\dfrac{\rho+(\gamma-1)\cdot(\alpha_K-\delta-\tau)}{\gamma}\cdot\dfrac{W}{K} \end{pmatrix}\cdot K\cdot dt$$
$$+ (1-z)\cdot\beta_K \cdot K \cdot dB$$

$$(3.20) \quad dD = \begin{pmatrix} (\alpha_K - \delta - \tau)\cdot W + \beta_K^2\cdot\gamma\cdot\dfrac{K^2}{W} \\[2mm] -(\beta_K^2\cdot\gamma + (1-z)\cdot\alpha_K - \delta)\cdot K \end{pmatrix}\cdot dt + z\cdot\beta_K\cdot K\cdot dB$$

$$(3.21) \quad dW = \left(\dfrac{\alpha_K - \delta - \tau - \rho}{\gamma}\cdot W - \beta_K^2\cdot K + \dfrac{1}{2}\cdot(1+\gamma)\cdot\beta_K^2\cdot\dfrac{K^2}{W} \right)\cdot dt$$
$$+ \beta_K \cdot K \cdot dB$$

The system of SDEs (3.19) - (3.21) describes the model dynamics in reduced form. Any arbitrary pair of the variables W, K and D forms hereby a set of possible state variables that automatically determines the third. For reasons to become clear later on, we decide to choose W and K as state variables and express the debt dynamics depending on W and K. The dynamics of the state variables is thus captured by the equations (3.19) and (3.21). Since both state variables show nonlinear dynamics, we face a two-dimensional nonlinear diffusion process as the appropriate description of the model dynamics. This is a quite remarkable feature. Most stochastic macroeconomic models try to avoid nonlinearity and higher dimensions regarding their reduced-form dynamics. The reason is that linear, one-dimensional dynamics are easy to solve in closed-form. However, it is well known that linear dynamics cannot account for many interesting real-world phenomena. Moreover, linearity turns out to be a special case in our model, namely when the risk vanishes, i.e. for $\beta_K = 0$. In this case the stochastic, nonlinear dynamics tend exactly to those deterministic, linear dynamics derived and discussed in Chapter 2. We thus note that the introduction of risk does not only add a stochastic part to the model dynamics but also complicates its deterministic part considerably.

Principally, we could now embark on investigating the accumulation dynamics of capital and public debt in order to study the issues of economic

86

growth and public indebtedness more closely. Before doing so, however, we need to develop parameter conditions that guarantee viability of model economy. The detailed scrutiny of economic growth and public indebtedness will therefore be postponed to Chapter 5 and 6.

Using (3.17a-b) and (3.18) in order to eliminate the price process components from (3.5a), we get the equilibrium consumption function:

$$(3.22) \qquad C = \frac{\rho + (\gamma - 1) \cdot (\alpha_K - \delta - \tau)}{\gamma} \cdot W + (\gamma - 1) \cdot \beta_K^2 \cdot K \cdot \left(\frac{1}{2} \cdot \frac{K}{W} - 1 \right)$$

We see that consumption, contrary to what is suggested by the functional form of (3.5a), is in fact a nonlinear function of private wealth. Moreover, it is a function of the two state variables K and W. Both features are in contrast to traditional results (see for example Merton (1971)), where consumption depends only linearly on the single state variable private wealth. The 'classical' result, however, can also be derived here as a special case, namely when the stochasticity of the model degenerates to certainty (i.e. when $\beta_K = 0$) or when the marginal elasticity of substitution, γ, equals unity (implying a logarithmic utility function). In the latter case, consumption simplifies to a share ρ of private wealth W [14]. Hence, risk considerations play no role in the consumption decision of a logarithmic-utility household. The parameter dependencies of consumption are quite clear: a higher rate of time preference ρ and a higher instantaneously expected return on capital α_K - δ increase, while higher tax rates decrease consumption. Only the effect of an increase in the elasticity of substitution γ is ambiguous.

Given the explicit consumption function (3.22), we now derive a parameter condition that guarantees positive consumption and sufficiency of the household optimum. We saw in Appendix 3.1 that the strict negativity of the indirect utility function coefficient a_1 guarantees positive consumption. Proposition 3.1 provides now the desired parameter constraint under which both positive consumption and sufficiency of the household optimum, as

---

[14] Ingersoll (1987, p. 257-258) calls this consumption behavior 'myopic'.

determined in (3.6), is satisfied. We first state this condition and turn then to Proposition 3.1:

$$(3.23) \qquad \tau < \alpha_K - \delta + \frac{\rho}{\gamma - 1} - \frac{1}{2} \cdot \gamma \cdot \beta_K^2$$

Proposition 3.1:

If the tax rate obeys the condition (3.23) and private wealth remains always positive [15], then the sufficiency condition for the household's optimization problem, (3.6), holds and consumption is always positive.

Proof: **see Appendix 3.2.**

There is a clear restriction regarding the tax policy of the government. If the government were to set up a tax policy violating this tax constraint, this would prohibit the private household from carrying out optimal consumption and portfolio decisions. The condition is the stochastic counterpart of condition (2.20) in the last chapter. If risk vanished in this model ($\beta_K = 0$), then (3.23) would become (2.20).

The effects of the model parameters on the right-hand side of (3.23) are as expected: an increase in α_K and ρ increases the right-hand side and thus softens the constraint. This is easily understandable: the higher the instantaneously expected marginal product of capital, the higher the expected output for a given stock of capital. The government can thus tax private wealth at a higher rate without running into trouble that it disables households to finance future consumption. A higher rate of time preferences implies that households discount future consumption more. Increasing the tax rate, the resulting consequences on future consumption are felt less painfully by the private sector. An increase in β_K, δ and γ decrease the right-hand side of (3.23) and harden the constraint. These effects can be

---

[15] The question whether the sign of private wealth is always positive has to be postponed to Proposition 3.4 in Section 6. The reason is that in order to answer this question we first need to determine the short-term interest rate dynamics. We will thus assume here that private wealth remains always positive.

understood as follows: higher volatility in the rate of return on capital, β_K, as well as higher risk aversion induces risk-averse households to shift from more to less risky investment. This reduces capital accumulation. Since lower capital accumulation deteriorates future consumption possibilities, a harsher tax rate constraint is imposed on the government in order to enable households to maintain future consumption. The same reasoning is clearly at work for rising depreciation rate.

Finally, the question arises how the tax policy constraint (3.23) is related to the transversality condition since it was the transversality condition in the deterministic model of Chapter 2 that provided us with a condition similar to (3.23). Corollary 3.1 gives the answer:

Corollary 3.1:

Given that the fiscal policy constraint (3.23) holds and assuming that wealth remains positive, then the transversality condition holds, too.

Proof: see Appendix 3.3.

The implication of Corollary 3.1 is that the validity of the transversality condition and the holding of both household's sufficient optimality condition and positive consumption imply each other mutually. Thus, we could have derived (3.23) also from the transversality condition.

Two further remarks have to be made regarding restriction (3.23): first, this restriction concerns only the tax rate and does thus not say anything about government expenditure. This may seem strange at first sight since what really matters is how much output the government 'confiscates' for its own, unproductive use. However, the household does only 'feel' the taxes as the way how the government finances public spending, not the spending itself. It will become clear in Proposition 3.3 and 3.4 of Section 6, that there are additional constraints on government expenditure imposed by the requirement that fiscal policy may not drive the stock of capital to zero. The second remark concerns the feasibility of tax policy: if the right hand side of (3.23) were equal to or smaller than zero, then tax policy would turn into subsidization policy for the tax rate became negative then. Throughout this chapter we will thus assume that the household and technology parameters are such that equation (3.23) right hand side always remains positive so that there is indeed some leeway for tax policy.

3.6 Stochastic dynamics and boundary behavior of the short-term interest rate

We now want to calculate and investigate the stochastic dynamics driving the short-term interest rate r_D. We then use these dynamics to derive the still missing public expenditure constraints. This is done by examining whether the interest rate process can 'commute' between certain areas of its state space. Finally, we show that the stochastic dynamics tend to a stochastic kind of steady-state. Making use of this allows us to examine long run effects of fiscal policy on the short-term interest rate. Apart from these specific purposes, it is important to understand the qualitative features of the short-term interest rate dynamics for it will play an important role in all chapters to come later on.

In order to derive the dynamics, we need to apply Ito's Lemma using $(3.18)^{16}$. After some tedious algebraic manipulations, we eventually get:

$$
dr_D = \left(\begin{array}{l} \left(\rho + (\gamma - 1) \cdot (\alpha_K - \delta - \tau) \right) \cdot \beta_K^2 \\[2mm] + \left((\gamma - 1) \cdot \beta_K^2 - z \cdot \alpha_K + \dfrac{\rho + \tau + (\gamma - 1) \cdot (\alpha_K - \delta)}{\gamma} \right) \cdot (r_D - \alpha_K + \delta) \\[2mm] + \dfrac{1}{2} \cdot (\gamma - 1 - 2 \cdot z) \cdot \dfrac{(r_D - \alpha_K + \delta)^2}{\gamma} - \dfrac{1}{2} \cdot (\gamma - 1) \cdot \dfrac{(r_D - \alpha_K + \delta)^3}{\gamma^2 \cdot \beta_K^2} \end{array} \right) \cdot dt
$$
$$
+ (r_D - \alpha_K + \delta) \cdot \left(\dfrac{r_D - \alpha_K + \delta}{\gamma \cdot \beta_K} + (1 - z) \cdot \beta_K \right) \cdot dB
$$

Factoring out coefficients in order to simplify notation, we get:

---

[16] Since (3.18) shows that r_D is a smooth, twice differentiable function of the two diffusion processes for K and W, calculating the SDE for r_D using Ito's Lemma is the proper procedure to derive the dynamics.

$$dr_D = \begin{pmatrix} \alpha_0 + \alpha_1 \cdot (r_D - \alpha_K + \delta) + \alpha_2 \cdot (r_D - \alpha_K + \delta)^2 \\ + \alpha_3 \cdot (r_D - \alpha_K + \delta)^3 \end{pmatrix} \cdot dt$$

(3.24a)

$$\underbrace{}_{\text{drift term}}$$

$$+ \underbrace{\Big(\big(\beta_0 + \beta_1 \cdot (r_D - \alpha_K + \delta)\big) \cdot (r_D - \alpha_K + \delta) \Big)}_{\text{diffusion term}} \cdot dB$$

with the following coefficient definitions[17]:

$$\beta_0 = (1 - z) \cdot \beta_K \geq 0$$

(3.24b)

$$\beta_1 = \frac{1}{\beta_K \cdot \gamma} > 0$$

$$\alpha_0 = \big(\rho + (\gamma - 1) \cdot (\alpha_K - \delta - \tau)\big) \cdot \beta_K^2 > 0$$

$$\alpha_1 = (\gamma - 1) \cdot \beta_K^2 - z \cdot \alpha_K + \frac{\rho + \tau + (\gamma - 1) \cdot (\alpha_K - \delta)}{\gamma}$$

(3.24b)

$$\alpha_2 = \frac{\gamma - 1 - 2 \cdot z}{2 \cdot \gamma}$$

$$\alpha_3 = -\frac{\gamma - 1}{2 \cdot \beta_K^2 \cdot \gamma^2} < 0$$

Equation (3.24a) shows that the stochastic dynamics of r_D depend only on the different model parameters and r_D itself. In contrast to many single-factor term structure models from mathematical finance, where the ad-hoc assumed drift and diffusion coefficients of the SDE driving the short-term interest rate are mainly linear (see, for example, Merton (1970), Vasicek (1977), Dothan (1978) or Ho/Lee (1986)), our short-term interest rate model exhibits nonlinear drift and diffusion coefficients [18]. Furthermore, we note that the

---

[17] The sign of α_0 can be derived using the tax policy constraint (3.23), other signs are obvious. We have omitted the sign when it was ambiguous.

[18] This feature could probably help to better understand observed interest rate behavior which remains unexplained when using the usual linear ad-hoc specifications of the short-term interest rate. These shortcomings recently prompted some researchers (for example Ait-Sahalia (1995)) to call for nonlinear specifications of stochastic interest rate dynamics. Remaining in the tradition of mathematical finance, such nonlinear extensions had to be introduced arbitrarily without getting conscious of their economic meaning. Our model,

influence of fiscal policy is reflected in four of the six coefficients of (3.24b). This really shows that fiscal policy has an impact on interest rate dynamics and thus on the whole term structure of interest rates. This impact has been neglected so far by all finance models.

The first question that always arises when one is confronted with an SDE is whether globally a solution exists and whether this solution is unique. Recalling General Appendix 2, we have to admit that the Lipschitz and growth conditions, which are essential for existence and uniqueness of solutions, do not hold globally (i.e. for $r_D \in [-\infty, \infty]$) owing to the nonlinearity that is inherent in both the drift and diffusion term of the interest rate process (3.24a). However, assuming that the condition (3.23) together with two other conditions that will be developed soon holds we are able to prove that the interest rate process will always remain within a certain bounded interval. Hence it will never tend to either positive or negative infinite values. It can easily be seen that in such a bounded interval both the Lipschitz and the growth condition locally hold therefore guaranteeing that a solution of (3.24a-b) exists and is unique.

The next question, given that a solution truly exists and uniqueness holds, is whether we can find a closed-form solution. This is never a problem as long as the considered SDE is linear. If it is nonlinear, the situation becomes different: referring to Kloeden/Platen (1992, Chapter 4), it is almost hopeless to find a closed-form solution when there is no chance of reducing a nonlinear SDE to a solvable one by means of a suitable variable transformation. Following Kloeden/Platen, one can show that the reducibility condition they give for such a transformation to exist (see Kloeden/Platen (1992), p. 116, formula (3.13)) is in general not fulfilled for our dynamics (3.24a). Thus, it is almost certain that no closed-form solution of (3.24a) can be found. In that situation, there are at least two possible ways to proceed when one absolutely needs an approximate solution in terms of a closed formula (for example, in order to do comparative statics or dynamics with regard to interesting model parameters): one can proceed according to the

---

however, makes clear where such nonlinearities may come from and is thus an important alternative to the usual ad-hoc specification.

lines of Gardiner (1983, Chapter 6.2) [19]. The other way is outlined in Kloeden/Platen (1992) and consists of numerically solving the SDE [20]. For our purposes, it is not indispensable to have a closed-form solution for the short-term interest rate since the whole boundary analysis as well as the analysis of transitional (i.e. short run) and asymptotic (i.e. long run) behavior of the interest rate process can be carried out using tools from diffusion process theory. In the following course, we will introduce and use these tools for our qualitative analysis.

Before we proceed to analyze the interest rate dynamics (3.24a-b) further, we need to say a few words what boundary analysis is all about. Since we are unable to derive a closed-form solution of (3.24a-b) explicitly, we have to get a 'picture' what values the diffusion process r_D can attain. In principle, r_D could reach values on the whole interval $[-\infty, \infty]$. These two infinite boundaries, however, imply zero wealth and either positive or negative capital stocks (see (3.18)). Such situations are economically irrelevant. Or take $r_D = \alpha_K - \delta$. When the short-term interest rate attains this value, then (3.18) implies that the stock of capital has to become zero. For a closed economy, where no capital can be imported, this has the consequence that output is no longer produced and consumption becomes zero for all time. Hence, the analysis whether the interest rate process can reach such points called 'boundaries' in the state space $[-\infty, \infty]$ becomes indispensable. In the following, we will first define the notion of 'regularity of a diffusion process', since all theorems and lemmata we need later on rely on the fact that a diffusion process will be regular:

---

[19] He proposes perturbation type methods to obtain approximate formulas. The crucial thing with this approach is that one cannot simply assess whether a special approximation, that still has to be simple enough for comparative statics or dynamics purposes, performs well in terms of being a good approximation to the original problem.

[20] In so doing, one has to discretize the SDE according to some suitable discretization scheme so that a stochastic difference equation results. Unfortunately, this is a very special method since it requires the numerical specification of all parameter values and hence looses generality.

Definition 3.1: Regularity of a diffusion process (Karlin/Taylor 1981)

A diffusion process is said to be regular on a state space Λ if the probability to reach any arbitrary point in Λ from any given starting point in Λ is greater than zero.

The value of this definition lies in the fact that it helps to sort out all points in the state space of a diffusion process which are not regular. Irregular points share one crucial feature: the diffusion term of a SDE (in our case, this is the term in (3.24a) that stands in front of the Brownian motion differential dB) becomes zero at these points. The consequence is that the state space of a regular diffusion process must be such that nowhere within the interior of this space the diffusion term becomes zero, except for the left and right boundary. Points with vanishing diffusion term are irregular according to Definition 3.1 owing to the following heuristically intuitive argument: assume that the drift term is zero when the diffusion process reaches an irregular point coming from the left, say. The diffusion process will then remain in this point forever [21]. This implies, that all the points right from this fixed point will never be reached when starting at some point left from this point. The probability of reaching any point right from this irregular point is zero if the process starts left from this point. This clearly contradicts Definition 3.1. If the drift term at such an irregular point is not zero but, for example, negative then the diffusion process is 'catapulted' back to the left region coming from left. Being left from the irregular point means never again being able to return to points right from it. The respective probability is zero, the point is seen to be irregular. This heuristic argumentation shows that irregular points with non-zero drift term constitute boundaries a diffusion process can only cross in one direction. If the drift term of an irregular point is additionally zero, then the irregular point has a fixed point (or equilibrium point) property. The reason why such boundaries may occur in diffusion processes is that their trajectories have, per definition, the property to be continuous with probability 1. Thus, the process cannot 'jump' over such boundaries. As a consequence, the state space of a diffusion process has to be divided into

---

[21] Such a case is the stochastic analog to the notion of a fixed point in deterministic dynamics.

subspaces which do not contain irregular points in order to preserve validity of Definition 3.1. In order to gain insight about the qualitative properties of the interest rate dynamics, we will then examine whether and under what circumstances r_D can 'commute' between these single areas. This analysis will finally deliver the required parameter restrictions in terms of constraining the government expenditure ratio z. Additionally, we will see that these conditions assure that private wealth will never reach zero let alone negative values. This property is needed to guarantee positive consumption, sufficiency of the household optimum and the validity of the transversality condition.

Looking at (3.24a-b), we see that there are indeed two values of the short-term interest rate that drive the diffusion term to zero:

(3.25)
$$r_{D,1} = \alpha_K - \delta - \frac{\beta_0}{\beta_1} \equiv \alpha_K - \delta - (1-z) \cdot \gamma \cdot \beta_K^2$$
$$r_{D,2} = \alpha_K - \delta$$

Thus, we decompose the state space for the short-term interest rate into three subspaces:

$$I_1 = [-\infty, \alpha_K - \delta - (1-z) \cdot \gamma \cdot \beta)$$
$$I_2 = (\alpha_K - \delta - (1-z) \cdot \gamma \cdot \beta_K^2, \alpha_K - \delta)$$
$$I_3 = (\alpha_K - \delta, \infty]$$

On each of these three intervals, the short-term interest rate process is regular due to Definition 3.1. Of special interest is hereby interval I_3: when the interest rate process reaches the left boundary of I_3, $r_{D,2} = \alpha_K - \delta$, corresponding to a zero capital stock (see (3.18)), then its diffusion term gets zero and its drift term equals α_0 (see (3.24b)). But α_0 is positive owing to (3.23) and thus the interest rate process enters the interior of I_3. Since α_0 is positive and the interest rate process is a diffusion process (i.e. cannot have 'jumps'), it can never again leave I_3. It follows that $r_{D,2} = \alpha_K - \delta$ is a 'reflecting boundary' for the interest rate process being within I_3 [22]. However, I_3 corresponds to a negative capital stock. Since negative values of capital are economically senseless, we exclude this possibility by just concentrating on I_1 and I_2 as possible areas for the short-term interest rate process to stay. As a consequence, we have to show under which conditions $r_{D,2} = \alpha_K - \delta$ and hence the whole interval I_3 cannot be reached from the interior of I_2. It should be further noted, that the interest rate process cannot start in $r_{D,2} = \alpha_K - \delta$ or right from it since we assume a positive initial stock of private capital and wealth.

In order to embark on our qualitative examination of the interest rate process behavior at the different boundaries, we have to calculate the so called 'scale function' associated with (3.24a) [23]:

(3.26)

$$
S(1,x] = \int_1^x \left((x - \alpha_K + \delta)^{-\frac{2\cdot(\alpha_1\cdot\beta_0 - 2\cdot\alpha_0\cdot\beta_1)}{\beta_0^3}} \cdot \left(\frac{(x-\alpha_K+\delta)\cdot\beta_1}{+\beta_0} \right)^{-\frac{2\cdot(\alpha_3\cdot\beta_0^3 - \alpha_1\cdot\beta_0\cdot\beta_1^2 + 2\cdot\alpha_0\cdot\beta_1^3)}{\beta_0^3\cdot\beta_1^2}} \right.
$$
$$
\left. \cdot e^{-2\cdot\frac{\alpha_3\cdot\beta_0^3 - \alpha_2\cdot\beta_1\cdot\beta_0^2 + \alpha_1\cdot\beta_0\cdot\beta_1^2 - \alpha_0\cdot\beta_1^3}{\beta_0^2\cdot\beta_1^2\cdot(\beta_0 + (x-\alpha_K+\delta)\cdot\beta_1)}} \cdot e^{2\cdot\frac{\alpha_0}{\beta_0^2\cdot(x-\alpha_K+\delta)}} \right) \cdot dx
$$

The purpose of this scale function is to provide us with a measure by which we can determine whether a certain boundary is attracting or not. The scale function is hence our main tool for the boundary analysis to come.

---

[22] Note that this could also be shown more rigorously according to the lines of Proposition 3.2 and 3.3.

[23] See the General Appendix 2 for a general definition and discussion of the meaning of the scale function. An additional remark may be due here: if the interest rate process is in I_1, then the first two terms inside the integral of the scale function become negative for any $x \in I_1$. Since this could yield complex-valued outcomes instead of real-valued ones, we will, for the use in the later Propositions 3.3 and 3.4, normalize (3.26) appropriately so that the scale function remains real-valued. Such a normalization, which is equivalent to a multiplication with a scalar, does not falsify the conclusions drawn later on since the only thing that really matters is whether the scale function is unbounded (∞) or bounded ($< \infty$) for specific boundaries.

The natural question arises: under what parameter conditions can a boundary be reached? In order to answer this question, one needs the following lemma which states the condition for a boundary to be attracting by the use of the scale function (3.26):

Lemma 3.1: Attraction of a boundary (Karlin/Taylor 1981)

A boundary l is said to be attracting a regular diffusion process defined on an interval [l, r] if $S(l, x] < \infty \; \forall x \in (l, r)$ holds. This definition holds in a equivalent way for the right boundary, r, too.

Thus one has 'only' to calculate the scale function and show that, for arbitrary points x from within the investigated area, the upper inequality holds. This guarantees attraction to the boundary considered. We first concentrate on the interval I_2 and examine whether the right boundary, $r_{D,2}$, can be reached. This yields Proposition 3.2:

Proposition 3.2:

The right boundary of I_2, $r_{D,2} = \alpha_K - \delta$, is attracting due to (3.23) from the interior of I_2.

Proof: see Appendix 3.4.

Proposition 3.2 has the following important feature: starting within I_2 means that there is always a positive probability for the short-term interest rate to reach $r_{D,2} = \alpha_K - \delta$ and thus I_3. Even if the left boundary of I_2,

$$r_{D,1} = \alpha_K - \delta - \frac{\beta_0}{\beta_1} \equiv \alpha_K - \delta - (1 - z) \cdot \gamma \cdot \beta_K^2, \text{ was also attracting, we could}$$

not exclude the probability that the interest rate process does not reach $r_{D,2}$ ultimately driving the capital stock to zero and eventually to negative values. If $r_{D,1}$ is not attracting, then $r_{D,2}$ will be reached almost surely, i.e. with probability 1. Since we want to exclude the situation that the capital stock will ultimately be driven into negative values, we have to assume that the short-term interest rate process will indeed start within interval I_1. This, however, holds only if the initial interest rate is smaller or equal to $r_{D,1}$ which leads to the following condition:

(3.27)

$$\alpha_K - \delta - \gamma \cdot \beta_K^2 \cdot \frac{K_0}{K_0 + D_0} \le \alpha_K - \delta - (1-z) \cdot \gamma \cdot \beta_K^2$$

$$\Rightarrow z \ge 1 - \frac{K_0}{K_0 + D_0} = \frac{D_0}{K_0 + D_0}$$

The government expenditure ratio has to be at least as high as the initial stock of public debt per initial private wealth. The validity of condition (3.27) guarantees that the initial short-term interest rate is smaller or equal to the 'critical' value $r_{D,1} = \alpha_K - \delta - (1-z) \cdot \gamma \cdot \beta_K^2$. The interest rate process will start within I_1 or at least at its right boundary. (3.27) can be viewed as setting a lower ceiling for government expenditure ratio z which, at least at first sight, seems very surprising. Economic intuition would tell us that, the lower z, the 'easier' capital accumulation should become. Additionally, lower expenditure ratios usually reduce the deficit burden. Other things being equal, this, in turn, should lead to lower interest rates. Lower interest rates shift the risk-return relationship between bonds and capital so that more capital should be demanded and accumulated. This view of the model is obviously too short for we have not considered the influence of risk so far. Lower values for z also lead to an increase in the volatility of the growth rate of capital (see (3.19)). This means that a series of negative productivity shocks now has a much stronger impact on capital accumulation and impairs it more strongly than in a situation with quite high expenditure ratios. Government expenditure, although being intrinsically useless to the private sector, thus act as a damping mechanism and hence as a kind of 'insurance' against negative productivity shocks. The lower boundary for z accordingly has an economic justification.

Note that condition (3.27) is sufficient, but not necessary to guarantee that r_D will never reach the interior of I_2. This is so because equality of (3.27) means that we start at $r_{D,1}$ and from there the interest rate process can, in principle, again enter I_2 with all the economic consequences described so far. Thus, we have to derive a necessary condition that guarantees that the interest rate process can never cross $r_{D,1}$ when it starts in I_1 even if it starts exactly at $r_{D,1}$. This condition is the following:

$$\alpha_0 - \alpha_1 \cdot \frac{\beta_0}{\beta_1} + \alpha_2 \cdot \left(\frac{\beta_0}{\beta_1}\right)^2 - \alpha_3 \cdot \left(\frac{\beta_0}{\beta_1}\right)^3 < 0$$

(3.28)
$$\Rightarrow \alpha_0 - \alpha_1 \cdot (1-z) \cdot \gamma \cdot \beta_K^2 + \alpha_2 \cdot (1-z)^2 \cdot \gamma^2 \cdot \beta_K^4$$
$$- \alpha_3 \cdot (1-z)^3 \cdot \gamma^3 \cdot \beta_K^6 < 0$$

Proposition 3.3 shows that (3.28) is the necessary condition that 'forces' the short-term interest rate dynamics into the interval I_1:

Proposition 3.3:

If (3.28) holds, then the right boundary of I_1, $r_{D,1} = \alpha_K - \delta - (1-z) \cdot \gamma \cdot \beta_K^2$, is not attracting from the interior of I_1.

Proof: see Appendix 3.5.

(3.28) imposes an upper boundary on z. This upper boundary feature of (3.28) is clear from an economic standpoint but it is not clear at first sight by looking at (3.28). Let us consider the left-hand side of (3.28) as a function $f(z)$. We note that $f(z)$ is a cubic polynomial in z. A cubic polynomial always has three roots, either three real-valued or one real-valued and two complex-valued roots. Moreover, we can easily verify that at $z = 0$ the function $f(z)$ is smaller than zero so that (3.28) holds. Inserting $z = 1$ yields a value of $f(z)$ bigger than zero so that (3.28) no longer holds. According to the mean value theorem of standard calculus, we thus have at least one root of $f(z)$ within the interval $(z = 0, z = 1)$. Since $f(z)$ tends to $-\infty$ for $z \to +\infty$ and $f(z)$ tends to $+\infty$ for $z \to -\infty$ (note that $-\alpha_3$ is positive), we see that there is also at least one change in the sign of $f(z)$ on each of the intervals $(z = -\infty, z = 0)$ and $(z = 1, z = \infty)$. Since we have three intervals on which the sign of $f(z)$ changes and simultaneously we have three roots of $f(z)$, we can conclude from the mean value theorem that there is exactly one root of $f(z)$ on each of the following intervals: $(z = -\infty, z = 0)$, $(z = 0, z = 1)$ and $(z = 1, z = \infty)$. Moreover, $f(z)$ increases monotonically within the interval $(z = 0, z = 1)$. As long as z is therefore smaller than the root lying within ($z = 0$, $z = 1$), constraint (3.28) holds. This imposes an upper value of z which is exactly given by the root on the interval ($z = 0$, $z = 1$).

Back to the meaning of (3.28): if (3.28) was violated, then z would be too big to leave the private sector enough resources to maintain capital accumulation. Thus, (3.28) has to hold as a necessary condition in order to make sure that the economy does not collapse into a zero capital stock. Together with (3.27), it implies that if the short-term interest rate process starts within I_1, then it will always stay within I_1. This guarantees positive capital stocks forever. Furthermore, (3.28) together with (3.23) and (3.27) constrains the choice of fiscal policy (i.e. the set of (τ, z)) the government can carry out.

In principle, it is now possible to calculate the root of the left-hand side of (3.28) for $z \in (0, 1)$ in order to do comparative statics. However, the result becomes too complicated to interpret it economically so that we do not examine this issue further.

The last question that remains open regarding the boundary behavior of the short-term interest rate process is the question whether the left boundary of I_1, $-\infty$, will be reached or not. The answer to this question is important for the following reason: reaching $-\infty$ implies that private wealth becomes zero (see (3.18)). This possibility was excluded until now for it could undermine the whole analysis carried out so far. Moreover, a zero stock of private wealth could cause problems with the transversality condition. Fortunately, it is quite easy to show that, under the parameter assumptions made, the stock of private wealth will always remain positive. This important fact is implied by the non-attracting behavior of $r_D = -\infty$.

Proposition 3.4:

The left boundary of I_1, $r_D = -\infty$, is non-attracting and guarantees that private wealth W will always remain positive.

Proof: see Appendix 3.6.

The description of the boundary behavior of the short-term interest rate process is now complete. If the fiscal policy constraints (3.23), (3.27) and (3.28) hold, then the short-term interest rate process remains in the interval $I_1 = (-\infty, \alpha_K - \delta - (1-z) \cdot \gamma \cdot \beta)$ forever without ever settling down on the left or on the right boundary of this interval [24]. Moreover, the non-attracting behavior of the left boundary, $-\infty$, implies that the stock of public debt can become negative so that the government would become the creditor of its own private sector. However, the amount of a possibly negative stock of public debt cannot exceed the amount of private capital.

3.7 Transitional and asymptotic analysis of the short-term interest rate

After we have pinned down the boundary behavior of the short-term interest rate process by deriving the fiscal policy constraints (3.23), (3.27) and (3.28), we now want to analyze the transitional (i.e. short run) and asymptotic (i.e. long run) behavior of this interest rate process. As an integral part of this analysis, we will examine the short- and long run effects on the short-term interest rate dynamics induced by changes in the fiscal policy parameters. By 'short run' we mean the instantaneous effect (i.e. the effect that happens over the next, infinitesimally small time period) on the interest rate dynamics triggered by a parameter change. 'Long run' means that we study the effect on the interest rate dynamics at the end of the infinite time horizon. For this purpose, we will show and use the property that the interest rate dynamics attains a 'stochastic steady state' associated with a stationary probability distribution.

In the last section, the stochastic interest rate dynamics has been shown to have the following form:

$$(3.24a) \qquad dr_D = \mu(r_D) \cdot dt + \sigma(r_D) \cdot dB$$

---

[24] Note that, if (3.27) holds as an equality, then the short-term interest rate starts at the right boundary. Owing to (3.28), however, it leaves it immediately and never reaches it any more.

$$\mu(r_D) \equiv \alpha_0 + \alpha_1 \cdot (r_D - \alpha_K + \delta) + \alpha_2 \cdot (r_D - \alpha_K + \delta)^2$$

with:
$$+ \alpha_3 \cdot (r_D - \alpha_K + \delta)^3$$

$$\sigma(r_D) \equiv \left(\beta_0 + \beta_1 \cdot (r_D - \alpha_K + \delta) \right) \cdot (r_D - \alpha_K + \delta)$$

where $\mu(r_D)$ is called 'drift' and $\sigma(r_D)$ stands for 'diffusion' which is sometimes also called 'volatility'. The drift denotes the instantaneously expected change of r_D, i.e. the difference between the value of the interest rate at the next, infinitesimally small time period and right now when the stochastic shock is zero (which equals the shock's expected value). The diffusion denotes the instantaneous standard deviation of r_D, i.e. the standard deviation of the difference between the value of the interest rate at the next, infinitesimally small time period and right now. In finance literature, the term 'volatility' is often used to denote the 'instantaneous variance of r_D' instead of the 'instantaneous standard deviation of r_D'. In order to avoid confusions, we will thus call $\sigma(r_D)$ 'diffusion' and $\sigma(r_D)^2$ 'volatility'.

Before we embark on discussing the short run effects of τ and z on the dynamics of r_D, we first examine the shape of both the drift and the diffusion term of (3.24a). We begin with the diffusion which is a quadratic function in r_D. As we already have seen in equation (3.25), $r_{D,1} = \alpha_K - \delta - (1-z) \cdot \gamma \cdot \beta_K^2$ and $r_{D,2} = \alpha_K - \delta$ are the two roots of this quadratic function. The boundary analysis showed that the first root acts as the right boundary of the interval I_1 on which the short-term interest rate process stays. The second root can never be reached given our fiscal policy parameter constraints (3.23), (3.27) and (3.28). Calculating the derivative $\sigma'(r_D)$ and setting it equal to zero delivers the solution $r_{D,3} = \alpha_K - \delta - 0.5 \cdot (1-z) \cdot \gamma \cdot \beta_K^2$. As the second derivative of $\sigma(r_D)$ is positive, this solution corresponds to a minimum of $\sigma(r_D)$ and lies between $r_{D,1}$ and $r_{D,2}$. Therefore, it also does not belong to I_1. Since $r_{D,3}$ is the only extreme point of the diffusion, we can conclude that the diffusion is monotonically decreasing and always positive on the interval $I_1 = (-\infty, r_{D,1})$. It would reach positive infinity if r_D tended to minus infinity. As a consequence, the diffusion grows quadratically for decreasing values of r_D.

This means that the short-term interest dynamics shows higher volatility when it starts at lower initial values.

In contrast to the quadratic diffusion, the drift is a cubic equation in r_D and has thus three roots. Although these roots could be calculated explicitly, the result would become too messy to have any use. Thus, we confine ourselves to qualitatively describing these roots. Due to the negative sign of parameter function α_3, the drift tends to plus infinity when r_D tends to minus infinity and vice versa. Since the drift is positive at $r_{D,2}$ (owing to (3.23)) and negative at $r_{D,1}$ (owing to (3.28)), we can conclude that there are at least three changes in the sign of the drift: at least one in each of the following intervals: $(-\infty, r_{D,1})$, $(r_{D,1}, r_{D,2})$ and $(r_{D,2}, \infty)$. Since a cubic polynomial has three roots, we can conclude that in each of the just mentioned intervals there must exist exactly one root of the drift. Calling the root within I_1 r_{II}, we face the following behavior of the drift within I_1: the drift is positive in $(-\infty, r_{II})$, zero at r_{II} and negative in $(r_{II}, r_{D,1})$. This means that the interest rate process tends to move around this root, being continuously perturbed through the non-vanishing diffusion term. Moreover, the drift can be shown to have a minimum at a point smaller than $r_{D,2}$ and a maximum at a point bigger than $r_{D,2}$. Whether this minimum is in I_1 or not depends on the particular parameter values.

In order to get a visual impression of the drift and diffusion terms, we plot them in the following graphics using as parameter values: $\alpha_K = 7.5\%$, $\beta_K = 5\%$, $\delta = 1.5\%$, $\gamma = 5$, $\rho = 10\%$, $\tau = 7\%$ and $z = 40\%$ [25]. The drift is depicted as the dashed curve, the diffusion is drawn as the solid curve and the vertical line stands for the right boundary of I_1, $r_{D,1}$. For this parameter constellation, the drift has its minimum at $r_D = 3.77\%$ and a root at $r_{II} = 2.21\%$. Between $r_{D,1} = 5.25\%$ and r_{II}, the drift is negative, left from r_{II} it becomes positive. At r_{II}, the process 'looses' its drift, so that its local behavior is just governed by the diffusion. These results imply that the short-term interest rate tends to

---

[25] We have chosen these parameter values in order to guarantee that the state space of the short-term interest rate becomes reasonable given empirical observations. Moreover, these parameter values do not violate the fiscal policy restrictions (3.23) and (3.28).

move around r_{II}. Such behavior is called 'mean-reverting' which is a very desirable feature that fits with empirical observation.

The diffusion is positive on the whole interval (-∞, 5.25 %) so that positive productivity shocks in the production function are transmitted into increasing short-term interest rates and vice versa. Since the diffusion depends quadratically on the short-term interest rate, we note that the 'amplifier effect' of a productivity shock on the short-term interest rate is hence level-dependent.

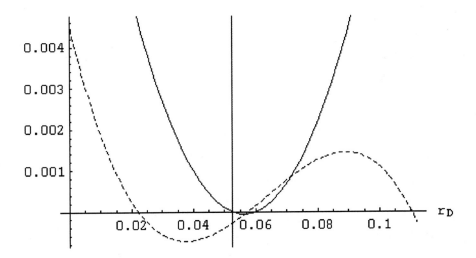

Figure 3.1: Drift and diffusion of the short-term interest rate dynamics.

Now, we can calculate the short run effects on r_D induced by changes in either the tax rate τ or the government expenditure ratio z:

(3.29)
$$\frac{d\sigma(r_D)}{d\tau} = 0$$
$$\frac{d\mu(r_D)}{d\tau} = -(\gamma - 1) \cdot \beta_K^2 + \frac{r_D - \alpha_K + \delta}{\gamma} < 0$$

(3.30)
$$\frac{d\sigma(r_D)}{dz} = -\beta_K \cdot (r_D - \alpha_K + \delta) > 0$$

(3.30)
$$\frac{d\mu(r_D)}{dz} = -(r_D - \alpha_K + \delta) \cdot \left(\alpha_K + \frac{r_D - \alpha_K + \delta}{\gamma} \right) < 0$$
$$\Leftrightarrow r_D < \alpha_K \cdot (1 - \gamma) - \delta$$

(3.29) shows that an increase in the tax rate has no influence on the diffusion of the interest rate process but diminishes its drift. This means that the short-term interest rate declines in the short run without a change in volatility. Both effects are not astonishing: since the tax rate does neither impact on the diffusion of the capital nor on the diffusion of the debt accumulation process, there is also no effect on the interest rate diffusion and thus on volatility. On the other hand, a rising tax rate increases the drift of the capital process and diminishes the drift of the debt process; the capital-debt ratio grows in the short run and reduces the interest rate via its drift as can be seen from the equilibrium condition (3.18).

The short run effects of a change in z are more complicated: first of all, an increase in z leads always to a rise in interest rate diffusion. This is not surprising since a higher government expenditure ratio results in a higher diffusion of primary government expenditure in the short run. This translates to increasing volatility of primary deficit, to a higher diffusion coefficient and hence to higher volatility of interest rates. In contrast to this unambiguous sign of the diffusion effect, the drift term effect may depend on the interest rate level as can be seen from (3.30). If $r_D < \alpha_K \cdot (1 - \gamma) - \delta$ holds, then this effect is always negative. For $r_D = \alpha_K \cdot (1 - \gamma) - \delta$, the effect becomes zero; if $r_D < \alpha_K \cdot (1 - \gamma) - \delta$ holds, the effect becomes positive. The only situation where the effect is unambiguously negative occurs for $\alpha_K \leq (1 - z) \cdot \beta_K^2$. The reason is that for this parameter constellation all interest rate values, that theoretically drive the drift term effect either to zero or positive values, are bigger than $r_{D,2}$. In the boundary behavior analysis, however, we have seen that, given the set of fiscal policy constraints (3.23), (3.27) and (3.28), bigger values than $r_{D,2}$ are never possible. Consequently, the validity of $\alpha_K \leq (1 - z) \cdot \beta_K^2$ alone guarantees a unique negative sign of the effect the government expenditure ratio has on the drift of the short-term interest rate. Since $\beta_K < \alpha_K < 1$ will usually prevail, we have to admit that

$\alpha_K \leq (1-z) \cdot \beta_K^2$ will almost never hold so that the non-uniqueness of the sign of this effect is the rule rather than the exception. What could be an economic explanation for such an ambiguous sign? Looking at the equilibrium short-term interest rate (3.18), we note that the short run effect of a change in z on the short-term interest rate is determined by the reaction of the capital wealth ratio. Since wealth does not change in the short run because z does not directly affect wealth (see (3.20)), this reaction is simply driven by the behavior of capital in response to a changing government expenditure ratio. The effect of z on K is, however, ambiguous since z reduces both drift and diffusion of K. Additionally, both drift and diffusion are dependent on the level of K. As a consequence, the sign of the short run effect on the interest rate drift is determined by the stochastic shock accompanying a change in z. The magnitude of this effect depends on the capital wealth ratio and hence on the interest rate level itself (via (3.18)).

Summarizing the transitional analysis, we saw that changes in the tax rate as well as in the government expenditure ratio affect the interest rate dynamics in the short run. This triggers completely different trajectories of the short-term interest rate, independent from whether the fiscal policy changes are temporary or permanent. To see this, we plot the difference between two simulated short-term interest rate trajectories in weekly frequency [26]. Figure 3.2 shows the differences between the benchmark and the second trajectory (the solid curve) as well as between the benchmark and the third trajectory (the dashed curve).

---

[26] For both trajectories an identical series of stochastic shocks is used. The necessary calculation is done by firstly discretizing the original SDE (3.24a) according to the so-called 'Euler-scheme' (see Kloeden/Platen (1992), Kloeden/Platen/Schurz (1994)) which yields a stochastic difference equation. We then simulate this equation week by week using the same parameter values as above together with a sample of standard normally distributed numbers [26] (one for each week with 254 weeks at total) and an initial value for $r_D = 4$ %. This delivers the 'benchmark' short-term interest rate trajectory. Then, we calculate a second trajectory with a temporary tax rate decrease which means that in the first time period the tax rate is reduced to 6 % and from then on again set to 7 %. Finally, we calculate a third trajectory with a permanent tax rate decrease happening in the first time period where the tax rate is permanently reduced to 6 %.

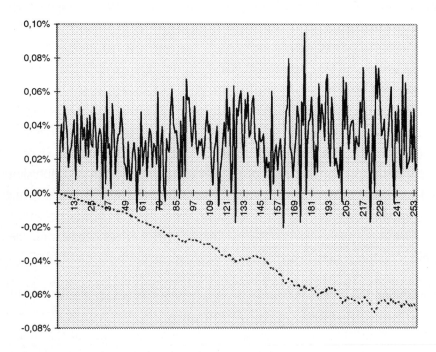

Figure 3.2: Temporary versus permanent tax rate decreases: absolute differences between short-term interest rate trajectories simulated on a weekly basis.

If neither a temporary nor a permanent change in the tax rate altered the interest rate dynamics (apart from the above-shown short-term effect on drift and diffusion) then we should see both differences fluctuating around the horizontal axis. However, the plot shows, at least for the parameter constellation chosen, that both the temporary as well as the permanent tax rate reduction lead to substantial changes of the interest rate level over the whole period. Moreover, the temporary tax rate reduction leads to a significant enhancement of the variance compared to the benchmark trajectory. This shows that the interest rate dynamics react very sensitively on fiscal policy, both in terms of level and variance. Understanding the short run effects is therefore necessary but not sufficient for a complete understanding of the dynamics. We now turn to the asymptotic analysis of the interest rate dynamics in reaction to fiscal policy changes.

We have already seen during the boundary behavior analysis that there is no fixed point towards which the stochastic dynamics of the short-term interest rate converges. Now we look for some 'weaker form' of an attracting set which characterizes long run behavior of the interest rate dynamics. This means that we examine whether the diffusion process is ergodic in the sense that the probability distribution associated with the diffusion process converges to a stationary (i.e. time-independent) probability distribution. This kind of convergence of the probability distribution instead of the process variable itself can be thought of a 'stochastic steady state'. This stands in contrast to deterministic dynamics, where a variable usually has to attain a fixed value so that we speak about a steady state. Proposition 3.5 shows now:

Proposition 3.5:

If a stationary probability distribution of the short-term interest rate dynamics exists, then it is characterized by the following time-independent probability density (3.31):

(3.31)

$$p(r^S) = m \cdot \left(\alpha_K - \delta - r^S\right)^{\omega} \cdot \left(\beta_1 \cdot (\alpha_K - \delta - r^S) - \beta_0\right)^{\xi} \cdot \exp\left(\dfrac{\dfrac{\psi}{r^S - \alpha_K + \delta} + \zeta}{\beta_0 + \beta_1 \cdot (r^S - \alpha_K + \delta)}\right)$$

with:

$$\omega = -2 + \frac{2 \cdot (\alpha_1 \cdot \beta_0 - 2 \cdot \alpha_0 \cdot \beta_1)}{\beta_0^3}$$

$$\xi = -\left(1 + \gamma + \frac{2 \cdot (\alpha_1 \cdot \beta_0 - 2 \cdot \alpha_0 \cdot \beta_1)}{\beta_0^3}\right)$$

$$\psi = -\frac{2 \cdot \alpha_0}{\beta_0^2} < 0$$

$$\zeta = \frac{2 \cdot (\alpha_3 \cdot \beta_0^3 - \beta_1 \cdot (\alpha_2 \cdot \beta_0^2 + \beta_1 \cdot (-\alpha_1 \cdot \beta_0 + \alpha_0 \cdot \beta_1)))}{\beta_0^2 \cdot \beta_1^2} > 0$$

Proof: see Appendix 3.7.

Before we start to examine this probability density, we must first prove that the stationary probability distribution characterized by (3.31) really exists. This is quite easy since we have already shown in the preceding section that our short-term interest rate process 'lives' on the interval $I_1 = (-\infty, r_{D,1})$ without ever reaching any of the two boundaries of I_1 given the fiscal policy constraints (3.23), (3.27) and (3.28). Making use of Theorem 1.17 of Skorohod (1989), we know that if the probability density given by (3.31) is integrable over I_1, then the stationary probability distribution exists. The probability distribution of the short-term interest rate converges to this ergodic distribution as time tends to infinity. In order to prove existence, one has just to prove that the stationary probability density is integrable. This is done in Appendix 3.8.

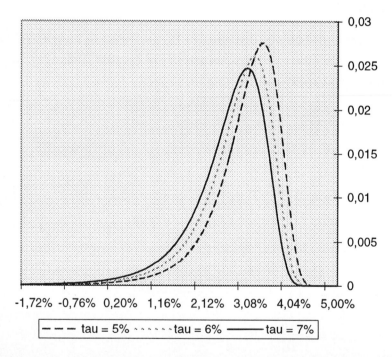

Figure 3.3: Stationary short-term interest rate probability densities for different τ-values.

As a consequence of Proposition 3.5 and Appendix 3.8, the long run behavior of the short-term interest rate dynamics is completely characterized by the probability density (3.31). Unfortunately, we are unable to further explore the properties of this stationary probability density analytically since the results would be just too lengthy to give them an economically reasonable meaning. Therefore, we numerically calculate and plot the stationary probability densities for different values of both the tax rate and the public expenditure ratio. As underlying parameter values, we choose again: $\alpha_K = 7.5\%$, $\beta_K = 5\%$, $\delta = 1.5\%$, $\gamma = 5$ and $\rho = 10\%$. Figure 3.3 shows three density curves associated with different tax rate values: $\tau = 7\%$ (left curve), 6% (middle curve) and 5% (right curve) as well as an identical public expenditure ratio of $z = 40\ \%$. Figure 3.4 also depicts three density curves, but for three different public expenditure ratios: $z = 35\%$ (left curve), 40% (middle curve) and 45% (right curve) with identical tax rate $\tau = 7\%$ for all three densities.

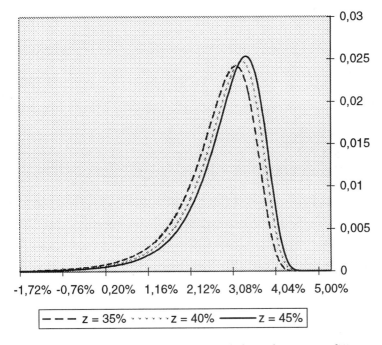

Figure 3.4: Stationary short-term interest rate probability densities for different z-values.

From a pure probabilistic standpoint, it is remarkable that all plotted density functions are single-peaked and hence possess a unique local maximum. This is due to the fact that our fiscal policy constraints (3.23) and (3.28) rule out two of three roots of the short-term interest rate's drift term so that these roots are not attainable for the short-term interest rate process. As a consequence, the stationary density function becomes unimodal instead of multimodal. Additionally, all distributions are characterized by the ranking: expected value < median < maximum likelihood value. Thus, the distributions are not symmetrical but left-skewed. Exact values of certain characteristic features (for example location parameters) of the different distributions are listed in Table 3.1 and 3.2 below.

Table 3.1: Some characteristic values of the density plotted in Figure 3.3.

	$\tau = 5\,\%$	$\tau = 6\,\%$	$\tau = 7\,\%$
Expected value	2.96 %	2.75 %	2.57 %
Median	3.11 %	2.91 %	2.74 %
Maximum likelihood value	3.35 %	3.17 %	3.01 %
Probability mass between $r^s = 2\%$ and $r^s = 4\%$	88.1 %	85.0 %	80.3 %
Stand. Deviation	0.76 %	0.81 %	0.86 %

The essential economic lesson seems to lie in the observation, that the higher τ or the smaller z, the more the probability density shifts to the left so that smaller interest rate values gain and higher interest rate values loose probability. Consequently, a probability shift to high interest rates in the long run is triggered either by high values of z or low values of τ or both. Additionally, densities for low values of τ or high values of z are 'slim' compared to the other densities, which can be seen by recognizing their lower standard deviation and their higher values measuring how much probability mass lies between interest rate values of 2 % and 4 %. Recalling the short run effects of fiscal policy on the interest rate dynamics given by (3.29) and (3.30), we note that the long run effects show quite much in the

Table 3.2: Some characteristic values of the density plotted in Figure 3.4.

	z = 35 %	z = 40 %	z = 45 %
Expected value	2.45 %	2.57 %	2.70 %
Median	2.62 %	2.74 %	2.87 %
Maximum likelihood value	2.89 %	3.01 %	3.13 %
Probability mass between $r^S = 2\%$ and $r^S = 4\%$	76.6 %	80.3 %	83.5 %
Stand. Deviation	0.88 %	0.86 %	0.84 %

same direction, at least as long as we only compare them with the short run drift effects. The diffusion effects in the short run, however, are different from the effects on the standard deviation (which may stand as a proxy for diffusion) in the long run. We cannot offer good intuition for this difference. One should be aware, however, that in the case of nonlinear, stochastic dynamics initially triggered effects do not have to be carried over into 'final' effects automatically. Such a feature holds only for linear, deterministic dynamics. Most important, since we are talking about probabilities only, the determination of clear-cut fiscal policy effects in the short- as well as long run does not imply that all interest rate trajectories reflect these effects in the same way. It is the specific series of shocks together with these effects that finally determines the whole trajectory of interest rates.

3.8 Short summary

By formulating and solving the households intertemporal stochastic optimization problem, we have derived the consumption function as well as the asset demands. Compared to Chapter 2, we note that the introduction of risk in form of stochastic shocks on productivity altered the qualitative results substantially. General market equilibrium is characterized by a nonlinear, two-dimensional system of stochastic differential equations in the state variables K and W. Using these equations, we derived the equilibrium interest rate dynamics. The resulting short-term interest rate process was seen to be an autonomous and strongly nonlinear stochastic differential equation. This is in contrast to all available results in finance literature so far but in accordance to what has been called for in recent finance literature (see, for example, Ait-Sahalia (1995)) in view of empirical evidence. We derived parameter constraints in terms of the two fiscal policy parameters so that the economy always has positive stocks of capital and remains viable for all time. These constraints were seen to ensure that the short-term interest rate moves within a bounded interval only. Finally, we derived and analyzed the short run and long run effects of fiscal policy changes on the interest rate dynamics. In order to do that, we first had to prove the existence of a stationary probability distribution toward which the interest rate dynamics converges and to calculate the respective density function. Our theoretical finding was that fiscal policy effects are qualitatively important. Numerical calculations showed that they are not only of marginal magnitude. The consequence for policy design is that repercussion effects on interest rates should not be neglected.

After setting up our basic model of a stochastic economy and having analyzed the dynamics of the short-term interest rate as well as the influence of fiscal policy on it, we will deepen the analysis of three main issues in the next chapters: the influence of fiscal policy on the term structure of interest rates (Chapter 4); the influence of fiscal policy on economic growth (Chapter 5) and the dynamics of public indebtedness in response to fiscal policy and financial market interaction (Chapter 6).

Appendix 3.1: Derivation of the optimal solution of the household problem (3.4)

Applying the method of dynamic programming to the optimization problem (3.4) yields the so-called Bellman equation:

$$(A3.1.1) \qquad 0 = \max_{C,K,F} E\left[e^{-\rho \cdot t} \cdot \frac{C^{1-\gamma}-1}{1-\gamma} \cdot dt + dV(W,t) \middle| \mathfrak{I}_t \right]$$

Intuitively spoken, (A3.1.1) means that an optimal policy at time t is characterized by generating an expected value for the 'flow of total utility' of zero over the infinitesimally small period [t, t+dt]. Flow of total utility consists of the instantaneous utility flow plus a change in the indirect utility function which measures all discounted future utility given the optimal choices. Applying Ito's Lemma in order to calculate the change of indirect utility, dV, delivers then [27]:

$$(A3.1.2)\, 0 = \max_{C,K,F} E\left[e^{-\rho \cdot t} \cdot \frac{C^{1-\gamma}-1}{1-\gamma} \cdot dt + V_t \cdot dt + V_W \cdot dW + \frac{1}{2} \cdot V_{WW} \cdot d\langle W \rangle \middle| \mathfrak{I}_t \right]$$

Plugging (3.3b) into (A3.1.2), making use of the fact that the quadratic variation of the semimartingale dW equals the square of its diffusion term (i.e. the term in front of dB in (3.3b)) times dt, taking expectations, dividing by dt and letting dt tend to zero yields the following so called Hamilton-Jacobi-Bellman (HJB) equation:

$$(A3.1.3)\, 0 = \max_{C,K,F} \left[\begin{array}{l} e^{-\rho \cdot t} \cdot \dfrac{C^{1-\gamma}-1}{1-\gamma} + V_t + \dfrac{1}{2} \cdot V_{WW} \cdot (K \cdot \sigma_K + F \cdot \sigma_F)^2 \\[2mm] + V_W \cdot \left(K \cdot (\mu_K - r_D) + F \cdot (\mu_F - r_D) + W \cdot (r_D - \tau) - C\right) \end{array} \right]$$

---

[27] In order to simplify notation, we omit the arguments of the indirect utility function V and denote its partial derivatives with subscripts. Likewise, we write in the subscripts t for t_0 and W for W_0.

114

Since the utility function is time-separable and the time horizon is infinite, it can be shown (compare Ingersoll (1987) p. 274 ff.) that the indirect utility function is also time-separable:

(A3.1.4)
$$V(W,t) = e^{-\rho t} \cdot Z(W) \Rightarrow V_t(W,t) = -\rho \cdot e^{-\rho t} \cdot Z(W)$$
$$\Rightarrow V_W(W,t) = e^{-\rho t} \cdot Z'(W) \Rightarrow V_{WW}(W,t) = e^{-\rho t} \cdot Z''(W)$$

Plugging the results of (A3.1.4) into (A3.1.3), we get [28]:

$$(A3.1.5)\ \rho \cdot Z = \max_{C,K,F} \left[\begin{array}{c} \dfrac{C^{1-\gamma}-1}{1-\gamma} + \dfrac{1}{2} \cdot Z''\cdot(K \cdot \sigma_K + F \cdot \sigma_F)^2 \\[2mm] + Z'\cdot\big(K \cdot (\mu_K - r_D) + F \cdot (\mu_F - r_D) + W \cdot (r_D - \tau) - C\big) \end{array} \right]$$

Using (A3.1.5) and assuming the existence of interior optima only, we are now able to derive the set of first-order optimality conditions:

(A3.1.6)
$$C^{-\gamma} - Z' = 0$$
$$Z'(\mu_K - r_D) + Z''\big(K \cdot \sigma_K + F \cdot \sigma_F\big) \cdot \sigma_K = 0$$
$$Z'(\mu_F - r_D) + Z''\big(K \cdot \sigma_K + F \cdot \sigma_F\big) \cdot \sigma_F = 0$$

Solving for the single control variables, these conditions yield:

(A3.1.7a - c)
$$C = Z'^{-\frac{1}{\gamma}}$$
$$K = -\frac{\sigma_F}{\sigma_K} \cdot F - \frac{Z'(\mu_K - r_D)}{Z'' \cdot \sigma_K^2}$$
$$\frac{\mu_F - r_D}{\sigma_F} = \frac{\mu_K - r_D}{\sigma_K}$$

For the optimality conditions (A3.1.7a - c) to characterize a maximum, the following sufficient optimality condition (second-order condition) has to hold:

---

[28] Note that we are omitting the argument of Z and denoting derivatives of Z with respect to W using primes.

$$
\text{(A3.1.8)} \qquad (C,K,F) \cdot H(C,K,F) \cdot \begin{pmatrix} C \\ K \\ F \end{pmatrix} < 0
$$

with:
$$
H(C,K,F) = \begin{pmatrix} -\gamma \cdot Z'^{\frac{1+\gamma}{\gamma}} & 0 & 0 \\ 0 & Z'' \cdot \sigma_K^2 & Z'' \cdot \sigma_K \cdot \sigma_F \\ 0 & Z'' \cdot \sigma_K \cdot \sigma_F & Z'' \cdot \sigma_F^2 \end{pmatrix}
$$

$H(C, n_2, n_3)$ is the Hesse-Matrix evaluated at the optimally chosen policies. (A3.1.8) says that the quadratic form associated with the vector of optimal control variables and the Hessian evaluated at the optimal control variables has to be strictly negative (see Takayama (1993) p. 37). The quadratic form is then negative definite and assures a maximum. Plugging the first-order conditions into the Hessian and then both into equation (A3.1.8), we eventually get:

$$
\text{(A3.1.9)} \qquad -\gamma \cdot Z'^{\frac{\gamma-1}{\gamma}} + \frac{Z'^2}{Z''} \cdot \frac{(\mu_K - r_D)^2}{\sigma_K^2} < 0
$$

Since at this point we know neither the solution for the indirect utility function nor the equilibrium values for r_D, μ_K and σ_K, we will return to the implications of this condition later on.

Another issue that we have not discussed so far concerns the transversality condition that must also hold in order to assure the existence of optimal household policies. In our model, the transversality condition is given by:

$$
\text{(A3.1.10)} \qquad \lim_{t_0 \to \infty} V(W_{t_0}, t_0) = 0
$$

This means that the indirect utility vanishes asymptotically for optimal choices when time tends to infinity. Since further examination of this condition is impossible without knowing the solution of the indirect utility function, we postpone the analysis until that solution is found. The proof that the transversality condition really holds is given in Corollary 3.1 in Section 7 using the results of Propositions 3.1 and 3.4.

Back to the optimality conditions characterizing consumption and asset demands in (A3.1.7a-c): inserting these conditions into the Hamilton-Jacobi-Bellman equation (A3.1.5) yields a nonlinear differential equation whose solution gives the indirect utility function:

(A3.1.11)
$$0 = \rho \cdot Z + \frac{1}{1-\gamma} - \frac{\gamma}{1-\gamma} \cdot (Z')^{\frac{\gamma-1}{\gamma}} - Z' \cdot (r_D - \tau) \cdot W$$
$$+ \frac{1}{2} \cdot \frac{(\mu_K - r_D)^2}{\sigma_K^2} \cdot \frac{Z'^2}{Z''}$$

As was shown by Merton (1971), the indirect utility function as the solution of a dynamic portfolio optimization problem is structurally equivalent to the functional form of the utility function when the utility function belongs to the class of HARA (**H**yperbolic **A**bsolute **R**isk **A**version) functions. Since our chosen utility function belongs to this class, it is obvious to guess the following functional form for the indirect utility function:

(A3.1.12)
$$Z = a_1 \cdot W^{a_2} + a_3$$
$$Z' = a_1 \cdot a_2 \cdot W^{a_2 - 1}$$
$$Z'' = a_1 \cdot a_2 \cdot (a_2 - 1) \cdot W^{a_2 - 2}$$

where a_1 to a_3 are coefficients that do not depend on the state variable W and will be determined according to the method of undetermined coefficients after having replaced Z and its derivatives in (A3.1.11) by use of the relations in (A3.1.12). Doing so yields:

(A3.1.13)
$$\frac{1}{1-\gamma} + \rho \cdot a_3 = -\rho \cdot a_1 \cdot W^{a_2} + \frac{\gamma}{1-\gamma} \cdot (a_1 \cdot a_2)^{\frac{\gamma-1}{\gamma}} \cdot W^{\frac{(a_2-1)\cdot(\gamma-1)}{\gamma}}$$
$$+ a_1 \cdot a_2 \cdot (r_D - \tau) \cdot W^{a_2} - \frac{1}{2} \cdot \frac{(\mu_K - r_D)^2}{\sigma_K^2} \cdot \frac{a_1 \cdot a_2}{a_2 - 1} \cdot W^{a_2}$$

Equation (A3.1.13) is only fulfilled if the left hand side, which is independent of W, and the right hand side, which depends on W, both equal zero. Setting $a_2 = 1 - \gamma$ so that the exponents of all W terms become equal, we can then factor out W to the power of $1 - \gamma$ on the right hand side of the equation and get the following two equations from (A3.1.13):

$$\frac{1}{1-\gamma} + \rho \cdot a_3 = 0$$

(A3.1.14)
$$\frac{\gamma}{1-\gamma} \cdot (a_1 \cdot (1-\gamma))^{\frac{\gamma-1}{\gamma}} - \rho \cdot a_1 + a_1 \cdot (1-\gamma) \cdot (r_D - \tau)$$

$$+ \frac{1}{2} \cdot \frac{(\mu_K - r_D)^2}{\sigma_K^2} \cdot \frac{a_1 \cdot (1-\gamma)}{\gamma} = 0$$

These two equations have the following solutions:

$$a_1 = -\frac{1}{\gamma - 1} \cdot \frac{1}{\left(\frac{\gamma-1}{\gamma} \cdot (r_D - \tau) + \frac{\rho}{\gamma} + \frac{1}{2} \cdot \frac{(\mu_K - r_D)^2}{\sigma_K^2} \cdot \frac{\gamma-1}{\gamma^2} \right)^\gamma} < 0$$

(A3.1.15)
$$\Leftrightarrow \frac{\gamma-1}{\gamma} \cdot (r_D - \tau) + \frac{\rho}{\gamma} + \frac{1}{2} \cdot \frac{(\mu_K - r_D)^2}{\sigma_K^2} \cdot \frac{\gamma-1}{\gamma^2} > 0$$

$$a_3 = \frac{1}{\rho \cdot (\gamma - 1)} > 0$$

From the optimality condition (A3.1.7a), we can derive that a_1 has to be negative since this is the only way that guarantees positive consumption given that wealth does not become negative. Thus, the denominator of a_1 has to be strictly positive. This also excludes singularity of a_1. Under which conditions is the denominator of a_1 strictly positive? The answer to this question will be provided by Proposition 3.1 in Section 5 after we have solved for the short-term interest rate in equilibrium. It will then also become clear that the parameter constraint developed in Proposition 3.1 does also guarantee the sufficient (i.e. second-order) condition for the optimum (A3.1.9).

The last point in this appendix concerns the calculation of the first and second-order conditions using the solution of the indirect utility function (A3.1.12) and (A3.1.15). The first order-conditions look as follows:

(A3.1.16 a) $\quad C = \left(\dfrac{\gamma - 1}{\gamma} \cdot (r_D - \tau) + \dfrac{\rho}{\gamma} + \dfrac{1}{2} \cdot \dfrac{(\mu_K - r_D)^2}{\sigma_K^2} \cdot \dfrac{\gamma - 1}{\gamma^2} \right) \cdot W$

(A3.1.16 b) $\quad K = \dfrac{\mu_K - r_D}{\sigma_K^2 \cdot \gamma} \cdot W - \dfrac{\sigma_F}{\sigma_K} \cdot F$

(A3.1.16 c) $\quad \dfrac{\mu_F - r_D}{\sigma_F} = \dfrac{\mu_K - r_D}{\sigma_K}$

The second-order condition yields the following sufficiency condition for a maximum of the household's problem:

(A3.1.17) $\dfrac{\gamma \cdot \left(\dfrac{\gamma - 1}{\gamma} \cdot (r_D - \tau) + \dfrac{\rho}{\gamma} + \dfrac{1}{2} \cdot \dfrac{(\mu_K - r_D)^2}{\sigma_K^2} \cdot \dfrac{\gamma - 1}{\gamma^2} \right) + \dfrac{(\mu_K - r_D)^2}{\gamma \cdot \sigma_K^2}}{\left(\dfrac{\gamma - 1}{\gamma} \cdot (r_D - \tau) + \dfrac{\rho}{\gamma} + \dfrac{1}{2} \cdot \dfrac{(\mu_K - r_D)^2}{\sigma_K^2} \cdot \dfrac{\gamma - 1}{\gamma^2} \right)^{\gamma} \cdot W^{\gamma - 1}} > 0$

Equations (A3.1.16a-c) and (A3.1.17) are equations (3.5a-c) and (3.6) in the text.

Appendix 3.2: Proof of Proposition 3.1

The first part of the proof consists of showing that the indirect utility function parameter a_1 is always negative. This ensures positive consumption given that private wealth remains also positive. In the second part, it is shown that the condition derived in the first part does also imply sufficiency of the household optimum.

Looking at equation (A3.1.15), we see that negativity of a_1 requires that the denominator of a_1, $h(r_D)$, must be strictly positive:

$$h(r_D) \equiv \frac{\gamma-1}{\gamma} \cdot (r_D - \tau) + \frac{\rho}{\gamma} + \frac{1}{2} \cdot \frac{(\alpha_K - \delta - r_D)^2}{\beta_K^2} \cdot \frac{\gamma-1}{\gamma^2} > 0$$

$$\Leftrightarrow \tau < r_D + \frac{\rho}{\gamma-1} + \frac{1}{2} \cdot \frac{(\alpha_K - \delta - r_D)^2}{\gamma \cdot \beta_K^2} \equiv x(r_D)$$

This last inequality imposes a constraint on tax policy given the other model parameters together with the short-term interest rate r_D. We note that, the lower $x(r_D)$, the stronger is the restriction on tax policy. Thus, we are looking for a global minimum of $x(r_D)$, r_D^*, because if the tax constraint holds for this minimum, it will, of course, hold for all the other possible values of the short-term interest rate r_D. The global minimum of $x(r_D)$ is calculated as follows:

$$x(r_D) = r_D + \frac{\rho}{\gamma-1} + \frac{1}{2} \cdot \frac{(\alpha_K - \delta - r_D)^2}{\gamma \cdot \beta_K^2}$$

$$\Rightarrow \begin{cases} x'(r_D) = 1 - \dfrac{\alpha_K - \delta - r_D}{\gamma \cdot \beta_K^2} \\[2mm] x''(r_D) = \dfrac{1}{\gamma \cdot \beta_K^2} > 0 \Rightarrow r_D^* \text{ Minimum !} \end{cases}$$

$$x'(r_D) = 0 \Rightarrow r_D^* = \alpha_K - \delta - \gamma \cdot \beta_K^2$$

We see that a global minimum exists. As we will notice later on, this minimum is reached exactly when the stock of public debt equals zero. Hence, the constraint in r_D^* is the strongest over the whole range of values for the short-term interest rate. Plugging the minimum value r_D^* into the tax constraint derived above, we finally get:

$$(3.23) \quad \tau < \alpha_K - \delta + \frac{\rho}{\gamma-1} - \frac{1}{2} \cdot \gamma \cdot \beta_K^2$$

For this constraint, the denominator of a_1 is strictly positive, rendering a_1 strictly negative. As a consequence, consumption gets strictly positive given that private wealth remains positive. It is interesting to note that (3.23) is the stochastic counterpart of the transversality condition (2.20) in Chapter 2. This can be seen by letting β_K tend to zero in (3.23). The difference, however, is that (3.23) was not derived by using the transversality condition (which has not been examined so far), but by requiring non-negativity of consumption. The implications of the transversality condition will be scrutinized later on. Thus, the first step of the proof is completed.

For the second part of the proof to be carried out, we need to recall the sufficiency condition (3.6). Making use of equations (3.17a-b), the non-negativity of private wealth and simplifying the resulting expression, this condition looks as follows:

$$
-\frac{\gamma \cdot \left(\dfrac{\gamma-1}{\gamma} \cdot (r_D - \tau) + \dfrac{\rho}{\gamma} + \dfrac{1}{2} \cdot \dfrac{(\alpha_K - \delta - r_D)^2}{\beta_K^2} \cdot \dfrac{\gamma-1}{\gamma} \right) + \dfrac{(\alpha_K - \delta - r_D)^2}{\beta_K^2 \cdot \gamma}}{\left(\dfrac{\gamma-1}{\gamma} \cdot (r_D - \tau) + \dfrac{\rho}{\gamma} + \dfrac{1}{2} \cdot \dfrac{(\alpha_K - \delta - r_D)^2}{\beta_K^2} \cdot \dfrac{\gamma-1}{\gamma} \right)^\gamma} \cdot W^{1-\gamma} < 0
$$

Using the definition for the denominator of a $_1$, $h(r_D)$, this expression becomes:

$$
-\frac{\gamma \cdot h(r_D) + \dfrac{(\alpha_K - \delta - r_D)^2}{\beta_K^2 \cdot \gamma}}{h(r_D)^\gamma} < 0
$$

Since $h(r_D)$ was shown to be positive when the tax constraint (3.23) holds and W was assumed to be always positive, it can easily be seen that the sufficiency inequality holds. This completes the whole proof.

Appendix 3.3: Proof of Corollary 3.1

As already noted in Appendix 3.1, the transversality condition is given by:

(A3.1.10) $\displaystyle \lim_{t_0 \to \infty} V(W_{t_0}, t_0) = 0$

This means that the indirect utility function has to approach zero when initial time t_0 tends to infinity. Using equations (A3.1.4), (A3.1.12) and (A3.1.15), transversality condition (A3.1.10) becomes:

(A3.3.1)

$$\lim_{t_0 \to \infty} \left(-\frac{e^{-\rho \cdot t_0}}{\gamma - 1} \cdot \frac{W^{1-\gamma}}{\left(\frac{\gamma - 1}{\gamma} \cdot (r_D - \tau) + \frac{\rho}{\gamma} + \frac{1}{2} \cdot \frac{(\alpha_K - \delta - r_D)^2}{\beta_K^2} \cdot \frac{\gamma - 1}{\gamma^2} \right)^\gamma} + \frac{e^{-\rho \cdot t_0}}{\rho \cdot (\gamma - 1)} \right) = 0$$

$$\Rightarrow \lim_{t_0 \to \infty} \left(-\frac{e^{-\rho \cdot t_0}}{\gamma - 1} \cdot \frac{1}{W^{\gamma - 1}} \cdot \frac{1}{\left(\frac{\gamma - 1}{\gamma} \cdot (r_D - \tau) + \frac{\rho}{\gamma} + \frac{1}{2} \cdot \frac{(\alpha_K - \delta - r_D)^2}{\beta_K^2} \cdot \frac{\gamma - 1}{\gamma^2} \right)^\gamma} \right) = 0$$

From the last equation in (A3.3.1), we can see that the first term tends to zero in the time limit. The transversality condition is fulfilled when the second and third term remain bounded from above. The limiting behavior of these crucial terms is, of course, only determined by their denominators since boundedness from above means that these denominators must not approach zero. Assuming that private wealth W does not approach zero, the denominator of the third term plays the decisive role. We note that it is identical to the function $h(r_D)$ appearing in Appendix 3.2. There, it was shown that under validity of (3.23), $h(r_D)$ is strictly positive. Thus, the third term of (A3.3.1) is bounded from above so that the product of the second and the third term of the last equation of (A3.3.1) is also bounded from above. Since the first term tends to zero, the whole limit tends to zero. Hence, the transversality condition holds. This completes the proof.

Appendix 3.4: Proof of Proposition 3.2

We will first state the scale function (3.26) appropriately so that we can use it for our right boundary $r_{D,2} = \alpha_K - \delta$:

122

$$(*) \qquad S[x_0, r_{D,2}) = \int_{x_0}^{r_{D,2}} \left(\begin{array}{l} (\alpha_K - \delta - x)^{-\frac{2 \cdot (\alpha_1 \cdot \beta_0 - 2 \cdot \alpha_0 \cdot \beta_1)}{\beta_0^3}} \\ \cdot \left((x - \alpha_K + \delta) \cdot \beta_1 + \beta_0 \right)^{-\frac{2 \cdot (\alpha_3 \cdot \beta_0^3 - \alpha_1 \cdot \beta_0 \cdot \beta_1^2 + 2 \cdot \alpha_0 \cdot \beta_1^3)}{\beta_0^3 \cdot \beta_1^2}} \\ \cdot e^{-2 \cdot \frac{\alpha_3 \cdot \beta_0^3 - \alpha_2 \cdot \beta_1 \cdot \beta_0^2 + \alpha_1 \cdot \beta_0 \cdot \beta_1^2 - \alpha_0 \cdot \beta_1^3}{\beta_0^2 \cdot \beta_1^2 \cdot (\beta_0 + (x - \alpha_K + \delta) \cdot \beta_1)}} \cdot e^{2 \cdot \frac{\alpha_0}{\beta_0^2 \cdot (x - \alpha_K + \delta)}} \end{array} \right) \cdot dx$$

First, we show that $S[x_0, r_{D,2}) < \infty$ holds. We know that integrability on any finite interval \qquad $[x_0, r_{D,2}]$ is always possible for any given integrand if and only if this integrand is smooth and has no singularities. Singularity means that the integrand must not tend to plus or minus infinity at each point within the integration interval. As one can see at first sight from (*), smoothness is certainly not the problem. Additionally, we recognize that over $[x_0, r_{D,2}]$ the only possibility of a singularity may occur at $r_{D,2} = \alpha_K - \delta$, namely when

$e^{2 \cdot \frac{\alpha_0}{\beta_0^2 \cdot (x - \alpha_K + \delta)}}$ tends to infinity for $x \to r_{D,2} = \alpha_K - \delta$. The critical question is thus: how does $\frac{2 \cdot \alpha_0}{\beta_0^2 \cdot (x - \alpha_K + \delta)}$ behave for $x \to r_{D,2} = \alpha_K - \delta$? Since x tends to $r_{D,2}$ from the left, the denominator of $\frac{2 \cdot \alpha_0}{\beta_0^2 \cdot (x - \alpha_K + \delta)}$ is negative tending to zero. Since the numerator of $\frac{2 \cdot \alpha_0}{\beta_0^2 \cdot (x - \alpha_K + \delta)}$ is positive due to the tax rate constraint (3.23), $\frac{2 \cdot \alpha_0}{\beta_0^2 \cdot (x - \alpha_K + \delta)}$ tends to minus infinity for $x \to r_{D,2} = \alpha_K - \delta$. Thus, $e^{2 \cdot \frac{\alpha_0}{\beta_0^2 \cdot (x - \alpha_K + \delta)}}$ tends to zero. Although the first term of (*) could still tend to infinity for $x \to r_{D,2} = \alpha_K - \delta$, L'Hospital's rule tells us that the integrand in (*) remains bounded for $x \to r_{D,2} = \alpha_K - \delta$. Hence, we have shown that at any point within $[x_0, r_{D,2}]$, the integrand is bounded from above and positive, thus rendering $S[x_0, r_{D,2}) < \infty$. $r_{D,2}$ is hence attracting and the proof is complete.

Appendix 3.5: Proof of Proposition 3.3

Again, we first have to state the scale function (3.26) appropriately so that we can use it for the right boundary $r_{D,1} = \alpha_K - \delta - (1 - z) \cdot \gamma \cdot \beta_K^2$:

$$(**) \quad S[x_0, r_{D,1}] = \int_{x_0}^{r_{D,1}} \left(\begin{array}{c} (\alpha_K - \delta - x)^{-\frac{2\cdot(\alpha_1\cdot\beta_0 - 2\cdot\alpha_0\cdot\beta_1)}{\beta_0^3}} \\ \cdot ((\alpha_K - \delta - x)\cdot\beta_1 - \beta_0)^{-\frac{2\cdot(\alpha_3\cdot\beta_0^3 - \alpha_1\cdot\beta_0\cdot\beta_1^2 + 2\cdot\alpha_0\cdot\beta_1^3)}{\beta_0^3\cdot\beta_1^2}} \\ \cdot e^{-2\cdot\frac{\alpha_3\cdot\beta_0^3 - \alpha_2\cdot\beta_1\cdot\beta_0^2 + \alpha_1\cdot\beta_0\cdot\beta_1^2 - \alpha_0\cdot\beta_1^3}{\beta_0^2\cdot\beta_1^2\cdot(\beta_0 + (x - \alpha_K + \delta)\cdot\beta_1)}} \cdot e^{2\cdot\frac{\alpha_0}{\beta_0^2\cdot(x - \alpha_K + \delta)}} \end{array} \right) \cdot dx$$

Now, we have to show that $S[x_0, r_{D,1}] < \infty$ does not hold. In order to show this, we just have to verify that there is at least one singularity within $[x_0, r_{D,1}]$, i.e. one point at which the integrand of (**) is unbounded. We recognize that over $[x_0, r_{D,1}]$, the only possibility of a singularity may occur at $r_{D,1} = \alpha_K - \delta - (1 - z)\cdot\gamma\cdot\beta_K^2$, namely when $e^{-2\cdot\frac{\alpha_3\cdot\beta_0^3 - \alpha_2\cdot\beta_1\cdot\beta_0^2 + \alpha_1\cdot\beta_0\cdot\beta_1^2 - \alpha_0\cdot\beta_1^3}{\beta_0^2\cdot\beta_1^2\cdot(\beta_0 + (x - \alpha_K + \delta)\cdot\beta_1)}}$ tends to infinity for $x \to r_{D,1} = \alpha_K - \delta - (1 - z)\cdot\gamma\cdot\beta_K^2$. The critical question is thus:

how does $-2\cdot\frac{\alpha_3\cdot\beta_0^3 - \alpha_2\cdot\beta_1\cdot\beta_0^2 + \alpha_1\cdot\beta_0\cdot\beta_1^2 - \alpha_0\cdot\beta_1^3}{\beta_0^2\cdot\beta_1^2\cdot(\beta_0 + (x - \alpha_K + \delta)\cdot\beta_1)}$ behave for

$x \to r_{D,1} = \alpha_K - \delta - (1 - z)\cdot\gamma\cdot\beta_K^2$? Since x tends to $r_{D,1}$ from the left, the

denominator of $-2\cdot\frac{\alpha_3\cdot\beta_0^3 - \alpha_2\cdot\beta_1\cdot\beta_0^2 + \alpha_1\cdot\beta_0\cdot\beta_1^2 - \alpha_0\cdot\beta_1^3}{\beta_0^2\cdot\beta_1^2\cdot(\beta_0 + (x - \alpha_K + \delta)\cdot\beta_1)}$ is negatively tending to zero. Since

the numerator of $-2\cdot\frac{\alpha_3\cdot\beta_0^3 - \alpha_2\cdot\beta_1\cdot\beta_0^2 + \alpha_1\cdot\beta_0\cdot\beta_1^2 - \alpha_0\cdot\beta_1^3}{\beta_0^2\cdot\beta_1^2\cdot(\beta_0 + (x - \alpha_K + \delta)\cdot\beta_1)}$ is positive if (3.28) holds, the

whole fraction $-2\cdot\frac{\alpha_3\cdot\beta_0^3 - \alpha_2\cdot\beta_1\cdot\beta_0^2 + \alpha_1\cdot\beta_0\cdot\beta_1^2 - \alpha_0\cdot\beta_1^3}{\beta_0^2\cdot\beta_1^2\cdot(\beta_0 + (x - \alpha_K + \delta)\cdot\beta_1)}$ tends to plus infinity [29] for

$x \to r_{D,1} = \alpha_K - \delta - (1 - z)\cdot\gamma\cdot\beta_K^2$. Thus, $e^{-2\cdot\frac{\alpha_3\cdot\beta_0^3 - \alpha_2\cdot\beta_1\cdot\beta_0^2 + \alpha_1\cdot\beta_0\cdot\beta_1^2 - \alpha_0\cdot\beta_1^3}{\beta_0^2\cdot\beta_1^2\cdot(\beta_0 + (x - \alpha_K + \delta)\cdot\beta_1)}}$ tends to

plus infinity. Although the second term of the integrand in (**) could still tend to zero for $x \to r_{D,2} = \alpha_K - \delta$, L'Hospital's rule tells us that the integrand in (**) becomes unbounded for $x \to r_{D,2} = \alpha_K - \delta$. Thus, $S[x_0, r_{D,2}) = \infty$ holds and $r_{D,1}$ is hence not attracting. This completes the proof of Proposition 3.3.

---

[29] The fraction itself would tend to minus infinity but since it has to be multiplied with -2, it finally tends to plus infinity.

124

Appendix 3.6: Proof of Proposition 3.4

As in the two appendices before, we first state the scale function (3.26) appropriately so that we can use it for the left boundary $r_D = -\infty$:

$$(***)\quad S(-\infty, x_0] = \int_{-\infty}^{x_0} \left(\begin{array}{l} (\alpha_K - \delta - x)^{-\frac{2\cdot(\alpha_1\cdot\beta_0 - 2\cdot\alpha_0\cdot\beta_1)}{\beta_0^3}} \\ \cdot ((\alpha_K - \delta - x)\cdot\beta_1 - \beta_0)^{-\frac{2\cdot(\alpha_3\cdot\beta_0^3 - \alpha_1\cdot\beta_0\cdot\beta_1^2 + 2\cdot\alpha_0\cdot\beta_1^3)}{\beta_0^3\cdot\beta_1^2}} \\ \cdot e^{-2\cdot\frac{\alpha_3\cdot\beta_0^3 - \alpha_2\cdot\beta_1\cdot\beta_0^2 + \alpha_1\cdot\beta_0\cdot\beta_1^2 - \alpha_0\cdot\beta_1^3}{\beta_0^2\cdot\beta_1^2\cdot(\beta_0+(x-\alpha_K+\delta)\cdot\beta_1)}} \cdot e^{2\cdot\frac{\alpha_0}{\beta_0^2\cdot(x-\alpha_K+\delta)}} \end{array} \right) \cdot dx$$

The strategy for the proof is similar to the one before in Proposition 3.3: here, we will show that at $r_D = -\infty$, the integrand of (***) tends to infinity thus rendering $S(-\infty, x_0]$ unbounded. This, in turn, implies that $r_D = -\infty$ is non-attracting. Note that both arguments in the exponential functions in the integrand of (***) tend to zero if r_D (i.e. x) tends to minus infinity. This implies that both exponents tend to 1 and we have thus just to look at the product of the first two terms in the integrand. These terms can be written as follows:

$$f(x) = (\alpha_K - \delta - x)^{-\frac{2\cdot(\alpha_1\cdot\beta_0 - 2\cdot\alpha_0\cdot\beta_1)}{\beta_0^3}} \cdot ((\alpha_K - \delta - x)\cdot\beta_1 - \beta_0)^{-\frac{2\cdot(\alpha_3\cdot\beta_0^3 - \alpha_1\cdot\beta_0\cdot\beta_1^2 + 2\cdot\alpha_0\cdot\beta_1^3)}{\beta_0^3\cdot\beta_1^2}}$$

$$\Rightarrow f(x) = (\alpha_K - \delta - x)^{-\frac{2\cdot(\alpha_1\cdot\beta_0\cdot\beta_1^2 - 2\cdot\alpha_0\cdot\beta_1^3)}{\beta_0^3\cdot\beta_1^2}} \cdot ((\alpha_K - \delta - x)\cdot\beta_1 - \beta_0)^{\frac{2\cdot(\alpha_1\cdot\beta_0\cdot\beta_1^2 - 2\cdot\alpha_0\cdot\beta_1^3)}{\beta_0^3\cdot\beta_1^2}}$$

$$\cdot ((\alpha_K - \delta - x)\cdot\beta_1 - \beta_0)^{-\frac{2\cdot\alpha_3\cdot\beta_0^3}{\beta_0^3\cdot\beta_1^2}}$$

$$\Rightarrow f(x) = \left(\frac{(\alpha_K - \delta - x)\cdot\beta_1 - \beta_0}{\alpha_K - \delta - x}\right)^{\frac{2\cdot(\alpha_1\cdot\beta_0\cdot\beta_1^2 - 2\cdot\alpha_0\cdot\beta_1^3)}{\beta_0^3\cdot\beta_1^2}} \cdot ((\alpha_K - \delta - x)\cdot\beta_1 - \beta_0)^{-\frac{2\cdot\alpha_3}{\beta_1^2}}$$

In order to simplify notation, we introduce $y = \alpha_K - \delta - x$. Sending x to minus infinity implies that y is being sent to plus infinity. Then we obtain:

$$(****) \quad f(y) = \left(\frac{y \cdot \beta_1 - \beta_0}{y} \right)^{\frac{2 \cdot (\alpha_1 \cdot \beta_0 \cdot \beta_1^2 - 2 \cdot \alpha_0 \cdot \beta_1^3)}{\beta_0^3 \cdot \beta_1^2}} \cdot (y \cdot \beta_1 - \beta_0)^{-\frac{2 \cdot \alpha_3}{\beta_1^2}}$$

$$\Rightarrow f(y) = \left(\beta_1 - \frac{\beta_0}{y} \right)^{\frac{2 \cdot (\alpha_1 \cdot \beta_0 \cdot \beta_1^2 - 2 \cdot \alpha_0 \cdot \beta_1^3)}{\beta_0^3 \cdot \beta_1^2}} \cdot (y \cdot \beta_1 - \beta_0)^{-\frac{2 \cdot \alpha_3}{\beta_1^2}}$$

Considering the limit $y \to \infty$, we note that the first term of $f(y)$ tends to a fixed number. The second term, however, is unbounded in the limit if and only if the argument of the power, $-\frac{2 \cdot \alpha_3}{\beta_1^2}$, is positive. Since α_3 is negative due to (3.24b), the argument is indeed positive and renders the second term of $f(y)$ and also $f(y)$ equal to infinity. Therefore, $S(-\infty, x_0]$ becomes infinite, too, and $r_D = -\infty$ is thus non-attracting. This completes the proof.

Appendix 3.7: Calculation of the stationary probability density associated with the short-term interest rate process:

The evolution of a diffusion process like the short-term interest rate in our model can be described in two ways. The first consists of describing the evolution of the process variable itself by means of a stochastic differential equation (SDE). This is what we did so far. The second way is to specify the transitional probability distribution associated with the diffusion process. The transitional probability distribution is characterized as a conditional probability density that indicates the probability p for the process attaining a value of, say, y at time t when it started at a value of y_0 at time 0. It can then be shown (see, for example, Karlin/Taylor (1981), Gardiner (1983), Sobczyk (1991) or Risken (1996)) that this conditional probability density p has to satisfy a certain partial differential equation (PDE) called 'Kolmogoroff forward equation' or 'Fokker-Planck equation'. In order to show the connection between a SDE and its associated PDE, we consider the following SDE for an arbitrary diffusion process Y[30]:

---

[30] 'Y' here denotes an arbitrary diffusion process and has nothing to do with output Y! Additionally, we distinguish the process Y from values y out of the state space of Y in order not to confuse the process with its values.

(A3.7.1) $dY = \mu(Y) \cdot dt + \sigma(Y) \cdot dB$

The conditional probability density p that is associated with the evolution of Y is then described by the Fokker-Planck equation:

$$(A3.7.2a) \quad \frac{\partial p(y, t|y_0, 0)}{\partial t} = \frac{1}{2} \cdot \frac{\partial^2}{\partial y^2} \left(\sigma(y)^2 \cdot p(y, t|y_0, 0) \right) - \frac{\partial}{\partial y} \left(\mu(y) \cdot p(y, t|y_0, 0) \right)$$

with the initial condition[31]:

(A3.7.2b) $p(y, 0|y_0, 0) = \delta(y - y_0)$

Here, 'δ' stands for the Dirac-Delta function. It equals one if its argument is zero (i.e. y equals y_0) and zero otherwise. The meaning of this initial condition is that, when time t equals zero, the whole 'probability mass' of the process Y is concentrated at its initial value, y_0. The solution of (A3.7.2a-b) then yields the unique conditional probability density of the process Y.

Given (A3.7.2a-b), we see that p(...) may reach a stationary state when it no longer depends on time t, i.e. when time t tends to infinity. Denoting the stationary probability density with $p(r^s)$, we then have to solve an ordinary instead of a partial differential equation:

$$(A3.7.3) \quad \frac{1}{2} \cdot \frac{d^2}{d(y^s)^2} \left(\sigma(y^s)^2 \cdot p(r^s) \right) = \frac{d}{dy^s} \left(\mu(y^s) \cdot p(r^s) \right)$$

Equation (A3.7.3) can now be integrated twice. This yields the following solution (by setting the first integration constant to zero without loss of generality):

$$(A3.7.4) \quad p(y^s) = \frac{m}{\sigma(y^s)^2} \cdot \exp\left(2 \cdot \int_\Theta \frac{\mu(y^s)}{\sigma(y^s)^2} \cdot dy^s \right)$$

---

[31] p(y, t|y_0, 0) should be read and understood as follows: the probability that the process Y attains a value of y at time t when it started with a value of y_0 at initial time 0.

Here, 'Θ' denotes the state space of y^S over which the integration is carried out. 'm' is a normalization constant so that $p(y^S)$ 'integrates' over Θ to 1:

(A3.7.5) $\qquad \int_\Theta p(y^S) \cdot dy^S = 1$

When we now apply (A3.7.4) to the dynamics of the short-term interest rate r_D, (3.24a-b), we get the following stationary probability density[32]:

(A3.7.6a)

$$p(r^S) = m \cdot (\alpha_K - \delta - r^S)^\omega \cdot \left(\beta_1 \cdot (\alpha_K - \delta - r^S) - \beta_0\right)^\xi \cdot \exp\left(\dfrac{\dfrac{\psi}{r^S - \alpha_K + \delta} +}{\dfrac{\zeta}{\beta_0 + \beta_1 \cdot (r^S - \alpha_K + \delta)}}\right)$$

with:

(A3.7.6b)

$$\omega = -2 + \frac{2 \cdot (\alpha_1 \cdot \beta_0 - 2 \cdot \alpha_0 \cdot \beta_1)}{\beta_0^3}$$

$$\xi = -1 - \gamma - \frac{2 \cdot (\alpha_1 \cdot \beta_0 - 2 \cdot \alpha_0 \cdot \beta_1)}{\beta_0^3}$$

$$\psi = -\frac{2 \cdot \alpha_0}{\beta_0^2} < 0$$

$$\zeta = \frac{2 \cdot (\alpha_3 \cdot \beta_0^3 - \beta_1 \cdot (\alpha_2 \cdot \beta_0^2 + \beta_1 \cdot (-\alpha_1 \cdot \beta_0 + \alpha_0 \cdot \beta_1)))}{\beta_0^2 \cdot \beta_1^2} > 0$$

'm' is calculated according to (A3.7.5):

(A3.7.6c) $\qquad \int_{-\infty}^{r_{D,1}} p(r^S) \cdot dr^S = 1$

with $r_{D,1} = \alpha_K - \delta - (1 - z) \cdot \gamma \cdot \beta_K^2$.

---

[32] Note that the signs of ψ and ζ are determined by the definitions (3.24b) and the government expenditure ratio constraint (3.28).

Since (A3.7.6a-c) are obviously quite complicated, we cannot compute the integral in (A3.7.6c) analytically so that the value of m has to be found numerically for given parameter constellations.

Appendix 3.8: Proof that the stationary probability density (3.31) is integrable:

The integrability condition for (3.31) is (see (A3.7.6c)):

(A3.8.1)
$$\int_{-\infty}^{\alpha_K - \delta - \frac{\beta_0}{\beta_1}} \left\{ \begin{array}{l} \left(\alpha_K - \delta - r^S\right)^\omega \cdot \left(\beta_1 \cdot (\alpha_K - \delta - r^S) - \beta_0\right)^\xi \\ \cdot \exp\left(\dfrac{\psi}{r^S - \alpha_K + \delta} + \dfrac{\zeta}{\beta_0 + \beta_1 \cdot (r^S - \alpha_K + \delta)}\right) \end{array} \right\} \cdot dr^S < \infty$$

How can one show integrability, especially when the integral cannot be evaluated explicitly as is the case here? We first substitute for the integration variable in order to transform the original, infinite integration area into a finite one. The resulting integral can then be shown to be integrable if and only if no singularity occurs. Considering the substitution:

(A3.8.2)
$$\alpha_K - \delta - r^S = \frac{1}{x}$$

Plugging it into (A3.8.1), then yields the integral:

(A3.8.3)
$$\int_0^{\frac{\beta_1}{\beta_0}} x^{-\omega} \cdot \left(\frac{\beta_1}{x} - \beta_0\right)^\xi \cdot \exp\left(-\psi \cdot x + \frac{\zeta \cdot x}{\beta_0 \cdot x - \beta_1}\right) \cdot \frac{dx}{x^2}$$

$$= \int_0^{\frac{\beta_1}{\beta_0}} x^{-(\omega + 2 + \xi)} \cdot \left(\beta_1 - \beta_0 \cdot x\right)^\xi \cdot \exp\left(-\psi \cdot x - \frac{\zeta \cdot x}{\beta_1 - \beta_0 \cdot x}\right) \cdot dx$$

(A3.8.3)
$$= \int_0^{\frac{\beta_1}{\beta_0}} x^{1 + \gamma} \cdot \left(\beta_1 - \beta_0 \cdot x\right)^\xi \cdot \exp\left(-\psi \cdot x - \frac{\zeta \cdot x}{\beta_1 - \beta_0 \cdot x}\right) \cdot dx$$

The last line of (A3.8.3) shows that the only potential singularity within $[0, \beta_1/\beta_0]$ may occur at the upper boundary $x = \beta_1/\beta_0$ for then the term „0^ξ exp($-\infty$)" remains. If ξ is nonnegative, then this term will be zero and the singularity vanishes. But what if ξ is negative? In this case '0/0' remains. But since we know that the exponential of minus infinity tends 'much faster' to zero than any polynomial x^a for $x = 0$ and positive 'a', we conclude that the integrand at $x = \beta_1/\beta_0$ remains bounded. Thus, the integrand within (A3.8.3) remains bounded at any point over the integration area. The integral must be bounded, too. As a result, the stationary probability distribution exists and the probability distribution associated with our short-term interest rate dynamics converges to this 'steady-state' ergodic distribution.

4 Term structure of interest rates and fiscal policy

4.1 Introduction

As already mentioned in great detail in Chapter 1, the whole mathematical finance literature dealing with the term structure of interest rates has abstracted from studying the influence of fiscal policy on the term structure. Usually, arbitrary stochastic dynamics for a given set of 'factors' [1] driving the term structure were introduced by postulating specific forms of diffusion processes representing the evolution of these factors. As a consequence of these ad-hoc approaches, the influence of fiscal policy was either completely neglected or introduced in an ad-hoc way, at best [2]. One can, of course, argue that the influence of fiscal policy is already integrated in the factor dynamics used, namely in the way the dynamics are parametrized. This implies that these parameters are seemingly policy invariant. When one argues that the influence of fiscal policy is already embedded in such arbitrary parameters with almost no economic meaning, then estimating these models is subject to criticism similar to the well-known 'Lucas Critique' [3]. As the respective introductory remarks in Chapter 1 should have made clear, we think that fiscal policy does matter for term structure considerations. We will now discuss the term structure of interest rate and the influence of fiscal policy in the macroeconomic setting laid down in the previous chapter.

The structure of this chapter is as follows: before embarking on analyzing the influence of fiscal policy on the term structure, we need to derive a bond price equation whose solution characterizes the term structure of interest rates. This is done in Section 2. We use the nonlinear diffusion process that describes the stochastic evolution of the short-term interest rate developed in

---

[1] The choice of how many and which factors to use is usually based on an analysis of available market data using a statistical procedure called 'Principal Component Analysis'. See f.e. Campbell/Lo/MacKinlay (1997), Chapter 6.4, or, for an application, Bühler (1996).

[2] As examples for such an ad-hoc integration compare Babbs/Webber (1996) or Tice/Webber (1997).

[3] See Lucas (1976).

the preceding chapter and combine it with the equilibrium equation of the private bond market. Then, we will show that doing so leads to a parabolic partial differential equation of second order with polynomial coefficients. The solution to this equation describes the price of a zero-coupon private bond.

Solving this equation is a highly complicated task. We show that the solution to the bond pricing equation can be represented using a classical tool in mathematical finance: the Feynman-Kac formula. Since evaluating this formula analytically requires knowledge of the probability distribution that renders the bond price a local martingale, it is not useful in getting a closed-form solution for our problem. We further argue that all other ways to obtain an analytical closed-form solution are likewise in vain. However, it is necessary to have a tractable formula when one wants to analytically study the impact of fiscal policy on the term structure. We therefore discuss some standard approximation approaches and justify the one we finally choose.

In Section 3, we will introduce our approximation scheme which is based on the linearization of our bond price valuation equation in such a way that we obtain a solution similar to the one calculated by Cox/Ingersoll/Ross (1985b). The arbitrary parameters introduced by the linearization will subsequently be determined by a so-called projection method. Using this solution, we then derive the yield curve and study the different characteristic term structure slopes with regard to their dependency on model parameters. We will carry out some comparative statics for this approximate solution by working out the conditions under which unanticipated changes concerning fiscal policy [4] change the term structure slope and thus the intertemporal conditions under which private households can lend and borrow. Since the calculations involved are still complicated, we have to concentrate on tax rate changes only. In order to illustrate the comparative statics results for the approximation scheme and to see the influence of changes in the public expenditure ratio, we will numerically examine these issues for a specific set of parameter values in Section 4. Section 5 summarizes the chapter.

---

[4] It should be noted that the model in its present form does not lend itself to an analysis what impact anticipated fiscal policy changes may have on the term structure. This would require a different set-up of the household's decision problem.

4.2 Derivation and discussion of the bond price valuation equation

In order to study the effects of changing fiscal policy (via changes in z and τ) on the term structure of interest rates, we first have to derive the term structure relationship. As already noted briefly in Section 3.3, the stock of private bonds the representative household holds sums up to zero since private bonds are by definition only traded between households. Therefore, they are said to be in 'net-zero-supply'. Recalling the third optimality condition (3.5c) and combining it with the equilibrium conditions (3.17a-b) delivers the equilibrium valuation equation for private bonds:

$$(4.1a) \qquad \frac{\mu_F - r_D}{\sigma_F} = \frac{\alpha_K - \delta - r_D}{\beta_K}$$

Such an equilibrium condition is standard in the finance literature (see for example Vasicek (1977)). It states that in equilibrium the price for one unit of risk of a private bond (the left side of (4.1)) has to equal the corresponding price for one unit of risk of capital (the right side of (4.1)). The price of risk is measured by the excess return of private bonds (capital) over the locally risk-free rate of return, $\mu_F - r_D$ ($\alpha_K - \delta - r_D$), per standard deviation of the return on bonds (capital), σ_F (β_K).

Using (4.1), we will now derive the price of a zero-coupon-bond and subsequently the term structure curve of the interest rates. For this purpose, we need to know μ_F and σ_F which were introduced in (3.2c). Plugging the short-term interest rate dynamics (3.24a) into (3.2c), we obtain the following expressions for expected value and standard deviation of the rate of return on the private bond:

$$(4.1b) \qquad \begin{aligned} \mu_F =& \left(\begin{array}{l} \alpha_0 + \alpha_1 \cdot (r_D - \alpha_K + \delta) + \alpha_2 \cdot (r_D - \alpha_K + \delta)^2 \\ + \alpha_3 \cdot (r_D - \alpha_K + \delta)^3 \end{array} \right) \cdot \frac{P_{r_D}}{P} \\ &+ \frac{1}{2} \cdot \left(\beta_0 + \beta_1 \cdot (r_D - \alpha_K + \delta) \right)^2 \cdot (r_D - \alpha_K + \delta)^2 \cdot \frac{P_{r_D r_D}}{P} + \frac{P_t}{P} \end{aligned}$$

$$(4.1b) \quad \sigma_F = \left(\beta_0 + \beta_1 \cdot (r_D - \alpha_K + \delta)\right) \cdot (r_D - \alpha_K + \delta) \cdot \frac{P_{r_D}}{P}$$

Note that we use P instead of P_F to denote the price of private bonds in (4.1b). Throughout this chapter, subscripts are used to denote partial derivatives of P with respect to the variable in the subscript.

The equilibrium valuation equation (4.1a) together with equations (4.1b) yield, after some algebraic manipulations, the following valuation equation for the price of private bonds $P(r_D,t)$:

$$(4.2a) \quad \begin{pmatrix} \alpha_0 + \alpha_1 \cdot (r_D - \alpha_K + \delta) + (\alpha_2 + \dfrac{\beta_0}{\beta_K}) \cdot (r_D - \alpha_K + \delta)^2 \\[2mm] + (\alpha_3 + \dfrac{\beta_1}{\beta_K}) \cdot (r_D - \alpha_K + \delta)^3 \end{pmatrix} \cdot P_{r_D}$$
$$+ \frac{1}{2} \cdot \left(\beta_0 + \beta_1 \cdot (r_D - \alpha_K + \delta)\right)^2 \cdot (r_D - \alpha_K + \delta)^2 \cdot P_{r_D r_D} + P_t - r_D \cdot P = 0$$

with terminal condition:

$$(4.2b) \quad P(r_D, T) = 1$$

(4.2b) says that at maturity date T, each private bond pays off 1 unit of the numeraire good for sure.

The valuation equation (4.2a-b) is an example of a parabolic partial differential equation (PDE) of second order [5]. Its solution yields the price of private bonds depending on the short-term interest rate r_D, time t and all model parameters inherent in the coefficient functions α_0 - α_3 and β_0 - β_1.

If we introduce 'time to maturity' $\hat{t} = T - t$ instead of 'time' t as the new second independent variable, then the former terminal condition (4.2b) will turn into an initial condition $P(r_D, 0) = 1$. We now face a so-called 'Cauchy-problem', a special problem of the class of the initial value problems (IVP):

---

[5] For a classification of second order partial differential equations see Vvedensky (1993).

$$(4.2c) \quad \begin{pmatrix} \alpha_0 + \alpha_1 \cdot (r_D - \alpha_K + \delta) + (\alpha_2 + \dfrac{\beta_0}{\beta_K}) \cdot (r_D - \alpha_K + \delta)^2 \\[2mm] + (\alpha_3 + \dfrac{\beta_1}{\beta_K}) \cdot (r_D - \alpha_K + \delta)^3 \end{pmatrix} \cdot P_{r_D}$$
$$+ \frac{1}{2} \cdot \left(\beta_0 + \beta_1 \cdot (r_D - \alpha_K + \delta) \right)^2 \cdot (r_D - \alpha_K + \delta)^2 \cdot P_{r_D r_D} - r_D \cdot P = P_t$$

with initial condition:

$$(4.2d) \quad P(r_D, 0) = 1$$

The PDEs (4.2a-b) or (4.2c-d) belong to a class of differential equations that is well-known to financial economists since the classical paper on option valuation by Black/Scholes (1973). But whereas the Black/Scholes PDE was quite easy to solve in closed form, this does not hold for our PDE. The reason for this lies in the lack of a so-called Lie point symmetry or, respectively, Lie group. Loosely speaking, a transformation of both dependent and independent variables of a given differential equation into new dependent and independent variables is called a Lie group if and only if this transformation is one-parametric and has the property of being a commutative group with respect to the group parameter. Applying this transformation to the original differential equation yields a differential equation in the transformed variables. If this new equation is structurally identical to the original one, then the transformation will generate a Lie point symmetry. The Lie group generating such a symmetry can then be used to construct a general solution for the original equation by eliminating the group parameter. This solution is called 'similarity solution'. Bluman (1980, 1983) and Hill (1982) have shown under which conditions a parabolic PDE of second order has a Lie point symmetry. Employing their results, one can easily show that (4.2a) or, equivalently, (4.2c) has no Lie point symmetry in general. But since the usual regularity conditions for the existence and uniqueness of solutions of PDEs are fulfilled [6] we know that there exists an economically meaningful solution to our PDE problem although we are not able to calculate a closed-form solution using Lie Group theory.

136

There are still two other ways to proceed: one can try and obtain a closed-form solution by the method of separating variables which delivers a solution in terms of an integral over the so-called 'Green's Function'. Green's Function is an infinite series including the eigenvalues and eigenfunctions of the so-called 'Sturm-Liouville problem' [7]. The Sturm-Liouville problem, in turn, is an eigenvalue problem for second order ordinary differential equations [8]. In order to solve the Sturm-Liouville problem we need to have two boundary conditions for the bond price at the lower and upper boundary of the short-term interest rate's definition interval. Unfortunately, these conditions are not at hand and introducing them in an ad-hoc way could falsify the result. For quite complicated problems like ours, it is, in addition, almost hopeless to get tractable analytical expressions of the eigenvalues and eigenfunctions of the Sturm-Liouville problem and thus a tractable Green's Function. Consequently, we will refrain from using this method.

Another way is to write the solution of (4.2c-d) down as a closed-form solution using the integral formula of Feynman and Kac [9].

$$(4.3a) \quad P(r_D, \hat{t}) = E_Q \left(e^{-\int_0^{\hat{t}} r_D(s) \cdot ds} \right)$$

where E_Q denotes expectation to be carried out under the 'risk-neutral' (i.e. equivalent martingale) probability measure associated with the following dynamics of r_D:

---

[6] See for example Fritz (1982), Evans (1994) or Vvedensky (1993).

[7] Polyanin/Zaitsev (1996, p. 378) briefly discuss the functional form of such a solution.

[8] Good references for these methods are Boyce/DiPrima (1997) or Courant/Hilbert (1993).

[9] For a more detailed discussion of the connections between PDEs and the Feynman-Kac formula see, for example, Duffie (1992, Appendix E), Baxter/Rennie (1996, Chapter 5) or Neftci (1996, Chapter 16).

$$
(4.3b) \quad dr_D = \begin{pmatrix} \alpha_0 + \alpha_1 \cdot (r_D - \alpha_K + \delta) + (\alpha_2 + \frac{\beta_0}{\beta_K}) \cdot (r_D - \alpha_K + \delta)^2 \\ + (\alpha_3 + \frac{\beta_1}{\beta_K}) \cdot (r_D - \alpha_K + \delta)^3 \end{pmatrix} \cdot dt
$$
$$
+ \Big(\beta_0 + \beta_1 \cdot (r_D - \alpha_K + \delta)\Big) \cdot (r_D - \alpha_K + \delta) \cdot dB
$$

(4.3a) has the intuitively understandable meaning that zero-coupon bond prices equal the expected value of properly discounted continuously compounded future short-term interest rates. In order to evaluate (4.3a), however, we need to solve for r_D explicitly from (4.3b). This was already seen to be impossible in the last chapter. Moreover, we would need to calculate the equivalent martingale measure which is likewise complicated. Although the meaning of (4.3a) is quite nice, we cannot use it for our further investigations since it does not provide us with a tractable formula in terms of exploitation of parameter dependencies.

Of course, we can ask ourselves: why should we try to find a closed-form solution when we are able to solve the problem numerically for any given set of parameter values, especially when we have access to a symbolic computer programs that easily provide us with appropriate numerical algorithms? The answer is that we want to examine in the most general way how the solution of our valuation equation adjusts to changes in the fiscal policy parameters. Obviously, we need a bond price formula for this investigation since one formula says more than a thousand numbers. An approximate solution is hence called for.

There are at least three promising ways to get such an approximate solution: the first employs the Cauchy-Kowalewska Theorem and uses it to derive a Taylor series solution around the initial condition (4.2d) (also called 'initial data') of the problem. The advantage of this method is that one can get solutions amenable to comparative statics analysis by just confining the steps within the Taylor series to a small number. The disadvantage is that this solution may then not match the true solution satisfactorily. Indeed, we face an intrinsic trade-off between 'amenability to further analysis' and 'goodness-of-fit'. However, this trade-off exists for any approximation scheme.

The second way consists of transforming the PDE (4.2a) or (4.2c) into its 'normal form' according to Bluman (1980, 1983). Employing a quadratic approximation of the term independent of the remaining derivatives in the normal form, one can subsequently find the corresponding Lie point symmetry and use this symmetry to calculate the similarity solution. Finally, one obtains the points around which the quadratic approximation is carried out using some projection method. This method seems to yield good results but the solution gets definitely too complicated for comparative statics so that we do not pursue it here any further.

The third way encompasses the linearization of those terms of (4.2a) or (4.2c) that are polynomial in the short-term interest rate r_D. Doing so introduces four different arbitrary parameters but the so-created PDE is structurally equivalent to the one solved successfully by Cox/Ingersoll/Ross (1985b). The trick behind the solution is to use an exponential 'educated guess', which is a special case of the separating variables method. The undetermined time-dependent functions within this 'educated guess' are subsequently found by solving a corresponding system of coupled ordinary differential equations. The arbitrary values showing up in the linearized PDE will finally be determined by the use of projection methods [10]. The procedure is to insert the solution back into the original PDE (4.2a) or (4.2c) yielding a residual function. If the solution of the linearized problem was the correct solution of the original problem, than the residual would be equal to zero. However, this will not be the case since we just solved the linearized problem and not the original one. So we must choose the different arbitrary values appearing in the linearized version of the original PDE in such a way that the solution of this linearized problem is 'as near as possible' to the true solution. 'As near as possible' means that the residual has to be close to zero given some mathematical norm measuring the distance. This is accomplished by choosing the parameters so that the mathematical norm of the residual over some appropriate subset of the definition space is minimized. We will use this method in our further analysis since it seems to show the best trade-off between approximation quality and tractability of the solution.

---

[10] See Gaspar/Judd (1997) and Judd (1998) for an extensive discussion of various projection methods, especially their applications in economics.

4.3 Term structure and fiscal policy analysis

4.3.1 The term structure relation

In this section, we will derive, discuss and visualize the term structure of interest rates using an approximate bond price solution obtained by the use of a combined linearization-projection solution method. The complete derivation of the approximate solution is presented in Appendix 4.1. The bond price solution is given as follows:

$$(4.4) \quad P(r_D, \hat{t}) = \exp\left(-\frac{2 \cdot \left(e^{2 \cdot \xi \cdot \hat{t}} - 1\right)}{\left(e^{2 \cdot \xi \cdot \hat{t}} + 3\right) \cdot \xi} \cdot r_D\right)$$

with: $\quad \xi = -2 \cdot \dfrac{\Omega_3}{\Omega_2} + \dfrac{1}{30} + \sqrt{\left(2 \cdot \dfrac{\Omega_3}{\Omega_2} - \dfrac{1}{30}\right)^2 + \left(8 \cdot \dfrac{\Omega_1}{\Omega_2} + \dfrac{4 \cdot \log 4}{45} \cdot \dfrac{\Omega_3}{\Omega_2}\right)}$

$$\Omega_1 = \frac{\gamma^3 \cdot \beta_K^8 \cdot \left(10 \cdot (1-z)^2 - 15 \cdot (1-z) + 6 - (1-z)^5\right)}{60}$$

$$\Omega_2 = \left(\gamma \cdot \beta_K^2 \cdot z + 2 \cdot (\alpha_K - \delta - \gamma \cdot \beta_K^2)\right) \cdot \gamma \cdot \beta_K^2 \cdot z$$

$$\Omega_3 = \alpha_0 \cdot \gamma \cdot \beta_K^2 \cdot z + \frac{\alpha_1 \cdot \gamma^2 \cdot \beta_K^4 \cdot z \cdot (z-2)}{2}$$
$$+ \frac{(1+\gamma) \cdot \gamma^2 \cdot \beta_K^6 \cdot ((1-z)^4 - 1)}{8} + \frac{(\alpha_2 + 1 - z) \cdot \gamma^3 \cdot \beta_K^6 \cdot (1 - (1-z)^3)}{3}$$

We note that the price of private bonds depends on the model parameters in a nontrivial way. Since we are interested in the term structure relation instead of the bond price, we now introduce the yield-to-return relationship $y(r_D, \hat{t})$ [11] describing the term structure of interest rates as follows:

---

[11] The graph of $y(r_D, t)$ is called „yield curve", a phrase that we will equivalently use sometimes for yield-to-return and term structure, too.

$$(4.5) \quad P(r_D, \hat{t}) = e^{-y(r_D, \hat{t}) \cdot \hat{t}} \Rightarrow y(r_D, \hat{t}) = -\frac{\ln\left(P(r_D, \hat{t})\right)}{\hat{t}}$$

We note that the yield-to-return relationship denotes the mean return on a zero-coupon default-free bond over its time to maturity. Inserting (4.4) into (4.5) delivers the yield-to-return relationship:

$$(4.6) \quad y(r_D, \hat{t}) = \frac{2 \cdot \left(e^{2 \cdot \xi \cdot \hat{t}} - 1\right)}{\left(e^{2 \cdot \xi \cdot \hat{t}} + 3\right) \cdot \xi \cdot \hat{t}} \cdot r_D$$

Since our approximation led us to a special case of the Cox/Ingersoll/Ross (CIR) solution, the yield curve is, as in CIR, linear in the only factor driving the term structure: the short-term interest rate r_D. All other things remaining constant, a change of the short-term interest rate translates thus only into an upward or downward shift of the yield curve. It does not change the structure of the yield curve in the time to maturity dimension. Changes in the short-term interest rate have thus only a level effect. Other approximation schemes, of course, could have delivered other, possibly nonlinear dependencies of the yield curve on the short-term interest rate. However, our main desire is to study theoretically possible changes in the slope of the yield curve regarding its dependence on time to maturity. Thus, we will further on abstract from the question whether nonlinear dependencies on r_D would have resulted in better approximations.

At first sight, (4.6) does not depend on the fiscal policy parameters directly. But a closer look reveals that there is such a dependence since ξ depends on Ω_1, Ω_2 and Ω_3 which, in turn, are influenced by the tax rate τ and the public expenditure ratio z. In the further analysis, we will therefore first study the influence of different values of ξ on the term structure and then examine how the fiscal policy parameters contribute to the determination of ξ.

Before we start to explore different slopes of the yield curve using (4.6), a natural question to settle concerns the term structure behavior at the 'boundaries' of time-to-maturity: using the rule of L'Hospital, it it straightforward to show that the yield curve tends to r_D when time to maturity approaches zero. This is a consistent result. The other extreme happens when time to maturity tends to infinity: again, one can use L'Hospital's rule to see that the yield curve now approaches zero. It is notable, however, that this does not mean that the long-term yields are always lower than short-term yields.

The most interesting question is how the yield curve depends on the coefficient ξ which is itself a function of the underlying model parameters. Before we start with this question, we will first visualize our approximate yield curve (4.6) to get an impression how it looks like. This is done in Figure 4.1 and 4.2. For this purpose, we plot in Figure 4.1 its three-dimensional surface for an initial value of the short-term interest rate r_D of 5% over a range of 30 years for time to maturity and over an interval of ξ between 0 and 1[12].

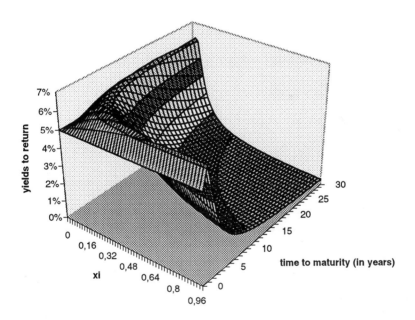

Figure 4.1: Approximate yields-to-return surface.

---

[12] The upper value for ξ in the plot is arbitrarily chosen.

For a value of $\xi = 0$, we see that the yield curve is completely flat. For increasing values of ξ the term structure becomes normal until a critical value of ξ is reached. For ξ values larger than the critical one, the term structure possesses a local maximum called 'hump'. We say that the term structure is 'hump-shaped'. For further increasing ξ, the hump is reached always earlier in terms of time to maturity. For arbitrarily high values of ξ, the time to maturity at which the hump occurs tends to zero. The still hump-shaped term structure is no longer distinguishable from an inverse term structure. In the asymptotic limit for ξ, the term structure finally becomes completely inverse. From this example we can see that our approximation gives us enough leeway for any of the 'classical' term structure characteristics: the flat, normal, hump-shaped and inverse term structure.

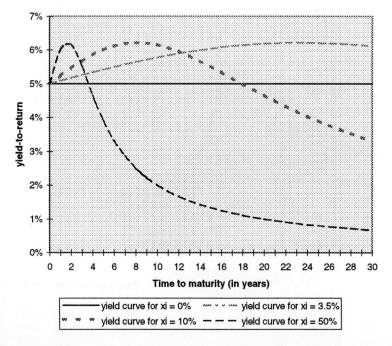

Figure 4.2: Different cross sections of the above approximate yields-to-return surface .

4.3.2 Conditions for the most characteristic term structure slopes

We now examine more closely how fiscal policy parameter changes can theoretically account for different characteristic slopes of the term structure. The above plots illustrated that different term structures are associated with different values of ξ. ξ is itself a function of τ and z, apart from the other model parameters. Since the purpose of the following formal discussion is to determine the conditions under which the yield curve changes its slope with regard to time to maturity, we will first discuss for which values of ξ we get different slopes of the term structure. Afterwards, we will discuss the influence of fiscal policy on ξ.

We calculate the first two derivatives of the yield-to-return function (4.6) with respect to time to maturity for they are important auxiliary functions in order to distinguish the different characteristic term structure slopes:

$$(4.7a) \qquad \frac{dy(r_D, \hat{t})}{d\hat{t}} = \frac{-2 \cdot e^{4 \cdot \xi \cdot \hat{t}} + 4 \cdot \left(4 \cdot \hat{t} \cdot \xi - 1\right) \cdot e^{2 \cdot \xi \cdot \hat{t}} + 6}{\left(e^{2 \cdot \xi \cdot \hat{t}} + 3\right)^2 \cdot \xi \cdot \hat{t}^2} \cdot r_D$$

$$(4.7b) \qquad \frac{d^2 y(r_D, \hat{t})}{d\hat{t}^2} = \frac{4 \cdot r_D}{\left(e^{2 \cdot \xi \cdot \hat{t}} + 3\right)^3 \cdot \xi \cdot \hat{t}^3} \cdot \left(\begin{array}{l} e^{6 \cdot \xi \cdot \hat{t}} - \left(8 \cdot \hat{t}^2 \cdot \xi^2 + 8 \cdot \hat{t} \cdot \xi - 5\right) \cdot e^{4 \cdot \xi \cdot \hat{t}} \\ + (24 \cdot \hat{t}^2 \cdot \xi^2 - 24 \cdot \xi \cdot \hat{t} + 3) \cdot e^{2 \cdot \xi \cdot \hat{t}} - 9 \end{array} \right)$$

Assuming as mentioned before that the term structure variable 'time to maturity' is confined to a range of $[0, \hat{t}_{max}]$, where $\hat{t}_{max} = 30$ is the value for the longest time to maturity a private bond can have [13], then the four main slopes of the term structure curve arising from empirical observations can now be distinguished as follows:

---

[13] The reason why we chose 30 years as the maximal time to maturity is that on most financial markets one does usually not find private bonds having time to maturity of more than 30 years.

144

1) The flat term structure

Flat term structure curve assumptions are often made in the business administration literature of investment under certainty. Finding a flat term structure relationship empirically is, however, a rare event. Nevertheless, we will consider this possibility explicitly, be it only for reason of completeness. Flat term structure means that for any time to maturity the yield-to-return is the same. The consequence is that the yield curve must not depend on time to maturity $\hat{t}$ which implies for our model:

$$(4.8a) \quad y(r_D, \hat{t}) = 0 \Leftrightarrow \xi = 0$$

(4.8a) shows that only ξ equal to zero accounts for a flat term structure. The question is now, whether there are admissible combinations of fiscal policy parameters so that $\xi = 0$ and hence a flat term structure results. In Appendix 4.1 we showed that the relation between ξ and the fiscal policy parameters is given by (A4.1.15). Simultaneously, we saw that the approximation leading to (A4.1.15) via (A4.1.14) is the better the higher ξ. Unfortunately, for $\xi = 0$ this approximation is too bad in order to match the true solution of (A4.1.13) in terms of ξ well enough. Thus, one should actually take (A4.1.13) and solve it numerically for ξ given all other parameter values. This, however, would prohibit us from analytically carrying out the analysis whether there are fiscal policy parameter constellations leading to $\xi = 0$. Since we think that this analytical analysis is insightful, we will just neglect this problem and use (A4.1.15) later on as appropriate relation between ξ and the fiscal policy parameters.

2) The normal term structure

The normal term structure implies that the yield-to-return increases with increasing time to maturity but the increases itself become smaller and smaller. Thus, the first derivative of the yield-to-return with respect to $\hat{t}$ has to be positive and the second derivative of the yield-to-return with respect to

$\hat{t}$ has to be negative over the whole time-to-maturity interval $[0, \hat{t}_{max}]$. Recalling (4.7a-b) and assuming ξ and r_D to be positive, this implies:

(4.9a)
$$\frac{-2 \cdot e^{4\xi\hat{t}} + 4 \cdot \left(4 \cdot \hat{t} \cdot \xi - 1\right) \cdot e^{2\xi\hat{t}} + 6}{\left(e^{2\xi\hat{t}} + 3\right)^2 \cdot \xi \cdot \hat{t}^2} \cdot r_D > 0$$
$$\Rightarrow f(\xi, \hat{t}) \equiv -2 \cdot e^{4\xi\hat{t}} + 4 \cdot \left(4 \cdot \hat{t} \cdot \xi - 1\right) \cdot e^{2\xi\hat{t}} + 6 > 0$$

(4.9b)
$$\frac{4 \cdot r_D \cdot \left(e^{6\xi\hat{t}} - \binom{8 \cdot \hat{t}^2 \cdot \xi^2}{+ 8 \cdot \hat{t} \cdot \xi - 5} \cdot e^{4\xi\hat{t}} + \binom{24 \cdot \hat{t}^2 \cdot \xi^2}{- 24 \cdot \xi \cdot \hat{t} + 3} \cdot e^{2\xi\hat{t}} - 9\right)}{\left(e^{2\xi\hat{t}} + 3\right)^3 \cdot \xi \cdot \hat{t}^3} < 0$$

$$\Rightarrow g(\xi, \hat{t}) \equiv e^{6\xi\hat{t}} - \left(8 \cdot \hat{t}^2 \cdot \xi^2 + 8 \cdot \hat{t} \cdot \xi - 5\right) \cdot e^{4\xi\hat{t}}$$
$$+ \left(24 \cdot \hat{t}^2 \cdot \xi^2 - 24 \cdot \xi \cdot \hat{t} + 3\right) \cdot e^{2\xi\hat{t}} - 9 < 0$$

Since we do no longer have to consider the case $\xi = 0$, which was exclusively linked to a flat term structure, the denominators of the fractions in (4.9a-b) are strictly positive. Hence, we can concentrate on the respective numerators $f(\xi, \hat{t})$ and $g(\xi, \hat{t})$ in order to study the sign of the yield curve derivatives. Before we examine these conditions closer, we will first turn to the description of the other characteristic term structure slopes.

3) The inverse term structure

This means that the slope of the term structure curve decreases and its increments become smaller with increasing $\hat{t}$. Hence, the first derivative of the yield-to-return with respect to $\hat{t}$ is negative and the second derivative is positive. This implies that the relevant conditions to hold are exactly of opposite sign as (4.9a-b):

$$\frac{-2 \cdot e^{4\xi\hat{t}} + 4 \cdot \left(4 \cdot \hat{t} \cdot \xi - 1\right) \cdot e^{2\xi\hat{t}} + 6}{\left(e^{2\xi\hat{t}} + 3\right)^2 \cdot \xi \cdot \hat{t}^2} \cdot r_D < 0$$

(4.10a) $\Rightarrow f(\xi,\hat{t}) \equiv -2\cdot e^{4\cdot\xi\cdot\hat{t}} + 4\cdot\left(4\cdot\hat{t}\cdot\xi - 1\right)\cdot e^{2\cdot\xi\cdot\hat{t}} + 6 < 0$

(4.10b) $\dfrac{4\cdot r_D \cdot\left(e^{6\cdot\xi\cdot\hat{t}} - \begin{pmatrix}8\cdot\hat{t}^2\cdot\xi^2\\+8\cdot\hat{t}\cdot\xi-5\end{pmatrix}\cdot e^{4\cdot\xi\cdot\hat{t}} + \begin{pmatrix}24\cdot\hat{t}^2\cdot\xi^2\\-24\cdot\xi\cdot\hat{t}+3\end{pmatrix}\cdot e^{2\cdot\xi\cdot\hat{t}} - 9\right)}{\left(e^{2\cdot\xi\cdot\hat{t}}+3\right)^3\cdot\xi\cdot\hat{t}^3} > 0$

$$\Rightarrow g(\xi,\hat{t}) \equiv e^{6\cdot\xi\cdot\hat{t}} - \left(8\cdot\hat{t}^2\cdot\xi^2 + 8\cdot\hat{t}\cdot\xi - 5\right)\cdot e^{4\cdot\xi\cdot\hat{t}}$$
$$+ \left(24\cdot\hat{t}^2\cdot\xi^2 - 24\cdot\xi\cdot\hat{t}+3\right)\cdot e^{2\cdot\xi\cdot\hat{t}} - 9 > 0$$

Finally, we will turn to the hump-shaped yield curve and after that we will discuss the implications of the conditions characterizing the different term structure slopes.

4) The hump-shaped term structure [14]

This means that the slope of the term structure curve increases until some maximum (minimum) is reached and then decreases (increases) usually accompanied by decreasing increments, too. Thus, the first derivative of the yield-to-return with respect to $\hat{t}$ possesses one root within $[0, \hat{t}_{max}]$ at which the second derivative is negative (positive). The second derivative usually has a root (i.e. a turning point of the yield curve) right from the (local) maximum. This turns into the conditions:

(4.11) $\exists t^* \in (0, \hat{t}_{max}) := \begin{cases} \left.\dfrac{dy(r_D,\hat{t})}{d\hat{t}}\right|_{\hat{t}=t^*} = 0 \\[2mm] \left.\dfrac{d^2 y(r_D,\hat{t})}{d\hat{t}^2}\right|_{\hat{t}=t^*} < 0 \end{cases}$

$\exists t^{**} > t^* := \left.\dfrac{d^2 y(r_D,\hat{t})}{d\hat{t}^2}\right|_{\hat{t}=t^{**}} = 0$

---

[14] Note that the 'hump' can, at least in principle, be thought to be either a local maximum or a local minimum of the yield curve. In most of the literature, however, local maxima are meant when talking about hump-shaped forms of the term structure.

4.3.3 Structural impact of fiscal policy on the term structure

Having characterized the mathematical conditions (4.8a-4.11) that guarantee the different term structures, we will now study the impact of fiscal policy on the term structure. The condition that accounts for a flat term structure is given by (4.8a). Using (A4.1.15) together with (4.8a) yields:

$$(4.8b) \quad \xi = 0 \Leftrightarrow 8 \cdot \frac{\Omega_1}{\Omega_2} + \frac{4 \cdot \log 4}{45} \cdot \frac{\Omega_3}{\Omega_2} = 0$$
$$\Leftrightarrow 90 \cdot \Omega_1(z) + \log 4 \cdot \Omega_3(\tau, z) \equiv f(\tau, z) = 0$$

The second line of (4.8b) shows the condition for the fiscal policy parameters that implies a flat term structure. Using this condition, we can now answer the question under which conditions fiscal policy changes 'destroy' a flat term structure. For reasons of simplicity, we will only consider fiscal policy changes in form of changes in the tax rate whereas the government expenditure ratio z remains fixed. As can be seen from the second line in (4.8b), the flat term structure does not change if and only if a change in τ does not change Ω_3 since Ω_1 does not depend on τ. This implies:

$$(4.8c) \quad \frac{d\xi}{d\tau}\bigg|_{\xi=0} = 0 \Leftrightarrow \frac{d\Omega_3(\tau, z)}{d\tau} = 0$$

(4.8c) implies that a change in the tax rate does not change the flat term structure if and only if there is no effect on the auxiliary function Ω_3. Using the definition of Ω_3, we can calculate the derivative of Ω_3 with respect to τ:

$$\frac{d\Omega_3}{d\tau} \equiv \gamma \cdot \beta_K^2 \cdot z \cdot \frac{d\alpha_0}{d\tau} + \frac{\gamma^2 \cdot \beta_K^4 \cdot z \cdot (z-2)}{2} \cdot \frac{d\alpha_1}{d\tau}$$
$$(4.8d) \quad \Rightarrow \frac{d\Omega_3}{d\tau} \equiv -\gamma \cdot (\gamma - 1) \cdot \beta_K^4 \cdot z + \frac{1}{2} \cdot \gamma \cdot \beta_K^4 \cdot z \cdot (z-2)$$
$$\Rightarrow \frac{d\Omega_3}{d\tau} \equiv \left(\frac{1}{2} \cdot z - \gamma\right) \cdot \gamma \cdot \beta_K^4 \cdot z < 0$$

Since the expenditure ratio z is confined to the interval (0;1) and elasticity of substitution γ is assumed to be bigger than one, the derivative in (4.8d) is negative so that (4.8c) cannot hold. The consequence is that changing the tax rate without changing the expenditure ratio will always 'destroy' a flat term structure in our model. The only situation where such a policy change does not impact on the term structure is in a world of no risk ($\beta_K = 0$): here, the term structure is always flat and does not respond to any change in fiscal policy. This coincides with our findings in Chapter 2.

We now discuss the implications of (4.9-4.11) for the three other types of term structure relations. These implications are critically driven by the question whether the auxiliary functions $f(\xi,\hat{t})$ and $g(\xi,\hat{t})$, which correspond to the numerators of the first two derivatives of the yield curve with respect to time to maturity, have roots. When we look at $f(\xi,\hat{t})$ and $g(\xi,\hat{t})$ we note that both functions depend on the product $\xi\cdot\hat{t}$. Replacing $\xi\cdot\hat{t}$ with a new variable y (which must not be confused with the yield-to-return) leads to:

$$(4.12a)\ f(y) \equiv -2\cdot e^{4y} + 4\cdot(4\cdot y - 1)\cdot e^{2y} + 6$$

$$(4.12b)\ g(y) \equiv e^{6y} - (8\cdot y^2 + 8\cdot y - 5)\cdot e^{4y} + (24\cdot y^2 - 24\cdot y + 3)\cdot e^{2y} - 9$$

The only thing we now have to do is to examine when f(y) and g(y) become positive, zero or negative. This determines the sign of the first two derivatives of the yield-to-return, (4.7a-b), and pins down for which values of $y = \xi\cdot\hat{t}$ the different term structures arise.

It is straightforward to see that both functions f and g are zero for y = 0. However, their behavior is different when y tends to infinity: f(y) tends then to minus infinity whereas g(y) tends to plus infinity. Moreover, both functions have just one root right from y = 0. The main difference between the two functions is that f(y) is positive left from its positive root and negative right from it. g(y) shows the exact opposite behavior. The numerical values of these roots can be calculated using a numerical nonlinear equation solver. Doing so yields the following results: f = 0 at y = 0.816 and g = 0 at y = 1.727. Using these results and replacing y by $\xi\cdot\hat{t}$, we can now state the range of the sign of the yield curve derivatives (4.7a-b):

(4.13a)
$$\frac{dy(r_D,\hat{t})}{d\hat{t}} := \begin{cases} >0 \Leftrightarrow \xi < \dfrac{0.816}{\hat{t}} \\[2mm] =0 \Leftrightarrow \xi = \dfrac{0.816}{\hat{t}} \\[2mm] <0 \Leftrightarrow \xi > \dfrac{0.816}{\hat{t}} \end{cases}$$

(4.13b)
$$\frac{d^2y(r_D,\hat{t})}{d\hat{t}^2} := \begin{cases} <0 \Leftrightarrow \xi < \dfrac{1.727}{\hat{t}} \\[2mm] =0 \Leftrightarrow \xi = \dfrac{1.727}{\hat{t}} \\[2mm] >0 \Leftrightarrow \xi > \dfrac{1.727}{\hat{t}} \end{cases}$$

Equations (4.13a-b) equip us now with the information we need in order to settle the question when the different yield curve slopes occur. Recalling the conditions for a normal term structure to hold, the first derivative of the yield (4.13a) has to be positive while its second derivative has to be negative. Looking at (4.13a-b), these two conditions are always fulfilled if ξ is smaller than 0.816 divided by time to maturity. Since this restriction on ξ has to hold for all different maturity dates and is the harder to fulfill the bigger $\hat{t}$ gets, we simply take the maximal time to maturity value and plug it in (4.13a-b). This maximal value was assumed to be 30 years. This yields a critical value of $\xi_{critical} = 0.027$. If ξ is smaller than this value, than the first derivative of the yield curve is always positive and the second derivative is always negative for all times to maturity. Continuing this kind of argumentation for the other two characteristic term structures, we can state the following important proposition:

Proposition 4.1:

The regions of different term structure slopes are given as follows:

1. Flat term structure $\Leftrightarrow \xi = 0$

2. Normal term structure $\Leftrightarrow \xi \in (0,0.027)$

3. Hump-shaped term structure $\Leftrightarrow \xi \in [0.027, \infty)$

4. Inverse term structure $\Leftrightarrow \xi \to \infty$

<u>Proof:</u> Using (4.13a-b) together with the definitions of the different term structure slopes (4.9) to (4.11) and the result (4.8a) the proposition is obvious.

Proposition 4.1 separates the state space of ξ such that any value is associated with a characteristic term structure of interest rates. For most values of ξ the term structure is hump-shaped. Nevertheless, all other important yield curve slopes are possible, at least theoretically. Since we know that the specific value of ξ is determined by all model parameters via (A4.1.15), we could now calculate ξ for any arbitrary numerical set of model parameters and decide via Proposition 4.1 about the associated term structure. For given values of the household and technology parameters, it is thus the specific choice of the two fiscal policy parameters that determines the corresponding term structure. This is a key result of this chapter and we illustrate it with a numerical example in the next section.

The economic reasoning behind the different term structure slopes and its link to fiscal policy is clear: the yield-to-return for any future date reflects the financial market expectations of averaged short-term interest rates until that date. Since the dynamic evolution of the short-term interest rate is crucially influenced by fiscal policy - as we have intensively discussed last chapter - the yield curve hence reflects directly the fiscal policy induced expected time paths of future interest rates. Depending on the specific policy combination, either continuously increasing, continuously decreasing or first continuously increasing and then decreasing time paths for the short-term interest rates are viewed to be possible. The first scenario corresponds to normal term structure, the second to inverse and the third to hump-shaped term structure.

It becomes further clear from Proposition 4.1 that there are three 'regime shifts' between the different term structure characteristics, namely from flat to normal term structure, from normal to hump-shaped term structure and from hump-shaped to inverse term structure. The first regime shift was already discussed above and the third one is only theoretically possible [15]. Therefore, we can concentrate on the second regime shift where ξ crosses 0.027 and the term structure changes from hump-shaped to normal or vice versa. An interesting question is whether an infinitesimal change in the tax rate at $\xi_{critical}$ leads to a regime shift in the term structure. For this purpose, we need to calculate the derivative of ξ with respect to τ. Making use of (4.4) and employing some algebraic manipulations we get the following condition for ξ:

$$(4.14)\quad h(\tau,z) \equiv \xi^2 - \frac{\xi}{15} + 4\cdot\frac{\Omega_3(\tau)}{\Omega_2}\cdot\left(\xi - \frac{\log 4}{45}\right) - 8\cdot\frac{\Omega_1}{\Omega_2} = 0$$

The question whether a tax rate change leads to a regime shift at $\xi_{critical}$ can be answered by showing whether it changes ξ in (4.14) or not. Taking derivatives with respect to τ in (4.14) thus implies:

$$(4.15)\quad \left(2\cdot\xi - \frac{1}{15} + 4\cdot\frac{\Omega_3(\tau)}{\Omega_2}\right)\cdot\frac{d\xi}{d\tau} + \frac{4}{\Omega_2}\cdot\frac{d\Omega_3(\tau)}{d\tau}\cdot\left(\xi - \frac{\log 4}{45}\right) = 0$$

Assume that ξ does indeed not change. Then its derivative with respect to τ is zero and the first term in (4.15) vanishes. The second term, however, remains:

$$(4.16)\quad \frac{4}{\Omega_2}\cdot\left(\xi - \frac{\log 4}{45}\right)\cdot\frac{d\Omega_3}{d\tau} = 0$$

(4.16) will always hold as long as at least one of its terms is zero. The first term can only become zero for infinite high Ω_2 what we exclude. From (4.8d) we know that the derivative of Ω_3 with respect to τ is negative. Thus, the third term is also not zero so that (4.16) can only hold if ξ equals log4/45

---

[15] However, for a value of $\xi = 100$, for example, the hump occurs at a time to maturity less than three trading days so that the hump would quite likely no longer be detectable in

which is 0.031. This means that an infinitesimal tax rate change does not impact on ξ and hence on the term structure if and only if $\xi = 0.031$ holds. Since ξ_{critical} is smaller than 0.031, we can conclude that a change in the tax rate happening at ξ_{critical} will lead to a new ξ thereby changing the slope of the yield curve from normal to hump-shaped or vice versa. This is an interesting result in view of the discussion of Chapter 3 where we have already seen that changes in fiscal policy impact on the short-term interest rate dynamics. The altered interest rate dynamics, however, do in our yield curve model only imply that the yield curve shifts above or below. It has thus just a level effect. (4.16) shows that there is a critical value of ξ at which an infinitesimal tax rate change additionally induces a structural change in the yield curve over time to maturity. Fiscal policy hence impacts twofold on the term structure: indirectly via its influence on r_D (a „vertical" impact in view of the yield curve plot) and directly via its influence on ξ (a „horizontal" impact).

The last question is whether a tax rate increase at ξ_{critical} will drive the term structure to the 'hump-shaped region' or to the 'normal region'. To answer this question, we have to look on (4.15) again:

$$(4.15) \quad \left(2\cdot\xi - \frac{1}{15} + \frac{4\cdot\Omega_3}{\Omega_2}\right)\cdot\frac{d\xi}{d\tau} = -\frac{4}{\Omega_2}\cdot\left(\xi - \frac{\log 4}{45}\right)\cdot\frac{d\Omega_3}{d\tau}$$

Since the bracket on the left-hand side of (4.15) is positive (compare (4.4)), we have to look on the term of the right-hand side to determine the sign of the effect on ξ: the first term is negative since Ω_2 is assumed to be positive, the second term (i.e. the bracket) is also negative since ξ_{critical} is smaller than $(\log 4)/45$ and the third term is negative, too, due to (4.8d). Thus, the right-hand side is negative rendering the derivative of ξ with respect to τ negative. This implies that when ξ equals ξ_{critical}, an infinitesimal increase in the tax rate lowers ξ and drives the term structure to the 'normal region'. Accordingly,

---

data and one would observe an inverse term structure although it would theoretically still be hump-shaped.

an infinitesimal decrease in the tax rate implies a hump-shaped term structure.

Using (4.15), we further note that the sign of the derivative changes to positive as soon as $\xi > 0.031$. This implies, however, that the sign of the effect of an infinitesimal tax rate change on the term structure is not unique when the yield curve is in the 'hump-shaped region'. Instead, this effect is positive for $\xi > 0.031$ and negative for $\xi < 0.031$. In the first case, a tax rate increase shortens the time period at which the hump occurs and in the second one this time period is lengthened. The simplest economic explanation employs a Laffer-curve argument: for $\xi < 0.031$ an infinitesimal tax rate increase damages the tax base, private wealth, more than in a situation where $\xi > 0.031$ holds. The result is that in the area of $\xi > 0.031$ the public deficit development as a consequence of the tax rate increase improves much faster than in the area where $\xi < 0.031$ holds. The highest expected short-term interest rate associated with the hump in the yield curve is hence reached earlier and, having reached the hump, the short-term interest rate is from then on expected to fall faster for $\xi > 0.031$.

4.4 A numerical example

Although we were able to derive an explicit approximate solution for the yield curve and thus the term structure of interest rates in the last section, we could not carry out all interesting results qualitatively owing to the still complicated form of the approximate solution. In order to illustrate the relationship between fiscal policy reflected in the public expenditure ratio and the term structure of interest rates, we will now use numerical values for the household as well as the technology parameters. Subsequently, we numerically calculate and analyze those subsets of the set of feasible fiscal policy that account for the different term structure slopes. As parameter values, we take the same one's as were already used in the last chapter: $\alpha_K = 7.5\%$, $\beta_K = 5\%$, $\delta = 1.5\%$, $\gamma = 5$, $\rho = 10\%$ and $r_D = 5\%$. When we additionally assume that the initial capital/output ratio is twice as high as the

154

initial debt/output ratio, then we get the following constraints on fiscal policy from (3.23), (3.27) and (3.28):

$$\tau < 0.07875$$

(4.17a-c) $\quad -6.25 \cdot z^2 - 0.9375 \cdot z^3 + z \cdot (15.6875 + 25 \cdot \tau) - 125 \cdot \tau < 0$

$$z \geq 0.333$$

Plotting (4.17a-c) within a z-τ diagram, we get the set of feasible fiscal policy parameters that does obey to (4.17a-c) as the shaded area [16].

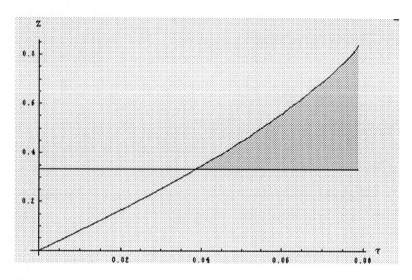

Figure 4.3: Set of feasible fiscal policy (shaded area).

Recalling (4.4), we can now calculate the values of ξ corresponding to any element of the feasible set of fiscal policy parameters in Table 4.1. We take a value range for the tax rate τ from 4% to 7.5% and for the public expenditure ratio z from 34% to 59%. A cross in the table below indicates that the corresponding combination of fiscal policy parameters is not feasible. From the results in Table 4.1 we learn that all values of ξ are higher than $\xi_{critical} = 0.027$. As a consequence, the term structure slope for this special parameter constellation is always in the hump-shaped area. A normal term

---

[16] Note that for tax rates somewhat smaller than 4% the set of feasible government expenditure ratios z becomes empty since the lower bound on z exceeds the upper bound on z.

structure can thus only be explained by choosing different household and technology parameters. Moreover, rising values of z always lead to sinking values of ξ and vice versa given unchanged values of tax rate τ.

Table 4.1: Values of ξ for different combinations of τ and z

	z=34%	z=39%	z=44%	z=49%	z=54%	z=59%
τ=4%	0.069	X	X	X	X	X
τ=4.5%	0.071	0.070	X	X	X	X
τ=5%	0.072	0.071	0.070	X	X	X
τ=5.5%	0.074	0.073	0.071	0.070	X	X
τ=6%	0.075	0.074	0.073	0.072	0.071	X
τ=6.5%	0.077	0.076	0.074	0.073	0.072	0.071
τ=7%	0.079	0.077	0.076	0.075	0.073	0.072
τ=7.5%	0.080	0.079	0.077	0.076	0.075	0.074

What does this imply for the impact of z on the term structure of interest rates? Before answering this question, we will illustrate the term structure again for $\xi \in (0.065, 0.085)$ and $r_D = 5\%$ in Figure 4.4.

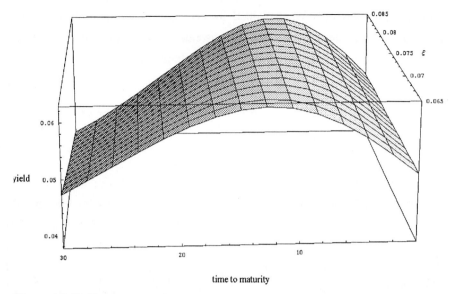

Figure 4.4: Yield-to-return surface.

The plot shows that the higher ξ, the earlier the hump occurs. Additionally, the yield-to-return prior to the hump is higher the higher ξ gets and the yield to return after the hump is lower the higher ξ becomes. Plugging these results together, we can conclude that rising public expenditure ratios z lead to the following three structural phenomena in the term structure of interest rates:

1. Later occurrence of the hump in the term structure.

2. Lower yields prior to the occurrence of the hump.

3. Higher yields after the occurrence of the hump.

Especially feature 2) looks surprising, at least at first sight, because conventional wisdom suggests that rising z should worsen primary deficits and enhance government's demand for credit as the only mean to finance the accruing deficit. In order to increase private credit supply simultaneously to achieve a new equilibrium on the public bond market, the short-term interest rate has to rise according to (3.18). This should then be reflected in higher yield curves. Obviously, an increase in z also affects capital accumulation directly (see equation (3.19)) and wealth accumulation indirectly via changing stocks of capital (see equation (3.21)). Since the capital stock enters the production function as the only input factor and production together with wealth, in turn, act as the 'bases' for government expenditure and revenue, it is not straightforward to see which effect has the biggest impact on the primary deficit. This holds even more when we recognize that rising z increases the drift of capital accumulation instantaneously but may 'in the next moment' decrease this drift via increasing public debt. Even if the effect of z on capital accumulation was clear, then it would still be parameter dependent whether wealth accumulation is promoted by an increase in capital or not. At the moment, we are unable to work out a unique sign of the effect of changing z on K and W, let alone the sign of the overall effect on the primary surplus. We are going to deal more closely with this question later on in Chapter 6. As the table above suggests, however, the overall effect of rising z on the primary surplus seems to be unambiguous: features 1) to 3) indicate, that, after an increase in z has happened, the hump occurs later with lower yields before and higher yields after. This implies that short-term interest rates in the aftermath of a rise in z are expected to increase slower, reach a maximum later and start to sink from then on again slower as prior to the change in z. In turn, this behavior can only be understood when we first assign more slowly growing expected primary deficits to an increase in z. Having reached a maximum, the expected primary deficit sinks thus improving the expected primary surplus of the public sector again, but also more slowly than under the old public expenditure ratio.

Generally, the following résumé holds: structural changes in the yield curve caused by changing fiscal policy are transmitted via the formation of expectations concerning the development of primary surpluses.

Before we close this section, a last remark may be appropriate here: the table above also shows that there are indeed many fiscal policy parameter constellations under which the term structure remains invariant to combined policy changes. Take, for example, the following fiscal policy combinations: 1) $\tau = 4.5\%$, $z = 39\%$, 2) $\tau = 5\%$, $z = 44\%$, 3) $\tau = 5.5\%$, $z = 49\%$. All these combinations result in $\xi = 0.07$. Since our whole analysis showed that ξ is

158

alone decisive for the slope of the term structure, we notice that any of these three fiscal policy combinations yield the same term structure. Although changes in a single fiscal policy instrument were seen to result almost always in structural changes of the yield curve, this needs not hold for a prudent and synchronized change in both fiscal policy instruments. A situation of such synchronized fiscal policy changes can, however, lead to different short-term interest rate dynamics. The future path of interest rates is then altered and hence the term structure, although remaining structurally identical, attains different levels compared to the situation prior to the fiscal policy change.

4.5 Short summary

We conclude this chapter by summarizing the main results: having stated the valuation equation for private bonds in form of a partial differential equation, we saw that we are not able to gain an appropriate closed-form solution. Thus, we developed an approximate solution for the bond price. We then analyzed how fiscal policy influences the different characteristic term structures. The influence of fiscal policy on the dynamic composition of the governments primary surplus and the resulting effect on public credit demand was seen to be an important transmission channel for the term structure. We were able to derive parameter conditions under which different, well-known characteristic slopes of the yield curve occur and how these slopes alter for tax rate changes. We found out critical parameter values that 'separate' different areas of term structure slopes and studied whether tax rate changes may lead to the transition from one term structure regime to another. In a numerical example, we studied the influence of the public expenditure ratio on the term structure and found that increasing it shifts the term structure towards an inverse term structure. Finally, we noted that a combined change in both fiscal policy instruments may leave the term structure invariant in contrast to changes in just a single instrument.

If our term structure model (4.6) was a good description of reality, then the mainly up- and downward shifts in the US yield curve during the first four months in 1980 depicted in Appendix 1.2 could be explained by stochastic shocks in the dynamics of the short-term interest rate only. The structural changes of the yield curve during summer and fall, however, must be explained due to changes in the model parameters. In this respect, a model like (4.6) may be able to deliver a plausible story for the US data in 1980. In order to settle the question whether the model is a good description of reality and, if it is, whether the structural yield curve changes are due to changing fiscal policy parameters, the model has to be tested rigorously using advanced econometric techniques. We refrained here from carrying out this task since our main interest was the examination of the theoretical effects of fiscal policy on the term structure.

In the next chapter, we will turn our attention to the question of economic growth and how financial markets affect it via the interest rate dynamics.

Appendix 4.1: Derivation of the bond price using a linearization-projection approach

In this appendix, we apply the work of Judd (1992) who develops the general projection method in a nice 'cook book' style. The first step is always to define the equation one wants to solve (i.e. (4.2a-b)) in form of an operator equation. This yields then:

(A4.1.1) $\Xi(P(r_D, t) = 0$

with the differential operator Ξ being defined as:

$$\Xi = \frac{1}{2} \cdot \left(\beta_0 + \beta_1 \cdot (r_D - \alpha_K + \delta)\right)^2 \cdot (r_D - \alpha_K + \delta)^2 \cdot \frac{\partial^2}{\partial r_D^2} + \frac{\partial}{\partial t} - r_D$$

$$+ \left(\begin{array}{l} \alpha_0 + \alpha_1 \cdot (r_D - \alpha_K + \delta) + (\alpha_2 + \frac{\beta_0}{\beta_K}) \cdot (r_D - \alpha_K + \delta)^2 \\ + (\alpha_3 + \frac{\beta_1}{\beta_K}) \cdot (r_D - \alpha_K + \delta)^3 \end{array} \right) \cdot \frac{\partial}{\partial r_D}$$

Since we cannot solve (A4.1.1) explicitly, we have to look for solutions that are as close as possible to the true one. Linearizing (A4.1.1) yields the following PDE depending on the yet undetermined parameters ψ, ζ, ω and ξ:

$$\frac{1}{2} \cdot (\psi + \zeta \cdot r_D) \cdot P_{r_D r_D} + (\omega + \xi \cdot r_D) \cdot P_{r_D} + P_t - r_D \cdot P = 0$$

The terminal condition does not change so that it is still given as:

$$P(r_D, T) = 1$$

Moreover, if we set $\psi = 0$, then we end up with:

$$\text{(A4.1.1a)} \qquad \frac{1}{2} \cdot \zeta \cdot r_D \cdot P_{r_D r_D} + (\omega + \xi \cdot r_D) \cdot P_{r_D} + P_t - r_D \cdot P = 0$$

and:

$$\text{(A4.1.1b)} \qquad P(r_D, T) = 1$$

Equation (A4.1a-b) is exactly the PDE describing the term structure in the model of Cox/Ingersoll/Ross (1985b). We also use their exponential guess to solve (A4.1a-b) exactly:

$$\text{(A4.1.2)}\; P(r_D, t) = A(t) \cdot e^{-B(t) \cdot r_D} \Rightarrow \begin{cases} P_t = (A'(t) - A(t) \cdot B'(t) \cdot r_D) \cdot e^{-B(t) \cdot r_D} \\ P_{r_D} = -A(t) \cdot B(t) \cdot e^{-B(t) \cdot r_D} \\ P_{r_D r_D} = A(t) \cdot B(t)^2 \cdot e^{-B(t) \cdot r_D} \end{cases}$$

Inserting (A4.1.2) into (A4.1.1a-b) and doing some algebraic manipulations yields the following differential equation:

$$\text{(A4.1.3)}\; A'(t) - \left(B'(t) - \frac{1}{2} \cdot \zeta \cdot B(t)^2 + \xi \cdot B(t) + 1 \right) \cdot A(t) \cdot r_D = \omega \cdot A(t) \cdot B(t)$$

In order to fulfill (A4.1.3) for any value of r_D, the following coupled system of ordinary differential equations for the two undetermined functions $A(t)$ and $B(t)$ has to hold:

(A4.1.4a) $B'(t) - \dfrac{1}{2} \cdot \zeta \cdot B(t)^2 + \xi \cdot B(t) + 1 = 0$

(A4.1.5a) $A'(t) - \omega \cdot A(t) \cdot B(t) = 0$

The terminal condition (A4.1.1b) together with the guess (A4.1.2) implies the following terminal conditions:

(A4.1.4b) $B(T) = 0$

(A4.1.5b) $A(T) = 1$

Our solution strategy is now as follows: we will first solve (A4.1.4a-b) which is a so-called Riccatti differential equation. We then plug the result into (A4.1.5a) and solve this equation using the terminal condition (A4.1.5b). The solution to (A4.1.5a-b) is given as (cp. Cox/Ingersoll/Ross (1985b) p. 393):

(A4.1.6) $B(t) = \dfrac{2 \cdot \left(e^{\sqrt{\xi^2 + 2 \cdot \zeta} \cdot (T-t)} - 1 \right)}{\left(\sqrt{\xi^2 + 2 \cdot \zeta} - \xi \right) \cdot \left(e^{\sqrt{\xi^2 + 2 \cdot \zeta} \cdot (T-t)} - 1 \right) + 2 \cdot \sqrt{\xi^2 + 2 \cdot \zeta}}$

Making use of solution (A4.1.6), we can now solve (A4.1.5a-b):

(A4.1.7) $A(t) = \left(\dfrac{2 \cdot \sqrt{\xi^2 + 2 \cdot \zeta} \cdot e^{\left(\sqrt{\xi^2 + 2 \cdot \zeta} - \xi\right) \frac{T-t}{2}}}{\left(\sqrt{\xi^2 + 2 \cdot \zeta} - \xi \right) \cdot \left(e^{\sqrt{\xi^2 + 2 \cdot \zeta} \cdot (T-t)} - 1 \right) + 2 \cdot \sqrt{\xi^2 + 2 \cdot \zeta}} \right)^{\frac{2 \cdot \omega}{\zeta}}$

This equation, together with (A4.1.2) and (A4.1.6), yields the complete solution for the bond price. For matter of convenience, we replace the time to maturity, $T - t$, by $\hat{t}$ and obtain the following bond price equation depending on r_D and $\hat{t}$:

$$P(r_D,\hat{t}) = \left(\frac{2 \cdot \sqrt{\xi^2 + 2 \cdot \zeta} \cdot e^{\left(\sqrt{\xi^2 + 2 \cdot \zeta} - \xi\right)\frac{\hat{t}}{2}}}{\left(\sqrt{\xi^2 + 2 \cdot \zeta} - \xi\right) \cdot \left(e^{\sqrt{\xi^2 + 2 \cdot \zeta} \cdot \hat{t}} - 1\right) + 2 \cdot \sqrt{\xi^2 + 2 \cdot \zeta}} \right)^{\frac{2 \cdot \omega}{\zeta}}$$

$$\cdot e^{-\frac{2\left(e^{\sqrt{\xi^2 + 2 \cdot \zeta} \cdot \hat{t}} - 1\right)}{\left(\sqrt{\xi^2 + 2 \cdot \zeta} - \xi\right)\left(e^{\sqrt{\xi^2 + 2 \cdot \zeta} \cdot \hat{t}} - 1\right) + 2\sqrt{\xi^2 + 2 \cdot \zeta}} \cdot r_D}$$

(A4.1.8)

As Cox/Ingersoll/Ross pointed out, this price equation has the economically convenient and meaningful feature that the bond price is a decreasing convex function of the short-term interest rate r_D and a decreasing function of time to maturity $\hat{t}$ given positive parameters ζ and ξ.

Having computed (A4.1.8) as the solution belonging to the linearized problem (A4.1.1a-b), we can now proceed with our projection method. Since (A4.1.8) will serve us as representation of the function base for our operator equation (A4.1.1) and since (A4.1.8) depends on $\hat{t}$ instead of t, we have to transform (A4.1.1) in an equivalent form depending also on $\hat{t}$ only. This gives:

(A4.1.9) $\quad \hat{\Xi}(P(r_D,\hat{t}) = 0$

with the new differential operator $\hat{\Xi}$ being defined as:

$$\hat{\Xi} = \frac{1}{2} \cdot \left(\beta_0 + \beta_1 \cdot (r_D - \alpha_K + \delta)\right)^2 \cdot (r_D - \alpha_K + \delta)^2 \cdot \frac{\partial^2}{\partial r_D^2} - \frac{\partial}{\partial \hat{t}} - r_D$$

$$+ \left(\begin{array}{l} \alpha_0 + \alpha_1 \cdot (r_D - \alpha_K + \delta) + (\alpha_2 + \frac{\beta_0}{\beta_K}) \cdot (r_D - \alpha_K + \delta)^2 \\[2mm] + (\alpha_3 + \frac{\beta_1}{\beta_K}) \cdot (r_D - \alpha_K + \delta)^3 \end{array} \right) \cdot \frac{\partial}{\partial r_D}$$

According to Judd, the next step in the projection method consists of choosing a function base and an inner product with which the projection is calculated. As appropriate function base, we take (A4.1.2) (keeping in mind the solutions for A(t) and B(t)) and plug it into (A4.1.9). This yields the residual function $R(r_D, \hat{t})$:

(A4.1.10)

$$R(r_D, \hat{t}) \equiv \left[\begin{array}{l} \dfrac{1}{2} \cdot (\beta_0 + \beta_1 \cdot (r_D - \alpha_K + \delta))^2 \cdot (r_D - \alpha_K + \delta)^2 \cdot A(\hat{t}) \cdot B(\hat{t})^2 \\[2mm] - A'(\hat{t}) + A(\hat{t}) \cdot B'(\hat{t}) \cdot r_D - A(\hat{t}) \cdot r_D \\[2mm] - \left(\begin{array}{l} \alpha_1 \cdot (r_D - \alpha_K + \delta) + (\alpha_2 + \dfrac{\beta_0}{\beta_K}) \cdot (r_D - \alpha_K + \delta)^2 \\[2mm] + \alpha_0 + (\alpha_3 + \dfrac{\beta_1}{\beta_K}) \cdot (r_D - \alpha_K + \delta)^3 \end{array} \right) \cdot A(\hat{t}) \cdot B(\hat{t}) \end{array} \right]$$

$$\cdot e^{-B(\hat{t}) \cdot r_D}$$

If (A4.1.8) was the correct solution, then the residual $R(r_D, \hat{t})$ would be identically zero. This implies that for any arbitrary choice of projection direction $pr(r_D, \hat{t})$ any arbitrary inner product over $R(r_D, \hat{t})$ and $pr(r_D, \hat{t})$, $\langle R(r_D, \hat{t}), pr(r_D, \hat{t}) \rangle$, has to be identical to zero. The idea of the projection procedure is now to choose a suitable projection direction and a suitable inner product. Then, one calculates values for the arbitrary parameters (here: ω, ξ and ζ) that make the inner product zero. For simplification, we make the following choices regarding inner product and projection direction:

(A4.1.11a) $\quad pr(r_D, \hat{t}) = \dfrac{e^{-B(\hat{t}) \cdot r_D}}{A(\hat{t})}$

(A4.1.11b) $\quad \langle R(r_D, \hat{t}), pr(r_D, \hat{t}) \rangle = \displaystyle\iint_\Lambda R(r_D, \hat{t}) \cdot pr(r_D, \hat{t}) \cdot dr_D \cdot d\hat{t}$

where Λ denotes some subspace of the definition space of the bond price $P(r_D, \hat{t})$. (A4.1.10) and (A4.1.11a-b) together yield:

164

(A4.1.12)

$$
\iint_{\Lambda} \left(\begin{array}{l} \dfrac{1}{2} \cdot \big(\beta_0 + \beta_1 \cdot (r_D - \alpha_K + \delta)\big)^2 \cdot (r_D - \alpha_K + \delta)^2 \cdot B(\hat{t})^2 + (B'(\hat{t}) - 1) \cdot r_D \\[2mm] - \left(\begin{array}{l} \alpha_0 + \alpha_1 \cdot (r_D - \alpha_K + \delta) + (\alpha_2 + \dfrac{\beta_0}{\beta_K}) \cdot (r_D - \alpha_K + \delta)^2 \\[3mm] + (\alpha_3 + \dfrac{\beta_1}{\beta_K}) \cdot (r_D - \alpha_K + \delta)^3 - \omega \end{array} \right) \cdot B(\hat{t}) \end{array} \right)
$$
$$
\cdot \, dr_D \cdot d\hat{t} = 0
$$

Taking Λ as $\Lambda := \left[0, \hat{t}_{max}\right] \times \left[\alpha_K - \delta - \gamma \cdot \beta_K^2, \alpha_K - \delta - \gamma \cdot \beta_K^2 \cdot (1 - z)\right]$, breaking the integrand into four parts for reasons of simplification and carrying out the double integration part by part results in the following four equations [17]:

$$
\int_{r_l}^{r_u} r_D \cdot \int_0^{\hat{t}_{max}} B'(\hat{t}) \cdot d\hat{t} \cdot dr_D = \frac{\left(e^{\sqrt{\xi^2 + 2 \cdot \zeta} \cdot \hat{t}_{max}} - 1\right) \cdot \left(\gamma \cdot \beta_K^2 \cdot z + 2 \cdot (\alpha_K - \delta - \gamma \cdot \beta_K^2)\right) \cdot \gamma \cdot \beta_K^2 \cdot z}{\left(\sqrt{\xi^2 + 2 \cdot \zeta} - \xi\right) \cdot \left(e^{\sqrt{\xi^2 + 2 \cdot \zeta} \cdot \hat{t}_{max}} - 1\right) + 2 \cdot \sqrt{\xi^2 + 2 \cdot \zeta}}
$$

$$
-\int_{r_l}^{r_u} \int_0^{\hat{t}_{max}} r_D \cdot d\hat{t} \cdot dr_D = -\frac{\left(\gamma \cdot \beta_K^2 \cdot z + 2 \cdot (\alpha_K - \delta - \gamma \cdot \beta_K^2)\right) \cdot \gamma \cdot \beta_K^2 \cdot z \cdot \hat{t}_{max}}{2}
$$

$$
\int_{r_l}^{r_u} \frac{1}{2} \cdot \big(\beta_0 + \beta_1 \cdot (r_D - \alpha_K + \delta)\big)^2 \cdot (r_D - \alpha_K + \delta)^2 \cdot \int_0^{\hat{t}_{max}} B(\hat{t})^2 \cdot d\hat{t} \cdot dr_D =
$$
$$
\frac{\gamma^3 \cdot \beta_K^8 \cdot \left(10 \cdot (1 - z)^2 - 15 \cdot (1 - z) + 6 - (1 - z)^5\right)}{60}.
$$

---

[17] $\hat{t}_{max}$ corresponds to the maximal time-to-maturity one can find on bond markets, for example 30 years.

$$\left(\frac{16 \cdot \sqrt{\xi^2 + 2 \cdot \zeta}}{\left(\sqrt{\xi^2 + 2 \cdot \zeta} - \xi \right) \cdot 2 \cdot \zeta \cdot \left(\xi + \sqrt{\xi^2 + 2 \cdot \zeta} + e^{\sqrt{\xi^2 + 2 \cdot \zeta} \cdot \hat{t}_{max}} \cdot \left(\sqrt{\xi^2 + 2 \cdot \zeta} - \xi \right) \right)} \right.$$

$$- \frac{8}{\left(\sqrt{\xi^2 + 2 \cdot \zeta} - \xi \right) \cdot 2 \cdot \zeta} + \frac{4 \cdot \hat{t}_{max}}{\left(\xi + \sqrt{\xi^2 + 2 \cdot \zeta} \right)^2}$$

$$+ \frac{4 \cdot \xi \cdot \log\left(\xi + \sqrt{\xi^2 + 2 \cdot \zeta} + e^{\sqrt{\xi^2 + 2 \cdot \zeta} \cdot \hat{t}_{max}} \cdot \left(\sqrt{\xi^2 + 2 \cdot \zeta} - \xi \right) \right)}{\zeta^2}$$

$$\left. - \frac{4 \cdot \xi \cdot \log\left(2 \cdot \sqrt{\xi^2 + 2 \cdot \zeta} \right)}{\zeta^2} \right)$$

$$\int_{r_u}^{r_l} \left(\omega + \alpha_0 + \alpha_1 \cdot (r_D - \alpha_K + \delta) + \left(\alpha_2 + \frac{\beta_0}{\beta_K} \right) \cdot (r_D - \alpha_K + \delta)^2 \right. \\ \left. + \left(\alpha_3 + \frac{\beta_1}{\beta_K} \right) \cdot (r_D - \alpha_K + \delta)^3 \right) \cdot \int_0^{\hat{t}_{max}} B(\hat{t}) \cdot d\hat{t} \cdot dr_D$$

$$= \left(\frac{2 \cdot \log\left(\xi + \sqrt{\xi^2 + 2 \cdot \zeta} + (\sqrt{\xi^2 + 2 \cdot \zeta} - \xi) \cdot e^{\sqrt{\xi^2 + 2 \cdot \zeta} \cdot \hat{t}_{max}} \right)}{\zeta} \right. \\ \left. - \frac{2 \cdot \hat{t}_{max}}{\sqrt{\xi^2 + 2 \cdot \zeta} + \xi} - \frac{2 \cdot \log\left(2 \cdot \sqrt{\xi^2 + 2 \cdot \zeta} \right)}{\zeta} \right) \cdot \beta_K^6 \cdot$$

$$\left(\frac{(\omega + \alpha_0) \cdot \gamma \cdot z}{\beta_K^4} + \frac{(\alpha_2 + 1 - z) \cdot \gamma^3 \cdot (1 - (1 - z)^3)}{3} \right. \\ \left. + \frac{\alpha_1 \cdot \gamma^2 \cdot z \cdot (z - 2)}{2 \cdot \beta_K^2} + \frac{(1 + \gamma) \cdot \gamma^2 \cdot ((1 - z)^4 - 1)}{8} \right)$$

Adding up these equations and setting the resulting equation equal to zero gives an equation that determines one of the three unknown parameters ω, ξ and ζ given the two others. In order to determine all three parameters, we need, in principle, two other equations which can be obtained by choosing two additional projection directions. We would then carry out the same calculations using the inner product in (A4.1.11b). Since the thus involved

166

calculations would be much more complicated than the previous one [18], we would end up with an extremely complicated three-dimensional systems of nonlinear algebraic equations that would have to be solved using other advanced numerical methods. Since nothing would be gained by this approach in terms of getting interpretable parameters, we take a slightly different approach which simplifies things substantially: we choose $\omega = 0$ and $\zeta = 1.5\,\xi^2$ [19]. The sum of the four equations from the last page is then:

(A4.1.13)

$$
\frac{\gamma^3 \cdot \beta_K^8 \cdot \left(10\cdot(1-z)^2 - 15\cdot(1-z) + 6 - (1-z)^5\right)}{60} \cdot \left(\frac{16\cdot \log\left(e^{2\cdot\xi\cdot\hat{t}_{max}} + 3\right)}{9\cdot\xi^3} + \frac{32}{3\cdot\xi^3 \cdot \left(e^{2\cdot\xi\cdot\hat{t}_{max}} + 3\right)} + \frac{4\cdot\hat{t}_{max}}{9\cdot\xi^2} - \frac{24 + 16\cdot\log 4}{9\cdot\xi^3} \right)
$$

$$
+ \frac{e^{2\cdot\xi\cdot\hat{t}_{max}} - 1}{e^{2\cdot\xi\cdot\hat{t}_{max}} + 3} \cdot \frac{\left(\gamma\cdot\beta_K^2 \cdot z + 2\cdot(\alpha_K - \delta - \gamma\cdot\beta_K^2)\right)\cdot \gamma\cdot\beta_K^2 \cdot z}{\xi} -
$$

$$
\left(\frac{4\cdot\log\left(\frac{1}{4}\cdot\left(3 + e^{2\cdot\xi\cdot\hat{t}_{max}}\right)\right)}{3\cdot\xi^2} - \frac{2\cdot\hat{t}_{max}}{3\cdot\xi} \right) \cdot \left(\alpha_0\cdot\gamma\cdot\beta_K^2 \cdot z + \frac{\alpha_1\cdot\gamma^2\cdot\beta_K^4 \cdot z\cdot(z-2)}{2} + \frac{(\alpha_2 + 1 - z)\cdot\gamma^3\cdot\beta_K^6 \cdot (1 - (1-z)^3)}{3} + \frac{(1+\gamma)\cdot\gamma^2\cdot\beta_K^6 \cdot ((1-z)^4 - 1)}{8} \right)
$$

$$
- \frac{\left(\gamma\cdot\beta_K^2 \cdot z + 2\cdot(\alpha_K - \delta - \gamma\cdot\beta_K^2)\right)\cdot \gamma\cdot\beta_K^2 \cdot z\cdot\hat{t}_{max}}{2} = 0
$$

---

[18] Note that the projection direction choice (A4.1.11a) was made in order to eliminate the exponential term of the residual. Other projection directions not eliminating the exponential term in the residual would result in extremely complex integrals, most of them having no closed-form antiderivative. Additional numerical techniques had to be employed to obtain solutions.

[19] In order to remain more general, we could also have taken an arbitrary positive constant for the relation between ζ and ξ instead of 1.5. The only necessary restriction is that negativity of the constant has to be ruled out for this could produce an exploding yield curve for any finite time-to-maturity value.

Equation (A4.1.13) determines the value of ξ as an implicit function of the underlying model parameters and the maximal time-to-maturity $\hat{t}_{max}$. (A4.1.13) looks quite formidable, but setting the maximum for time-to-maturity $\hat{t}_{max} = 30$ (which seems to be a reasonable value looking on bond markets in reality) allows us to simplify (A4.1.13) substantially using the following considerations: assume that ξ is a sufficiently large positive number. Then the exponential expression $e^{2\xi \cdot \hat{t}_{max}} + 3$ becomes so big that the sum of the two last terms within the brackets in the first line of (A4.1.13) does not contribute substantially to the value of this bracket. Omitting them does therefore introduce only a negligible error while it simplifies the bracket enormously. Furthermore, $e^{2\xi \cdot \hat{t}_{max}} + 3$ can be replaced by $e^{2\xi \cdot \hat{t}_{max}}$ owing to similar considerations. As a consequence, all logarithms within (A4.1.13) vanish. Eventually, the first fraction in line 3 of (A4.1.13), which consists of the exponential term $e^{2\xi \cdot \hat{t}_{max}}$ in the numerator as well as in the nominator, is approximately 1 for big values of $e^{2\xi \cdot \hat{t}_{max}}$. Employing these approximations and multiplying through by ξ^2 yields the following quadratic equation:

$$120 \cdot \Omega_1 + \Omega_2 \cdot \left(\xi - 15 \cdot \xi^2\right) + \Omega_3 \cdot \left(\frac{4 \cdot \log 4}{3} - 60 \cdot \xi\right) = 0$$

(A4.1.14)

$$\Rightarrow \xi^2 + \left(4 \cdot \frac{\Omega_3}{\Omega_2} - \frac{1}{15}\right) \cdot \xi - \left(8 \cdot \frac{\Omega_1}{\Omega_2} + \frac{4 \cdot \log 4}{45} \cdot \frac{\Omega_3}{\Omega_2}\right) = 0$$

with:

$$\Omega_1 = \frac{\gamma^3 \cdot \beta_K^8 \cdot \left(10 \cdot (1-z)^2 - 15 \cdot (1-z) + 6 - (1-z)^5\right)}{60} > 0 \quad \forall z \in (0;1)$$

$$\Omega_2 = \left(\gamma \cdot \beta_K^2 \cdot z + 2 \cdot (\alpha_K - \delta - \gamma \cdot \beta_K^2)\right) \cdot \gamma \cdot \beta_K^2 \cdot z$$

$$\Omega_3 = \alpha_0 \cdot \gamma \cdot \beta_K^2 \cdot z + \frac{\alpha_1 \cdot \gamma^2 \cdot \beta_K^4 \cdot z \cdot (z-2)}{2} + \frac{(\alpha_2 + 1 - z) \cdot \gamma^3 \cdot \beta_K^6 \cdot (1 - (1-z)^3)}{3}$$

$$+ \frac{(1+\gamma) \cdot \gamma^2 \cdot \beta_K^6 \cdot ((1-z)^4 - 1)}{8}$$

The solution of this quadratic equation is [20]:

$$(A4.1.15) \qquad \xi = -2 \cdot \frac{\Omega_3}{\Omega_2} + \frac{1}{30} + \sqrt{\left(2 \cdot \frac{\Omega_3}{\Omega_2} - \frac{1}{30}\right)^2 + \left(8 \cdot \frac{\Omega_1}{\Omega_2} + \frac{4 \cdot \log 4}{45} \cdot \frac{\Omega_3}{\Omega_2}\right)}$$

For most parameter values, Ω_1, Ω_2 and Ω_3 will be positive and ensure a positive ξ. Whether ξ is big enough to guarantee that (A4.1.14) is a good approximation of (A4.1.13) has to be determined by calculating the respective numerical value of ξ given all numerical parameter values. For the analysis in Section 3 we just assume that it is a good approximation.

We can now write down the complete approximate solution of the bond price equation. Recalling the general solution (A4.1.8) and making use of the assumptions regarding ω and ζ, we obtain equation (4.4) in the main text:

$$(4.4) \qquad P(r_D, \hat{t}) = \exp\left(-\frac{2 \cdot \left(e^{2 \cdot \xi \cdot \hat{t}} - 1\right)}{\left(e^{2 \cdot \xi \cdot \hat{t}} + 3\right) \cdot \xi} \cdot r_D\right)$$

$$\xi = -2 \cdot \frac{\Omega_3}{\Omega_2} + \frac{1}{30} + \sqrt{\left(2 \cdot \frac{\Omega_3}{\Omega_2} - \frac{1}{30}\right)^2 + \left(8 \cdot \frac{\Omega_1}{\Omega_2} + \frac{4 \cdot \log 4}{45} \cdot \frac{\Omega_3}{\Omega_2}\right)}$$

$$\Omega_1 = \frac{\gamma^3 \cdot \beta_K^8 \cdot \left(10 \cdot (1-z)^2 - 15 \cdot (1-z) + 6 - (1-z)^5\right)}{60}$$

$$\Omega_2 = \left(\gamma \cdot \beta_K^2 \cdot z + 2 \cdot (\alpha_K - \delta - \gamma \cdot \beta_K^2)\right) \cdot \gamma \cdot \beta_K^2 \cdot z$$

$$\Omega_3 = \alpha_0 \cdot \gamma \cdot \beta_K^2 \cdot z + \frac{\alpha_1 \cdot \gamma^2 \cdot \beta_K^4 \cdot z \cdot (z-2)}{2} + \frac{(\alpha_2 + 1 - z) \cdot \gamma^3 \cdot \beta_K^6 \cdot (1 - (1-z)^3)}{3}$$

$$+ \frac{(1+\gamma) \cdot \gamma^2 \cdot \beta_K^6 \cdot ((1-z)^4 - 1)}{8}$$

---

[20] We exclude the second solution since it is usually negative and smaller than the first one. This is in contradiction to our assumption that ξ is sufficiently high and positive.

5 Economic growth and fiscal policy

5.1 Introduction

Having explicitly examined the influence of fiscal policy on short-term interest rate dynamics and the term structure of interest rates in the last two chapters, we now want to turn to the second main question to be addressed within our model: how do fiscal policy and financial market interactions influence the evolution of output, income and hence economic growth? Since we already mentioned in Chapter 3 that our production function is known to produce endogenous growth, the question here is not whether growth reaches a steady state or not. The question is rather: does the interaction between interest rate dynamics and fiscal policy imply positive or negative growth rates in average? And are growth rates accelerating like in the deterministic setting (which did not automatically imply that they are positive)? Recalling the discussion in the introductory chapter, it is our aim to show that growth does not evolve independent of financial markets and fiscal policy settings.

Fur this purpose, we will first show that the economic growth process depends crucially on the evolution of the capital output ratio. Given the capital accumulation and output dynamics from Chapter 3, we derive the dynamics of the capital output ratio and find that it is described jointly together with the dynamics of the short-term interest rate in a nonlinear way. No explicit closed-form solutions can be found. We therefore analyze the dynamics of the capital output ratio qualitatively by using advanced concepts from multidimensional diffusion theory. The first insight that we gain is that the capital output ratio dynamics possesses a fixed point at a capital output ratio of zero. Using the concept of Lyapunov exponents - which is a generalization of the eigenvalue concept in deterministic dynamic systems to stochastic dynamic systems - we can show for certain constellations of the model parameters that this fixed point is unstable and will thus not be reached. Moreover, we can show that there are two regions in the state space of the capital output ratio in which the capital output process can stay.

Being in the first region implies relatively low values for the capital output ratio. Since low values of the capital output ratio are responsible for low growth rates in the average, we will call this region 'lower-growth region' (note that 'lower-growth region' should not be seen as a normative value judgment but as a mean to distinguish regions of relatively low and relatively high growth rates). Employing the fiscal policy restrictions derived in Chapter 3, we will then show that the capital output process can never leave the lower-growth region once it is in it. The question whether the lower-growth region may be entered by the capital output process when it has started outside (i.e. when it has started in the higher-growth region) is then assessed using the concept of 'effective dimensions'. This concept assigns a characteristic value to each point in state space of a multidimensional diffusion process. If these values fulfill a certain condition then one can conclude that there is zero probability for the process to hit some pre-specified point(s) in state space. We take the boundary that separates the lower- from the higher-growth region as the set of possible points the process may hit and show for some parameter constellations that there is a positive probability to reach the boundary. The conclusion is that the capital output process may always enter the lower-growth region with the consequence that it will then be trapped there forever. This whole discussion, which is contained in Section 2, serves to illustrate main qualitative properties of the dynamic behavior of the capital output ratio and economic growth.

In Section 3, we will then examine how changes in fiscal policy and interest rate dynamics affect capital output ratio and growth locally (i.e. in the short run) and globally (i.e. in the long run). The analysis will show that short- and long run effects are present and mainly coincide. We will see that the nature of these effects can be somewhat surprising in view of standard economic intuition. Moreover, we can show that the quality of these effects are often state variable dependent. This gives rise to nonlinear feedback effects between public policy, financial markets and economic growth. Additionally, we will identify and discuss the economic reasoning behind these effects. A brief summary of the results in Section 4 closes the chapter.

5.2 Local and global behavior of the capital output ratio and implications for economic growth

Recalling the output equation (3.1), we can rewrite it as a SDE describing the relative change of output. This relative change is the process which describes economic growth and it is given as follows:

(5.1a) $$\frac{dY}{Y} = \alpha_K \cdot \frac{K}{Y} \cdot dt + \beta_K \cdot \frac{K}{Y} \cdot dB = \alpha_K \cdot k \cdot dt + \beta_K \cdot k \cdot dB$$

where 'k' denotes the capital output ratio. From (5.1a) follows the locally expected growth rate as the instantaneously expected marginal product of capital, α_K, times the capital output ratio at any point in time:

(5.1b) $$\frac{E\left(\dfrac{dY}{Y}\right)}{dt} = \alpha_K \cdot k$$

(5.1a-b) shows that rising values of α_K and β_K clearly lead to increasing instantaneously expected growth rates and increasing instantaneous variances in the growth rates. Besides, (5.1b) implies that, the higher the capital output ratio, the higher instantaneously expected economic growth and instantaneous variance in growth rates. This means that bigger values of the capital output ratio do not only increase the drift $\alpha_K \cdot k$ but also enhance the diffusion $\beta_K \cdot k$ so that stochastic productivity shocks impact more strongly on growth. The growth rates are thus moving on higher levels when the capital output ratio gets bigger. An understanding of economic growth in our model requires a better understanding of the dynamics of the capital output ratio k since k is the determining factor for growth. Employing Ito's Lemma we can compute the dynamics of the capital output ratio as follows:

(5.2a) $$dk = d\left(\frac{K}{Y}\right) = k \cdot \frac{dK}{K} - k \cdot \frac{dY}{Y} + k \cdot \left\langle \frac{dY}{Y} \right\rangle - k \cdot \left\langle \frac{dK}{K}, \frac{dY}{Y} \right\rangle$$

Calculating the quadratic variation and covariation processes (i.e. the brackets in (5.2a)) using capital accumulation equation (3.19) and output

172

equation (5.1a) and replacing the remaining terms containing K and D by the equilibrium interest rate equation (3.18) yields:

(5.2b)
$$dk = \left(\begin{array}{c} (1-z)\cdot\alpha_K - \delta + (\gamma-1)\cdot\beta_K^2 - (\alpha_K + (1-z-k)\cdot\beta_K^2)\cdot k \\ + \dfrac{(\gamma-1)\cdot(r_D - \alpha_K + \delta)}{2\cdot\gamma} + \dfrac{(\rho + (\gamma-1)\cdot(\alpha_K - \delta - \tau))\cdot\beta_K^2}{r_D - \alpha_K + \delta} \end{array} \right) \cdot k\cdot dt$$

$$\underbrace{+ (1-z-k)\cdot k\cdot\beta_K \cdot dB}_{\text{diffusion of k}}$$

where the bracket term is labeled "drift of k".

(5.2b) shows that the dynamics of k depend on its own level as well as on the short-term interest rate r_D in a nonlinear way. Hence, economic growth is influenced by the interest rate dynamics. Moreover, fiscal policy impacts twice on capital output dynamics and growth: first, there is a direct influence since the fiscal policy parameters appear in the drift and the diffusion term of (5.2b). And second, there is an indirect impact via r_D since the analysis in Chapter 3 has shown the influence of fiscal policy on the short-term interest rate dynamics.

The stochastic dynamics of k is jointly given by the two-dimensional SDE in k and r_D, i.e. by the two-dimensional joint diffusion process (3.24a-b) and (5.2b). Since we were unable to solve the SDE (3.24a-b) of the short-term interest rate explicitly, we also cannot hope to get a closed-form solution of the system (3.24a-b) and (5.2b). Nevertheless, we can and will examine (5.2b) with regard to its qualitative behavior at certain boundaries etc.

The first question is: are there points on the definition interval of k, $[0, \infty]$ [1] at which k locally ceases to be a diffusion process implying that k becomes irregular? We have seen before in Chapter 3 that an answer to this question helps us 'sort out' certain regions on which a diffusion process can stay. The criterion for irregular points to appear is that the diffusion term $(1-z-k)\cdot k\cdot\beta_K$ has to vanish. Setting the diffusion term equal to zero delivers the following two irregular points k_1 and k_2:

---

[1] We assume k to start with a positive value so that it will start indeed within $[0, \infty]$. Later on, we will show that k can never leave this interval i.e. can never get negative.

(5.3a) $\quad (1-z-k)\cdot k\cdot\beta_K = 0 \Leftrightarrow k_1 = 0 \quad \vee \quad k_2 = 1-z$

Thus, we distinguish three regions on which k can stay: $I_1 = (-\infty,0)$, $I_2 = (0,1-z)$ and $I_3 = (1-z,\infty)$, with k_1 and k_2 being separating points or 'boundaries' between these regions. Due to Definition 3.1, the stochastic process for k is regular for any point within I_1, I_2 and I_3.

The next question is: are k_1 and k_2 equilibrium (or fixed) points and, if not, how does the drift behave at k_1 and k_2? The criterion for an equilibrium (or fixed) point is that the drift and diffusion term get zero at k_1 or k_2. Calculating the respective drifts yields:

(5.3b) $\quad$ drift of $k\big|_{k=k_1} = 0$

(5.3c) $\quad$ drift of $k\big|_{k=k_2} = \left(\dfrac{(\gamma-1)\cdot(r_D - \alpha_K + \delta + 2\cdot\gamma\cdot\beta_K^2)}{2\cdot\gamma} - \delta \right.$
$\left. + \dfrac{(\rho + (\gamma-1)\cdot(\alpha_K - \delta - \tau))\cdot\beta_K^2}{r_D - \alpha_K + \delta} \right)\cdot(1-z)$

(5.3b) tells us that k_1 is really an equilibrium point: the capital output ratio k does not change any more once having reached it. From an economic viewpoint, a zero capital output ratio has the unpleasant feature that economic growth also settles down to zero (see (5.1a)). If this equilibrium point were attained then we would end up with a steady state value for k and K like in the Solow-Swan model without population growth and technical progress. Starting with a positive capital output ratio, this also means that k_1 is a lower boundary of the capital output process: k can never become negative. Interval I_1 hence drops out as a possible subspace on which k could stay.

Does the fixed point property of $k_1 = 0$ mean that the capital output ratio will finally reach this equilibrium with the somewhat unpleasant consequence that it would stay there forever? In view of the results derived in Chapter 3, we suppose that this will certainly not happen because we have already shown under which conditions ((3.23), (3.27), (3.28)) the stock of capital, K, cannot approach zero. This alone, however, is in a strict mathematical sense not sufficient to ensure that k is also always different from zero: Y could theoretically become unbounded for large productivity shocks, thereby driving k to zero. We have thus to show that $k_1 = 0$ is an unstable equilibrium which, in turn, implies that this point will never be reached. The answer to the question whether an equilibrium point of a system of stochastic differential equations is unstable or not is intimately connected to the sign of the so-called 'top Lyapunov exponent' of the considered system. The Lyapunov exponents can be viewed as extensions of the concept of the real parts of the eigenvalues of a deterministic dynamic system. Since a detailed discussion of the related concepts requires a huge mathematical apparatus [2] and bursts the framework of our discussion, we will just state Proposition 5.1 and refer to Appendix 5.1 for a more detailed derivation and discussion of the results leading to it:

Proposition 5.1:

For the chosen parameter constellation $\alpha_K = 7.5\%$, $\beta_K = 5\%$, $\delta = 1.5\%$, $\gamma = 5$ and $\rho = 10\%$ the top Lyapunov exponent corresponding to $k_1 = 0$ is positive given that the tax rate and the public expenditure ratio obey the constraints (3.23) and (3.28). $k_1 = 0$ is hence an unstable equilibrium point.

Proof: see Table 5.1 together with Appendix 5.1.

We note that the top Lyapunov exponent is always positive, indicating that $k_1 = 0$ is an unstable equilibrium and will never be reached. The hyphens in the table indicate that the corresponding combination of τ and z does not obey the fiscal policy constraints derived in Chapter 3. Had we calculated the top Lyapunov exponents for these parameter constellations we would have found out that their signs are negative, indicating that $k_1 = 0$ is now a stable equilibrium point. We thus utter the conjecture that it is indeed the validity of the fiscal policy constraints (3.23) and (3.28) which provides that the capital

---

[2] See Arnold (1998) for a complete discussion of all questions regarding random dynamic systems which contains SDEs in the Ito sense as a special case.

output ratio will never reach zero, let alone negative values. Economic growth remains therefore feasible for all time.

Table 5.1: Top Lyapunov exponents

	$\tau = 1\%$	$\tau = 2\%$	$\tau = 3\%$	$\tau = 4\%$	$\tau = 5\%$	$\tau = 6\%$	$\tau = 7\%$
$z = 1\%$	0.031	0.035	0.038	0.040	0.043	0.045	0.047
$z = 6\%$	0.027	0.031	0.034	0.037	0.039	0.042	0.044
$z = 11\%$	-	0.027	0.030	0.033	0.036	0.038	0.041
$z = 16\%$	-	0.023	0.027	0.030	0.032	0.035	0.037
$z = 21\%$	-	-	0.023	0.026	0.029	0.032	0.034
$z = 26\%$	-	-	-	0.023	0.025	0.028	0.031
$z = 31\%$	-	-	-	0.018	0.022	0.025	0.027
$z = 36\%$	-	-	-	-	0.018	0.021	0.024
$z = 41\%$	-	-	-	-	0.015	0.018	0.021
$z = 46\%$	-	-	-	-	-	0.014	0.017
$z = 51\%$	-	-	-	-	-	0.011	0.014
$z = 56\%$	-	-	-	-	-	-	0.010
$z = 61\%$	-	-	-	-	-	-	0.007
$z = 66\%$	-	-	-	-	-	-	0.004

Let us now turn to the second irregular point at which the diffusion vanishes: $k_2 = 1 - z$. As already noted before, we have to distinguish between two areas where the capital output process can move on, namely $I_2 = (0, 1 - z)$ and $I_3 = $

$(1 - z, \infty)$. We will from now on call I_2 the „lower-growth region" and I_3 the „higher-growth region" (the higher k, the higher the expected instantaneous growth rate (5.1b)). k_2 is hence the 'separating boundary' between these regions. The question whether the capital output ratio can cross this boundary is crucial for the economic growth path since it determines whether the economy can shift between areas of relatively low and high growth. A word of caution is, however, necessary here: being in the higher-growth region does not automatically mean that the economy always enjoys higher growth rates than in the lower-growth region. The reason for this is that a series of strong negative productivity shocks (i.e. negative values of the Brownian motion driving technology in production function (3.1)) in the higher-growth region could well yield lower growth rates compared to a situation where a series of strong positive shocks happen in the lower-growth area. In average, however, the growth process in the higher-growth region will exceed growth rates in the lower-growth area.

From (5.3c) we know that the drift of k at $k_2 = 1 - z$ is given by the following expression which we will view as a function $f(r_D)$:

$$(5.3c) \quad f(r_D) = \left(\frac{(\gamma-1) \cdot (r_D - \alpha_K + \delta)}{2 \cdot \gamma} + (\gamma-1) \cdot \beta_K^2 - \delta \atop + \frac{(\rho + (\gamma-1) \cdot (\alpha_K - \delta - \tau)) \cdot \beta_K^2}{r_D - \alpha_K + \delta} \right) \cdot (1-z)$$

$$\equiv g(r_D) \cdot (1-z)$$

It is important to figure out whether the sign of $f(r_D)$ or, equivalently, $g(r_D)$ is unambiguous or not and how it depends on the short-term interest rate r_D. To illustrate the importance of this question, let us assume for the moment that the sign of $f(r_D)$ was negative and ask what this would imply. Obviously, the stochastic process driving k via (5.2b) could, once k_2 was reached coming from I_2, not enter the region I_3 because the negative drift at $k_2 = 1 - z$ would immediately 'bounce back' k_2 into region I_2. If, however, the economy started with an initial value of k in the high-growth region I_3 and the capital output process reached k_2, it would cross k_2 immediately thereby entering I_2. From then on, the capital output process would stay within the low-growth region I_2 forever since reaching k_2 again means being catapulted back into I_2. The economic meaning of such a situation is that the economy will finally be trapped in the low-growth region.

We start to examine $g(r_D)$ more closely considering the following limits first:

$$g(r_D) = \frac{(\gamma - 1) \cdot (r_D - \alpha_K + \delta)}{2 \cdot \gamma} + (\gamma - 1) \cdot \beta_K^2 - \delta$$

(5.4)
$$+ \frac{\left(\rho + (\gamma - 1) \cdot (\alpha_K - \delta - \tau)\right) \cdot \beta_K^2}{r_D - \alpha_K + \delta}$$

$$\Rightarrow \begin{cases} \lim_{r_D \to \pm\infty} g(r_D) = \pm\infty \\ \lim_{r_D \uparrow \alpha_K - \delta} g(r_D) = -\infty \\ \lim_{r_D \downarrow \alpha_K - \delta} g(r_D) = +\infty \end{cases}$$

(5.4) shows that $g(r_D)$ has a singularity at $r_{D,2} = \alpha_K - \delta$. The limit tends to $-\infty$ when r_D approaches $r_{D,2}$ from initially smaller values than $r_{D,2}$ and tends to $+\infty$ when r_D approaches $r_{D,2}$ from initially bigger values than $r_{D,2}$. However, we do not have to consider values for r_D bigger or equal to $r_{D,2}$ due to our discussion in Chapter 3. Since the limit of $g(r_D)$ tends to $-\infty$ for $r_D = -\infty$, we can conclude that there must be at least one local maximum within the interval $(-\infty, r_{D,2})$. In order to calculate this local maximum, we need the derivatives of $g(r_D)$:

(5.5)
$$g'(r_D) = \frac{\gamma - 1}{2 \cdot \gamma} - \frac{\left(\rho + (\gamma - 1) \cdot (\alpha_K - \delta - \tau)\right) \cdot \beta_K^2}{(r_D - \alpha_K + \delta)^2}$$

$$g''(r_D) = \frac{2 \cdot \left(\rho + (\gamma - 1) \cdot (\alpha_K - \delta - \tau)\right) \cdot \beta_K^2}{(r_D - \alpha_K + \delta)^3}$$

Using (5.5), we get the two candidate solutions for a local maximum (note that the unique sign in the second derivative is due to (3.23)):

(5.6a) $\quad r_{D,3} = \alpha_K - \delta + \sqrt{\dfrac{2 \cdot \gamma}{\gamma - 1} \cdot \left(\rho + (\gamma - 1) \cdot (\alpha_K - \delta - \tau)\right) \cdot \beta_K^2}$

$$(5.6a) \quad g''(r_{D,3}) = \frac{2 \cdot (\rho + (\gamma - 1) \cdot (\alpha_K - \delta - \tau)) \cdot \beta_K^2}{\sqrt{\frac{2 \cdot \gamma}{\gamma - 1} \cdot (\rho + (\gamma - 1) \cdot (\alpha_K - \delta - \tau)) \cdot \beta_K^2}^3} > 0$$

$$r_{D,4} = \alpha_K - \delta - \sqrt{\frac{2 \cdot \gamma}{\gamma - 1} \cdot (\rho + (\gamma - 1) \cdot (\alpha_K - \delta - \tau)) \cdot \beta_K^2}$$

$$(5.6b)$$

$$g''(r_{D,4}) = -\frac{2 \cdot (\rho + (\gamma - 1) \cdot (\alpha_K - \delta - \tau)) \cdot \beta_K^2}{\sqrt{\frac{2 \cdot \gamma}{\gamma - 1} \cdot (\rho + (\gamma - 1) \cdot (\alpha_K - \delta - \tau)) \cdot \beta_K^2}^3} < 0$$

Since solution (5.6a) is bigger than $r_{D,2}$, we can sort it out and solution (5.6b) remains the only local maximum. The value of $g(r_D)$ at $r_{D,4}$ is:

$$(5.7) \quad g(r_{D,4}) = (\gamma - 1) \cdot \beta_K^2 - \delta - 2 \cdot \sqrt{\frac{\gamma - 1}{2 \cdot \gamma} \cdot (\rho + (\gamma - 1) \cdot (\alpha_K - \delta - \tau)) \cdot \beta_K^2}$$

As we will see later on, a necessary condition for the sign of $g(r_D)$ to become positive at least over some subset of $(-\infty, r_{D,1})$, the state space of r_D, is that $g(r_{D,4})$ is positive.

Next, we calculate the roots of $g(r_D)$:

$$(5.8) \quad r_{D,5/6} - \alpha_K + \delta = \pm \sqrt{\underbrace{\left(\gamma \cdot \beta_K^2 - \frac{\gamma \cdot \delta}{\gamma - 1}\right)^2 - \frac{8 \cdot \gamma \cdot \beta_K^2 \cdot (\rho + (\gamma - 1) \cdot (\alpha_K - \delta - \tau))}{\gamma - 1}}_{\text{discriminant}}} - \underbrace{\left(\gamma \cdot \beta_K^2 - \frac{\gamma \cdot \delta}{\gamma - 1}\right)}_{A}$$

If the discriminant in (5.8) is negative, the roots get complex-valued so that there is no root of $g(r_D)$. This automatically implies that $g(r_D)$ is always negative over the whole state space of r_D, $(-\infty, r_{D,1})$, even at the local maximum $r_{D,4}$. This changes when the discriminant becomes positive: now both roots are either bigger or smaller than $r_{D,2}$, depending on whether the term A in (5.8) is negative or positive. Only for a positive discriminant and a positive term A we get two roots smaller than $r_{D,2}$. It can be shown that in this case $g(r_{D,4})$ is positive. But then one still has to show that the lower root is smaller than $r_{D,1}$ in order to assure that there are values of r_D for which $g(r_D)$ really gets positive.

These insights give the following conditions together with Proposition 5.2:

$$(5.9a) \quad \left(\gamma \cdot \beta_K^2 - \frac{\gamma \cdot \delta}{\gamma - 1}\right)^2 - \frac{8 \cdot \gamma \cdot \beta_K^2 \cdot (\rho + (\gamma - 1) \cdot (\alpha_K - \delta - \tau))}{\gamma - 1} > 0$$

$$(5.9b) \quad \gamma \cdot \beta_K^2 - \frac{\gamma \cdot \delta}{\gamma - 1} > 0$$

$$(5.9c) \quad \sqrt{\left(\gamma \cdot \beta_K^2 - \frac{\gamma \cdot \delta}{\gamma - 1}\right)^2 - \frac{8 \cdot \gamma \cdot \beta_K^2 \cdot (\rho + (\gamma - 1) \cdot (\alpha_K - \delta - \tau))}{\gamma - 1}}$$
$$+ z \cdot \gamma \cdot \beta_K^2 - \frac{\gamma \cdot \delta}{\gamma - 1} > 0$$

Proposition 5.2:

$g(r_D)$ is negative over the whole state space $(-\infty, r_{D,1})$ of r_D if at least one of the conditions (5.9a-c) fails to hold. The capital output ratio k then remains always in the low-growth region I_2 given that it starts therein. If all conditions (5.9a-c) hold, then $g(r_D)$ will be negative for $r_D \in (-\infty, r_{D,6})$, positive for $r_D \in (r_{D,6}, \min(r_{D,1}, r_{D,5}))$ and again negative for $r_D \in (\min(r_{D,1}, r_{D,5}), \max(r_{D,1}, r_{D,5}))$ where $r_{D,6}$ is the lower and $r_{D,5}$ the bigger root of (5.8) and $r_{D,1}$ is defined in (3.25).

Proof: Proposition 5.2 follows from the whole discussion above recognizing that (5.9c) was obtained by the requirement $r_{D,6} < r_{D,1}$.

The message of Proposition 5.2 is quite interesting: if all the parameter conditions (5.9a-c) hold, then there is a range of short-term interest rate values which acts as a „passage window" for the capital output ratio process. This window emerges between $r_{D,6}$ and $\min(r_{D,6}, r_{D,1})$ since the bigger root of

$g(r_D)$ may be bigger, equal to or smaller than $r_{D,1}$. Through this window, the capital output process can pass k_2 and enter the high-growth region I_3. Even if the process returns to k_2 again, it may stay within the high-growth region if and only if the short-term interest rate process r_D attains values on the window interval. Yet, the capital output process can also return to region I_2, thereby falling back into the low-growth region. This happens when r_D has either a lower value than $r_{D,6}$ or a higher value than $r_{D,5}$ given that $r_{D,5}$ is smaller than $r_{D,1}$ at the time when k hits k_2. Thus, the possibility exists that the capital output ratio process 'commutes' between the lower- and higher-growth areas I_2 and I_3.

However, this possibility is only a theoretical one as the following considerations make clear: the likelihood that condition (5.9a) holds is the higher, the lower the second term gets. The lowest values of this second term is reached when the fiscal policy constraint (3.23) becomes binding, i.e. when

$$\rho + (\gamma - 1) \cdot (\alpha_K - \delta - \tau) = \frac{1}{2} \cdot \gamma \cdot (\gamma - 1) \cdot \beta_K^2 \quad \text{holds. Plugging this into (5.9a)}$$

delivers after some algebraic steps:

(5.9a') $$\frac{\gamma^2 \cdot \delta^2}{(\gamma - 1)^2} > 3 \cdot \gamma^2 \cdot \beta_K^4 + \frac{2 \cdot \gamma^2 \cdot \delta \cdot \beta_K^2}{\gamma - 1}$$

From condition (5.9b) it follows:

(5.9b') $$\frac{\gamma^2 \cdot \delta^2}{(\gamma - 1)^2} < \gamma^2 \cdot \beta_K^4$$

(5.9a') and (5.9b') are clearly in contradiction to each other. Conditions (5.9a) and (5.9b) can thus never hold together when the fiscal policy constraint (3.23) becomes binding. When it does not bind, then the contradiction of (5.9a) and (5.9b) becomes even clearer. As a consequence, we state the following Corollary 5.1:

Corollary 5.1:

Given that the fiscal policy constraint (3.23) holds, $g(r_D)$ is negative over the whole state space $(-\infty, r_{D,1})$ with the consequence that the economy, once it has reached low-growth region I_2, remains there forever.

The conclusion of this corollary is that the economy is trapped in the low growth region $k \in (0, 1 - z)$ if it starts there or reaches it somewhere in time. Moreover, fiscal policy in form of the fixed public expenditure ratio can be seen to 'set a cap' on economic growth: the immediately expected growth rate within I_2 has a maximum value of $\alpha_K \cdot (1 - z)$ when the capital output ratio reaches its upper boundary k_2. One might conclude that fiscal policy aiming at enhancing economic growth should hence set the public expenditure ratio z equal to zero. This is, however, only seemingly correct since z at the same time affects the volatility of growth rates. This volatility gets the higher the smaller z becomes. High public expenditure does hence operate as a dampening mechanism for it provides a weaker transmission of both positive and negative productivity shocks on economic growth. This kind of mechanism is the same as already discussed in Chapter 3 when we studied the short-term interest dynamics. We conclude that there is a trade-off between the immediately expected and variance of growth rates in terms of setting the public expenditure ratio.

After we have seen that the capital output ratio and thus the economic growth process will be trapped within the lower-growth region I_2 once being in I_2, the following question appears: what happens if the capital output process starts in the higher-growth region I_3 corresponding to values of k higher than 1 - z? Are there any constellations under which the capital output ratio process will always remain in this higher-growth area, or is there always the possibility that the process hits k_2, enters the low-growth area I_2 and remains there forever? The answer is linked to the question whether the capital output ratio process k can reach the barrier $k_2 = 1 - z$ from I_3 or not. We check this by using a theorem stated in Durrett (1996). This theorem uses a special concept frequently employed in the theory of multidimensional diffusion processes: the so-called 'effective dimension'. If this effective dimension fulfills a certain requirement, then one knows that the process will not reach certain points. We first define the concept of an 'effective dimension' and then state the respective theorem:

Definition 5.1: Effective dimension of a multidimensional diffusion process

An m-dimensional diffusion process x may be given as the solution to the following stochastic differential equation:

$$dx = \mu(x) \cdot dt + \sigma(x) \cdot dB$$

where μ is an m-dimensional vector, σ is an $m \times n$ matrix and B is an n-dimensional vector of independent Brownian motions. Furthermore, we define the following auxiliary function:

$$\overline{a}(x) = \frac{1}{|x|^2} \cdot x^T \cdot \sigma^2(x) \cdot x$$

where '|...|' denotes the Euklidean norm, the superscript 'T' denotes the transpose of vector x and the square means the usual product of a matrix and its transpose $\sigma(x) \cdot \sigma^T(x)$. The effective dimension $d_e(x)$ is then given as:

$$d_e(x) = \frac{2 \cdot x^T \cdot \mu(x) + tr(\sigma^2(x))}{\overline{a}(x)}$$

where 'tr' denotes the trace of the square of matrix $\sigma(x)$. This completes the definition.

The theorem Durrett (1996, chapter 6.6c) stated is then the following:

Theorem 5.1: Hitting the zero-point with probability zero

If: 1) $d_e(x) \geq 2 (1 - \epsilon(|x|))$

and: 2) $\int_0^1 e^{-\int_y^1 \frac{\varepsilon(z)}{z} \cdot dz} \cdot \frac{dy}{y} = \infty$

holds, then $P_x(T_0 < \infty) = 0$.

The meaning of the theorem is the following: if a function ε depending on the Euklidean norm of the multidimensional diffusion process x can be found which fulfills inequality 1) and leads to non-existence of the integral 2), then the probability P_x that the multidimensional diffusion process x reaches the m-dimensional zero vector in finite time (i.e. $T_0 < \infty$ where T_0 denotes the time at which the zero vector is reached) is zero. By appropriately transforming our original diffusion process, Theorem 5.1 can be applied in order to assess whether the probability of the diffusion to reach a given point in the definition space is zero or not.

Having stated this theorem, one may ask: what is the meaning of an 'effective dimension'? Consider, for example, an m-dimensional Brownian motion. As Durrett (1996, Section 6.3) shows, it depends on the dimension of this Brownian motion whether it shows transient or recurrent behavior. Recurrence means that the process 'visits' any point of the state space at least once in finite time, transience corresponds to the opposite. A Brownian motion of dimension $m \le 2$ is recurrent and transient if $m > 2$ holds. Thus, a recurrent Brownian motion can always hit any point including the zero-point with positive probability. The question whether a multidimensional diffusion process is recurrent or transient and hits certain points with probability zero or with positive probability has hence to do with the dimension of the process. In this light, the effective dimension is obviously the characteristic measure for the question whether specific points in the state space of a diffusion process will not be hit and Theorem 5.1 states the conditions for this to hold.

The only problem in order to operationalize Theorem 5.1 and Definition 5.1 for our purposes is that the effective dimension $d_e(x)$ will usually depend on all components of the vector diffusion process x in such a way that these components cannot be easily eliminated using the Euklidean norm. This elimination, however, has to be done if we want to calculate condition 2) of Theorem 5.1 since we then need the ε-function depending on the Euklidean norm of the diffusion process x. There is a way out of this dilemma: assuming that $d_e(x)$ is a C^∞-function [3], we can use the Taylor-Theorem to develop a series expansion in terms of the Euklidean norm around arbitrary (vector-valued) points $\hat{x}$ of the diffusion's definition space. This yields:

$$(5.10) \quad d_e(x) = d_e(x)\Big|_{x=\hat{x}} + \sum_{j=1}^{m} \frac{\partial d_e(x)}{\partial x_j} \cdot \frac{dx_j}{d|x|^2}\Bigg|_{x=\hat{x}} \cdot |x|^2 + O(|x|^4)$$

$$\Rightarrow d_e(x) = \omega_0(\hat{x}) + \omega_1(\hat{x}) \cdot |x|^2 + O(|x|^4)$$

where $O(...)$ denotes the big Landau-symbol and the ω-functions are given as:

$$(5.11) \quad \omega_0(\hat{x}) = d_e(x)\Big|_{x=\hat{x}}$$

$$(5.12) \quad \omega_1(\hat{x}) = \sum_{j=1}^{m} \frac{\partial d_e(x)}{\partial x_j} \cdot \frac{dx_j}{d|x|^2}\Bigg|_{x=\hat{x}}.$$

Using these equations, we are able to state the following lemma:

Lemma 5.1: Hitting the zero-point with probability zero

If $\omega_0(\hat{x}) \equiv d_e(x)\Big|_{x=\hat{x}} \geq 2$ holds for arbitrary values $\hat{x}$ of the diffusion process x, then the probability that the zero vector will be reached in finite time is zero.

Proof: see Appendix 5.2

---

[3] This assumption can be shown to be true when the drift and diffusion terms of all components of the multidimensional diffusion are also C^∞-functions.

Using Theorem 5.1 together with Lemma 5.1, we can now examine whether there are parameter conditions guaranteeing non-attainability of the zero-point in finite time.

In order to apply Theorem 5.1, we first have to define which point we mean when we talk about 'hitting the zero point'. 'Zero point' in our case is the manifold in k-r_D space on which the capital output ratio k attains the value $k_2 = 1 - z$. Since this can, in principle, happen for any short-term interest rate value $r_D \in (-\infty, r_{D,1})$ we will not speak of a zero point but of a continuous family of zero points. Geometrically, this continuous family consists of a straight line of zero points constituting a linear manifold, a 'zero manifold'. The coordinates of this manifold are k $= 1 - z$, $r_D \in (-\infty, r_{D,1})$. We now introduce a transform from the old variables k and r_D into new variables $\hat{k}$ and $\hat{r}_D$. These new variables attain zero values any time when the original process in k and r_D reaches k_2 for any $r_D \in (-\infty, r_{D,1})$. These transforms are:

(5.13) $\quad \hat{k} = k - 1 + z$

(5.14) $\quad \hat{r}_D = r_D - \theta, \quad \theta \in (-\infty, r_{D,1})$

In (5.14) θ has to be chosen so that for any particular $r_D \in (-\infty, r_{D,1})$, $\hat{r}_D$ equals zero. Thus, (5.14) does not describe a point transformation like (5.13), but a continuous family of transformations since we have a continuous family of zero points. The stochastic dynamics of $\hat{k}$ and $\hat{r}_D$ can then be calculated as follows:

(5.15) $\quad d\hat{k} = \left(\begin{array}{c} (1-z) \cdot \alpha_K - \delta + (\gamma-1) \cdot \beta_K^2 - (\alpha_K - \beta_K^2 \cdot \hat{k}) \cdot (\hat{k} + 1 - z) \\ + \dfrac{(\gamma-1) \cdot (\hat{r}_D - \alpha_K + \delta + \theta)}{2 \cdot \gamma} + \dfrac{(\rho + (\gamma-1) \cdot (\alpha_K - \delta - \tau)) \cdot \beta_K^2}{\hat{r}_D - \alpha_K + \delta + \theta} \end{array} \right)$
$\qquad \cdot (\hat{k} + 1 - z) \cdot dt - \beta_K \cdot \hat{k} \cdot (\hat{k} + 1 - z) \cdot dB$

(5.16) $\quad d\hat{r} = \left(\begin{array}{c} \alpha_0 + \alpha_1 \cdot (\hat{r}_D - \alpha_K + \delta + \theta) + \alpha_2 \cdot (\hat{r}_D - \alpha_K + \delta + \theta)^2 \\ + \alpha_3 \cdot (\hat{r}_D - \alpha_K + \delta + \theta)^3 \end{array} \right) \cdot dt$

$$(5.16) \qquad + \left(\beta_0 + \beta_1 \cdot (\hat{r}_D - \alpha_K + \delta + \theta) \right) \cdot (\hat{r}_D - \alpha_K + \delta + \theta) \cdot dB$$

Using Definition 5.1 and Lemma 5.1, we can now compute the effective dimension:

$$
\begin{aligned}
(5.17) \qquad d_e(\hat{k}^*, \hat{r}_D{}^*) = {} & \frac{2 \cdot \left(\hat{k}^* \cdot \mu_1(\hat{k}^*, \hat{r}_D{}^*) + \hat{r}_D{}^* \cdot \mu_2(\hat{r}_D{}^*) \right)}{\left(\hat{k}^* \cdot \sigma_1(\hat{k}^*) + \hat{r}_D{}^* \cdot \sigma_2(\hat{r}_D{}^*) \right)^2} \cdot \left(\hat{k}^* + \hat{r}_D{}^* \right)^2 \\
& + \frac{\sigma_1^2(\hat{k}^*) + \sigma_2^2(\hat{r}_D{}^*)}{\left(\hat{k}^* \cdot \sigma_1(\hat{k}^*) + \hat{r}_D{}^* \cdot \sigma_2(\hat{r}_D{}^*) \right)^2} \cdot \left(\hat{k}^* + \hat{r}_D{}^* \right)^2 +
\end{aligned}
$$

with:

$$
\begin{aligned}
(5.18) \quad \mu_1(\hat{k}^*, \hat{r}_D{}^*) = {} & \left(\begin{array}{l} (1-z) \cdot \alpha_K - \delta + (\gamma - 1) \cdot \beta_K^2 - (\alpha_K - \beta_K^2 \cdot \hat{k}^*) \cdot (\hat{k}^* + 1 - z) \\ + \dfrac{(\gamma - 1) \cdot (\hat{r}_D{}^* - \alpha_K + \delta + \theta)}{2 \cdot \gamma} + \dfrac{\left(\rho + (\gamma - 1) \cdot (\alpha_K - \delta - \tau) \right) \cdot \beta_K^2}{\hat{r}_D{}^* - \alpha_K + \delta + \theta} \end{array} \right) \\
& \cdot (\hat{k}^* + 1 - z) \\[4pt]
\sigma_1(\hat{k}^*) = {} & -\beta_K \cdot \hat{k}^* \cdot (\hat{k}^* + 1 - z) \\[4pt]
\mu_2(\hat{r}_D{}^*) = {} & \left(\begin{array}{l} \alpha_0 + \alpha_1 \cdot (\hat{r}_D{}^* - \alpha_K + \delta + \theta) + \alpha_2 \cdot (\hat{r}_D{}^* - \alpha_K + \delta + \theta)^2 \\ + \alpha_3 \cdot (\hat{r}_D{}^* - \alpha_K + \delta + \theta)^3 \end{array} \right) \\[4pt]
\sigma_2(\hat{r}_D{}^*) = {} & \left(\beta_0 + \beta_1 \cdot (\hat{r}_D{}^* - \alpha_K + \delta + \theta) \right) \cdot (\hat{r}_D{}^* - \alpha_K + \delta + \theta)
\end{aligned}
$$

The asterisks for $\hat{k}, \hat{r}_D$ mean that any possible value of $\hat{k}, \hat{r}_D$ can be used to calculate the effective dimension. The formulae (5.17) and (5.18) clearly show that it is unfortunately impossible to explicitly determine and examine (in a comparative statics way) possible areas in $\hat{k}, \hat{r}_D$ -space for which the effective dimension fulfills the inequality of Lemma 5.1. This is due to the fact that the numerator as well as the denominator of the effective dimension (5.17) are polynomial functions of high degree in $\hat{k}, \hat{r}_D$. The only analytical method that is possibly helpful for this problem is the method of Gröbner Bases [4]. We tried to reduce the complexity of (5.17) using an algorithm of

---

[4] For a recent survey of the method of Gröbner Bases and its field of application, see Buchberger/Winkler (1998).

this method implemented in Mathematica 3.0. However, the algorithm did not yield a conclusive result. For that reason, we have to rely on a numerical example using the same parameter conditions as in Chapter 3, 4 and Proposition 5.1. Additionally, we choose $\tau = 7\%$ and $z = 50\%$ which fulfills the fiscal policy constraints (3.23) and (3.28). Choosing $r_D = 3\%$ as the short-term interest rate coordinate for the zero-point we get the zero-point coordinates: $k = 50\%$ and $r_D = 3\%$. Using (5.17), we can now calculate the effective dimension associated with any point within the $\hat{k} - \hat{r}_D$ state space. This yields Figure 5.1.

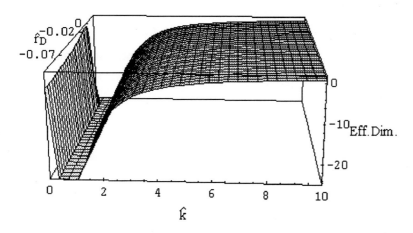

Figure 5.1: Effective dimension for the zero-point $r_D = 3\%$, $k = 50\%$.

It shows that for none of the points in the state space the effective dimension is higher than 2 as required for Theorem 5.1 to hold. Thus, there is always a positive probability that our original two-dimensional diffusion process in k and r_D starting in the higher-growth region reaches the zero-point after some time. Yet, we have to be cautious: this result holds for our assumed parameter constellation and describes just the probability of hitting boundary k_2 at $r_D = 3\%$. Since we have calculated many effective dimensions for lots of different r_D values and all showed the same qualitative behavior, we conjecture that our model parameter assumptions imply that there are no points in the k-r_D state space that show effective dimensions equal or larger than 2 given that the fiscal policy constraints hold. Hence, the capital output

188

ratio can attain k_2 from everywhere. When k has reached this boundary, then it will forever stay within lower-growth region I_2. Of course, it will certainly take much more time for the capital output ratio to reach k_2 if it starts with values well above k_2. In order to study this question, we would have to determine the expected time for k to reach k_2. This would require solving a complicated partial differential equation in two independent variables: short-term interest rate r_D and capital output ratio k [5]. Since we have already seen that finding an analytical solution of partial differential equations in two independent variables is a hard task, we will skip this question here. In future work, it would be interesting to estimate the model parameters on the basis of the endogenously derived dynamics given the abundance of time series data available for many variables. With the so-gained set of estimated model parameters, we could then numerically calculate such interesting measures like expected time for our diffusion processes to reach certain values within the state space like k_2.

5.3 Short and long run effects of fiscal policy and interest rates on capital output and growth

Having examined some qualitative features of the dynamic behavior of k, we now want to study the influence of financial market and fiscal policy interactions on the growth process. The influence of the financial market is reflected in the dependency of the capital output ratio's drift and diffusion term on the short-term interest rate r_D. The influence of fiscal policy is visible through the appearance of τ and z in the drift and diffusion term of (5.2b).

5.3.1 Short run effects

We first focus on the short run (i.e. instantaneous) effects by considering the influence of the corresponding variables and parameters on drift and diffusion of k. Recalling the drift and diffusion term of k, (5.2b), we can compute the following derivatives:

---

[5] See Schuss (1980, Chapter 5.4) for a derivation of the respective PDE.

(5.19a)
$$\frac{\partial(\text{drift of k})}{\partial r_D} = \left(\frac{\gamma-1}{2\cdot\gamma} - \frac{\left(\rho+(\gamma-1)\cdot(\alpha_K-\delta-\tau)\right)\cdot\beta_K^2}{(r_D-\alpha_K+\delta)^2} \right)\cdot k$$

(5.19b)
$$\frac{\partial(\text{diffusion of k})}{\partial r_D} = 0$$

(5.20a)
$$\frac{\partial(\text{drift of k})}{\partial \tau} = -\frac{(\gamma-1)\cdot\beta_K^2}{r_D-\alpha_K+\delta}\cdot k > 0$$

(5.20b)
$$\frac{\partial(\text{diffusion of k})}{\partial \tau} = 0$$

(5.21a)
$$\frac{\partial(\text{drift of k})}{\partial z} = \left(\beta_K^2\cdot k-\alpha_K\right)\cdot k$$

(5.21b)
$$\frac{\partial(\text{diffusion of k})}{\partial z} = -k\cdot\beta_K < 0$$

(5.19b) shows that r_D does not impact on the diffusion term of k. Thus, it does not influence the volatility of k. This is not surprising since r_D had no influence on the volatility of both capital accumulation and production. But r_D influences the drift of k in the following way: if the bracket in (5.19a) is positive, then the sign of the derivative is also positive and vice versa. The root of the bracket in (5.19a) is $r_{D,4}$ given in (5.6b). If the short-term interest rate is smaller than this root, then an increase in r_D renders the drift of k positive, otherwise negative. Other things remaining equal, an increasing drift of k rises k and enables higher growth rates, whereas a decreasing drift leads to lower growth rates in average. The explanation for this effect lies in the combination of two single economic effects: first, rising short-term interest rates make bonds more attractive for households than capital. This leads, other things being equal, to a lower proportion of wealth invested in capital. We will call this portfolio effect. However, rising short-term interest rates may simultaneously decrease current consumption. If this effect occurs, then more resources can be reinvested. If the consumption-induced increase in investment overcompensates the portfolio effect, then capital formation rises even with rising interest rates. This effect is referred to as crowding-in of capital. (5.19a) tells us that crowding-in of capital with rising interest rates happens only when short-term interest rates are lower than $r_{D,4}$. In case that they are higher, the usual crowding-out effect applies. The portfolio effect dominates then the consumption effect. Summarizing, we note that our model gives rise to the statement that crowding-in as well as crowding-out of capital formation and the corresponding effects on economic growth are possible depending which values the short-term interest rate attains. Thus, there is a strong link between interest rates and economic growth in our model. It is crucial on which level the short-term interest rate moves in order to assess whether crowding-out or crowding-in and hence positive or negative growth happens in the short run.

Turning to the influence of taxation, we see that an increasing tax rate has no influence on capital output ratio volatility (5.20b), but tends to enhance the drift of k, thus k and growth in the short run, other things being equal. This seems surprising, but there is an economic explanation for it. On the one hand, rising tax rates reduce consumption so that more resources are left for investing. On the other hand, rising tax rates reduce wealth accumulation thereby decreasing resources for investment. (5.20a) tells us that obviously the first effect overcompensates the second so that tax rate rises foster growth in the short run. This effect is higher the higher elasticity of substitution γ gets. A high elasticity of substitution implies that households prefer a uniformly equal consumption pattern over time. In order to maintain it with simultaneously rising taxes, they have to accumulate capital immediately. If the households had a rather low elasticity of substitution, then they would prefer to stick to an initially higher level of consumption accepting lower future consumption. The consequence is that in response to rising tax rates households would not foster capital accumulation that much.

We finally turn to the short run effect that is triggered by a change in the government expenditure ratio: an increase of z increases the drift of k, thus k and finally the immediately expected growth rate if and only if k exceeds α_K/β_K^2. This effect can be understood when we think of the coefficient α_K/β_K^2 as a measure whether the negative effect of rising z on disposable income and thus on capital formation ($- \alpha_K k$) is outweighed by the effect that a higher expenditure ratio dampens productivity shocks ($\beta_K^2 k^2$). This dampening effect can be understood as follows: if the government runs a higher expenditure policy via higher z and negative productivity shocks happen, then the government confiscates less resources compared to an expenditure policy associated with a lower value of z. As a consequence, in situations of negative productivity shocks the household can keep more of its output so that capital accumulation is fostered or at least less harmed than with less restrictive expenditure policy. Of course, in average high expenditure policies harm households more than low expenditure policies. Sufficiently risk averse households will nevertheless appreciate the dampening function of government expenditure so that this feature may foster higher capital output ratios and hence growth. Due to this dampening effect, rising z also diminishes the volatility of k and vice versa.

5.3.2 Long run effects

Turning to the long run effects of short-term interest rates and fiscal policy on k, we need to calculate the stationary probability density associated with k along the lines of Chapter 3 (where we did the same for the short-term interest rate r_D). Assuming that k enters, at least asymptotically, low-growth area I_2 we know from the boundary discussion above that it will stay there without reaching the boundaries 0 and 1-z ever again. From the theorem of Skorohod (see Proposition 3.6), we can now conclude that there exists a stationary probability distribution characterized by the probability density function if and only if this density function is integrable. The problem, however, is that the probability distribution of k is affected by r_D so that the joint probability distribution of k and r_D would have to be determined. Alas, this requires solving a complicated Fokker-Planck equation in three independent variables: k, r_D and time t. Even in its stationary version, it remains a partial differential equation in k and r_D and cannot be solved analytically. We thus apply the following trick: we pretend that r_D shall be fixed and treat it like a parameter. This enables us to write down a Fokker-Planck equation governing k which depends only on time t and capital output ratio k. Its stationary version can be solved directly by integration as we already showed in Chapter 3 (compare Appendix 3.7 and especially equation (A3.7.4)). We then get the stationary probability density for k, p(k):

(5.22a)
$$p(k) = \frac{m}{\beta_K^2} \cdot k^{\frac{a_1}{(1-z)^2 \cdot \beta_K^2} - 2} \cdot (1 - z - k)^{-\frac{a_1}{(1-z)^2 \cdot \beta_K^2}}$$
$$\cdot \exp\left(\frac{2 \cdot a_1}{(1-z) \cdot (1-z-k) \cdot \beta_K^2}\right)$$

were a_1 is given by:

(5.22b) $$a_1 = (\gamma - 1) \cdot \beta_K^2 - \delta + \frac{(\gamma - 1) \cdot (r_D - \alpha_K + \delta)}{2 \cdot \gamma} + \frac{\left(\rho + (\gamma - 1) \cdot (\alpha_K - \delta - \tau)\right) \cdot \beta_K^2}{r_D - \alpha_K + \delta}$$

In order to determine the integration constant 'm', we now treat r_D again as a variable and get:

(5.22c)
$$\int_{-\infty}^{r_{D,1}} \int_0^{1-z} p(k, r_D) \cdot dk \cdot dr_D = 1$$

Integral (5.22c) is too complicated to be evaluated analytically. Since m does not depend on r_D, however, we do not have to calculate (5.22c) in order to get m when investigating the long run effect of r_D on k. This situation changes if we are interested in the comparative statics with regard to τ and z since m usually depends on τ and z. We could solve (5.22c) numerically for any given set of parameter values, but then the results would hold only for the very specific parameter assumptions used. However, we can also directly derive the comparative static effect, namely by assuming that m does not depend on τ and z. This is, of course, only a rough approximation but hopefully justified in the light that it enables us to get analytical results. Taking the derivative of p(k) with respect to r_D yields:

(5.23)
$$\frac{\partial p(k)}{\partial r_D} = \frac{p(k)}{(1-z)^2 \cdot \beta_K^2} \cdot \left(\frac{\gamma - 1}{2 \cdot \gamma} - \frac{\left(\rho + (\gamma - 1) \cdot (\alpha_K - \delta - \tau)\right) \cdot \beta_K^2}{(r_D - \alpha_K + \delta)^2}\right)$$

$$(5.23) \qquad \cdot\left(\frac{2\cdot(1-z)}{1-z-k} - \ln\left(\frac{1-z-k}{k}\right)\right)$$

The sign of the derivative of (5.23) depends on the signs of the two brackets in (5.23). The first bracket equals the one in (5.19a). It has a positive sign if r_D is smaller than $r_{D,4}$ and vice versa. This means that the above mentioned short run effect (where the direct investment effect together with the consumption effect determined the sign) is also at work in the long run. In the long run, however, there are additional effects. The second bracket also changes its sign on $(0, 1 - z)$ which can be seen when we look at $k = 0$ and $k = 1 - z$. In the first case, the second bracket tends to minus infinity, in the second case to plus infinity. Moreover, by taking the derivative of the second bracket expression with respect to k, we can verify that this derivative is always positive indicating strong monotonicity. Hence, there is just one single root of the second bracket with regard to k. If k is bigger than this root, then the sign of the long run effect of r_D on k will be solely determined by the sign of the first bracket. Then the long run equals the short run effect. If, however, k is smaller than the root of the second bracket with regard to k, then the long run effect of r_D is reverse to the short run effect. The root of the second bracket in terms of k, however, cannot be calculated symbolically due to the transcendent form of the bracket. To overcome this problem we choose the following procedure: dividing the state space for z (i.e. $(0;1)$) into equally spaced intervals with distance 1%, we compute the root of the second bracket, k_3, for any value of z [6]. The corresponding plot in k_3-z space looks completely linear. Carrying out a linear regression produces the following relation for the root k_3:

$$(5.24) \quad k_3 = 0.098171\cdot(1-z)$$

The statistics of the linear regression (5.24) yield an R^2 - value of 1 and very high values for the corresponding t- and F-test values. The linear equation

---

[6] This calculation was done using the 'FindRoot' function from the computer algebra package 'Mathematica 3.0' As starting values we used $0.5(1 - z)$ which guarantees convergence since we have already shown that in the interval $(0, 1 - z)$ there is only one root.

(5.24) is thus an extremely well approximation to the true solution of the root of the second bracket in (5.23). With respect to the long run influence of r_D on k characterized by the change of the density function we get the following statements:

(5.25)
$$\frac{\partial p(k)}{\partial r_D} > 0 \Leftrightarrow r_D > r_{D,4}, k < k_3 \quad \vee \quad r_D < r_{D,4}, k > k_3$$

$$\frac{\partial p(k)}{\partial r_D} < 0 \Leftrightarrow r_D > r_{D,4}, k > k_3 \quad \vee \quad r_D < r_{D,4}, k < k_3$$

(5.25) tells us that the probability for low values of k ($k < k_3$) will rise with increasing r_D if r_D is relatively high ($r_D > r_{D,4}$). Simultaneously, the probability for high values of k ($k > k_3$) will sink for rising r_D if r_D is relatively high ($r_D > r_{D,4}$). If r_D is relatively low ($r_D < r_{D,4}$), then rising values of r_D will lead to sinking probability of relatively low values of k and increasing probability of relatively high values of k. How can this effect be explained? The analysis of the short run effect showed that higher interest rate values than $r_{D,4}$ imply less capital accumulation, thus lower values of k. The probability that k attains a relatively small value in the stochastic steady state given by the stationary probability distribution will therefore become bigger, the probability that higher values of k are reached gets accordingly smaller. The negative sign in (5.25) can be understood in the same way. The short run effect is thus still vivid in the long run: rising interest rates increase the probability for high (low) capital output ratios and growth rates if the interest rate lies below (above) the critical value of $r_{D,4}$. The Keynesian view of investment being suppressed by rising interest rates is in our model only valid in the high interest rate area; for low level interest rates, investment and hence capital accumulation is stimulated by rising interest rates. This is indeed a remarkable result.

Turning to the long run effects of fiscal policy, we calculate the following derivatives:

(5.26)
$$\frac{\partial p(k)}{\partial \tau} = -\frac{p(k)}{(1-z)^2 \cdot \beta_K^2} \cdot \frac{(\gamma-1) \cdot \beta_K^2}{r_D - \alpha_K + \delta} \cdot \left(\frac{2 \cdot (1-z)}{1-z-k} - \ln\left(\frac{1-z-k}{k} \right) \right)$$

$$(5.27) \quad \frac{\partial p(k)}{\partial z} = \frac{2 \cdot a_1 \cdot p(k)}{(1-z)^3 \cdot \beta_K^2} \cdot \left(\left(\frac{1-z}{1-z-k} \right)^2 + \frac{1}{2} \cdot \frac{1-z}{1-z-k} - \ln\left(\frac{1-z-k}{k} \right) \right)$$

Looking at (5.26), we note that the product of the first two fractions is positive so that the sign is determined by the bracket expression which is the same as in (5.25). For $k > k_3$, we thus get a positive sign of the respective derivative (5.26) and vice versa. (5.26) therefore implies that rising tax rates increase the probability of higher capital output ratios and growth and sinking tax rates increase the probability for lower capital output ratios and growth. Here, too, the already explained short run effect remains valid in the long run. The economic conclusion is that, unless the tax rate constraint (3.23) is binding, an increase in the tax rate may foster growth.

Finally, we look at the public expenditure ratio effect (5.27). The sign of the effect is determined by the sign of a_1 and the sign of the bracket expression. When we calculate the root of the bracket expression for k using the same procedure as for obtaining (5.24), we get [7]:

$$(5.28) \quad k_4 = 0.1304 \cdot (1-z)$$

Assuming that a_1 is negative, (5.27) tells us that an increase in z will increase (decrease) the probability of low (high) capital output ratios. The economic explanation is obvious. If a_1 is positive, then the opposite will hold. Again, the short run effect holds in the long run, implying that rising public expenditure ratios need not always be negative for growth. It is decisive how much the households appreciate the 'output smoothing' feature of public expenditure in situations of negative productivity shocks.

5.4 Short summary

We have seen that economic growth is described by a stochastic process that depends linearly on the capital output ratio k. The dynamics of the capital

---

[7] The linear regression statistics involved with (5.28) are of a similar quality than in the regression (5.24).

output ratio itself has an equilibrium point at k = 0. This point was shown to be unstable for a given parameter constellation. Growth will thus never cease. We also saw that the state space of k can be separated in two regions: a lower-growth region corresponding to lower values of k and a higher-growth region corresponding to larger values of k. Moreover, we were able to show that the capital output process and hence the growth process will always be confined to the lower-growth region once it is in that region. Assuming that the capital output process will indeed converge to this region, growth rates will decrease over time in the average. We then showed with a numerical example employing the concept of effective dimensions that there is always a positive probability that the capital output process will 'hit' the lower-growth region starting in the higher-growth region. This gives rise to the conjecture that with high probability the growth process will finally slow down, thereby reaching the lower-growth area and staying there forever. We also examined the short and long run influence of the short-term interest rate, the tax rate and the public expenditure ratio on capital output ratio and hence growth. The results were at least partially surprising: in the short run, increasing short-term interest rates and public expenditure ratios may stimulate growth via rising capital output ratios whereas rising tax rates definitely leads to higher growth. The long run effects point in a similar direction.

Appendix 5.1: Calculating the Lyapunov exponent for the equilibrium point $k_1 = 0$:

In this appendix, we discuss without any proofs the main concepts involved in calculating Lyapunov exponents. We follow Ariaratnam (1994), Kloeden/Platen (1992, Chapters 6.3 and 17.3) and Kloeden/Platen (1995).

Definition 1:

Consider an n-dimensional system of nonlinear SDEs written as follows:

$$(A5.1.1) \quad \begin{pmatrix} dx_1(t) \\ \cdots \\ dx_n(t) \end{pmatrix} = \begin{pmatrix} \mu_1(x(t)) \\ \cdots \\ \mu_n(x(t)) \end{pmatrix} \cdot dt + \begin{pmatrix} \sigma_{11}(x(t)) & \cdots & \sigma_{1m}(x(t)) \\ \cdots & \cdots & \cdots \\ \sigma_{m1}(x(t)) & \cdots & \sigma_{mm}(x(t)) \end{pmatrix} \cdot dw(t)$$

$$, x(0) = x_0 \in R^n$$

where x(t) is the vector of state variables in R^n ($x_1(t)$, ... $x_n(t)$), w(t) is a vector of Wiener processes (i.e. Brownian motions) in R^m and $x(0) = x_0$ is a (possibly random) vector of arbitrary initial values in R^n. Let us consider a stationary solution of the process x(t) and denote it as x^s [8]. Then the linearized version of (A5.1.1) is given as follows:

$$(A5.1.2) \quad \begin{pmatrix} dx_1(t) \\ \cdots \\ dx_n(t) \end{pmatrix} = \begin{pmatrix} \sum_{i=1}^{n} \dfrac{\partial \mu_1(x(t))}{\partial x_i(t)} \bigg|_{x(t)=x^s} \cdot x_i(t) \\ \cdots \\ \sum_{i=1}^{n} \dfrac{\partial \mu_n(x(t))}{\partial x_i(t)} \bigg|_{x(t)=x^s} \cdot x_i(t) \end{pmatrix} \cdot dt$$

$$+ \begin{pmatrix} \sum_{i=1}^{n} \dfrac{\partial \sigma_{11}(x(t))}{\partial x_i(t)} \bigg|_{x(t)=x^s} \cdot x_i(t) & \cdots & \sum_{i=1}^{n} \dfrac{\partial \sigma_{1m}(x(t))}{\partial x_i(t)} \bigg|_{x(t)=x^s} \cdot x_i(t) \\ \cdots & \cdots & \cdots \\ \sum_{i=1}^{n} \dfrac{\partial \sigma_{m1}(x(t))}{\partial x_i(t)} \bigg|_{x(t)=x^s} \cdot x_i(t) & \cdots & \sum_{i=1}^{n} \dfrac{\partial \sigma_{mm}(x(t))}{\partial x_i(t)} \bigg|_{x(t)=x^s} \cdot x_i(t) \end{pmatrix} \cdot dw(t)$$

The general solution of (A5.1.2), $x(t, x_0)$, can now be calculated explicitly and leads to the following definition of the so called 'Lyapunov exponent':

---

[8] Note that a 'stationary solution' in a deterministic context always corresponds to a fixed or equilibrium point. However, this concept is too narrow for stochastic processes since 'stationary solution' can now also mean that the probability distribution induced by the process becomes time independent and thus stationary. A stationary solution can hence exist even if no fixed points are present. This is important for our model since we have seen in Chapter 3 that the short-term interest rate process has no fixed point. But owing to the fact that we have shown the process to move on an open interval with zero probability of reaching the interval boundaries, one knows by a theorem of Skorokhod (1989) that the process must converge to a stationary solution if and only if its probability density exists and is integrable over the corresponding interval. In the further context, we use the fact that such a stationary solution for the short-term interest rate process exists.

198

(A5.1.3) $$\lambda = \limsup_{t \to \infty} \frac{\ln\|x(t, x^S)\|}{t}$$

where '$\|..\|$' denotes the Euklidean norm, 'ln' the natural logarithm and 'sup' the supremum.

The value of Definition 1 lies in the fact that we can use it to calculate the Lyapunov exponent, at least theoretically. The use of this concept, however, remains unclear unless one applies the celebrated Multiplicative Ergodic Theorem (MET) by Oseledets (1968). It states that for an n-dimensional dynamic system there are in general n Lyapunov exponents depending on the (possibly random) initial vector x_0. These exponents are deterministic, real numbers under mild ergodicity properties of the considered dynamic system. Moreover, the solution of the linearized system (A5.1.2) is stable if and only if the largest Lyapunov exponent (the so-called top Lyapunov exponent) is negative and unstable if and only if the largest Lyapunov exponent is positive. Furthermore, its stability properties imply the stability of the stationary solution being considered. Thus, the MET delivers the tool to decide whether a stationary solution is stable or not.

Back to our economic problem, namely the question whether $k_1 = 0$ is a stable equilibrium or not. For this purpose, we need to calculate the linearized versions of (3.24a) and (5.2b), where the stationary solution around which we linearize is $k_1 = 0, r_D = r^S$ (r^S denotes the stationary solution of r_D when r_D reaches its stationary probability distribution when time t tends to infinity):

(A5.1.4a)
$$dk = \varepsilon_1 \cdot k \cdot dt + \varepsilon_2 \cdot k \cdot dB$$
$$dr_D = \varepsilon_3 \cdot r_D \cdot dt + \varepsilon_4 \cdot r_D \cdot dB$$

with:

(A5.1.4b)
$$\varepsilon_1 = (1-z) \cdot \alpha_K - \delta + (\gamma-1) \cdot \beta_K^2 + \frac{(\gamma-1) \cdot (r^S - \alpha_K + \delta)}{2 \cdot \gamma}$$
$$+ \frac{(\rho + (\gamma-1) \cdot (\alpha_K - \delta - \tau)) \cdot \beta_K^2}{r^S - \alpha_K + \delta}$$

$$\varepsilon_2 = (1-z)\cdot\beta_K$$
$$\varepsilon_3 = \left(\alpha_1 + 2\cdot\alpha_2\cdot(r^S - \alpha_K + \delta) + 3\cdot\alpha_3\cdot(r^S - \alpha_K + \delta)^2\right)$$
$$\varepsilon_4 = \left(\beta_0 + 2\cdot\beta_1\cdot(r^S - \alpha_K + \delta)\right)$$

In principle, the solution of (A5.1.4a-b) is obtained by applying Ito's Lemma to each of the two equations in (A5.1.4a). This can be done since both equations are autonomous: their respective dynamics depend only on the own state variable. Unfortunately, these solutions alone do not help us calculate the Lyapunov exponent(s) in a form amenable to further analysis. The reason for this is that (A5.1.3) tells us that we need the log of the Euklidean norm over the vector made up by the solutions pertaining to (A5.1.4a-b). This yields a rather messy expression. In order to circumvent it, we thus introduce the following variable transformations into spherical coordinates. This procedure will finally yield a formula for the top Lyapunov exponent (see Kloeden/Platen(1995)):

(A5.1.5a)
$$R = \left\| \begin{pmatrix} r_D \\ k \end{pmatrix} \right\| \equiv \sqrt{r_D^2 + k^2}, \quad S_1 = \frac{r_D}{\sqrt{r_D^2 + k^2}}, \quad S_2 = \frac{k}{\sqrt{r_D^2 + k^2}}$$
$$\Rightarrow S_1^2 + S_2^2 \equiv 1$$

Applying Ito's Lemma to (A5.1.5a) using the equations (A5.1.4a-b) and the identity in (A5.1.5a), we get the following SDEs for R and S_1:

(A5.1.5b)
$$\frac{dR}{R} = \left(\left(\varepsilon_1 + \frac{\varepsilon_2^2}{2} - \varepsilon_3 + \frac{\varepsilon_4^2}{2} - \varepsilon_2\cdot\varepsilon_4\right)\cdot S_1^2 - \frac{(\varepsilon_2 - \varepsilon_4)^2}{2}\cdot S_1^4 + \varepsilon_3\right)\cdot dt$$
$$+ \left((\varepsilon_2 - \varepsilon_4)\cdot S_1^2 + \varepsilon_4\right)\cdot dB$$

(A5.1.5c)
$$dS_1 = \left(\begin{array}{c} \left(\varepsilon_3 - \varepsilon_1 + 4\cdot\varepsilon_2\cdot\varepsilon_4 - \frac{3\cdot\varepsilon_2^2}{2} - \frac{5\cdot\varepsilon_4^2}{2}\right)\cdot S_1^2 \\ + \frac{3\cdot(\varepsilon_2 - \varepsilon_4)^2}{2}\cdot S_1^4 + \varepsilon_1 - \varepsilon_3 - \varepsilon_2\cdot\varepsilon_4 + \varepsilon_4^2 \end{array} \right)\cdot S_1\cdot dt$$
$$+ (\varepsilon_2 - \varepsilon_4)\cdot(1 - S_1^2)\cdot S_1\cdot dB$$

Integrating (A5.1.5b) using Ito's Lemma yields[9]:

$$\text{(A5.1.6)} \quad \ln R = \int \left(\begin{array}{c} \left(\varepsilon_1 + \dfrac{\varepsilon_2^2}{2} - \varepsilon_3 + \dfrac{3 \cdot \varepsilon_4^2}{2} - 2 \cdot \varepsilon_2 \cdot \varepsilon_4 \right) \cdot S_1^2 \\ - (\varepsilon_2 - \varepsilon_4)^2 \cdot S_1^4 + \varepsilon_3 - \dfrac{1}{2} \cdot \varepsilon_4^2 \end{array} \right) \cdot dt$$
$$+ \int \left((\varepsilon_2 - \varepsilon_4) \cdot S_1^2 + \varepsilon_4 \right) \cdot dB$$

We can now calculate the top Lyapunov exponent using (A5.1.3) and (A5.1.6):

$$\lambda = \limsup_{t \to \infty} \frac{\ln R}{t}$$

$$\text{(A5.1.7)} \quad \Rightarrow \lambda = \lim_{t \to \infty} \frac{\int \left(\begin{array}{c} \left(\varepsilon_1 + \dfrac{\varepsilon_2^2}{2} - \varepsilon_3 + \dfrac{3 \cdot \varepsilon_4^2}{2} - 2 \cdot \varepsilon_2 \cdot \varepsilon_4 \right) \cdot S_1^2 \\ - (\varepsilon_2 - \varepsilon_4)^2 \cdot S_1^4 + \varepsilon_3 - \dfrac{1}{2} \cdot \varepsilon_4^2 \end{array} \right) \cdot dt}{t}$$
$$+ \lim_{t \to \infty} \frac{\int \left((\varepsilon_2 - \varepsilon_4) \cdot S_1^2 + \varepsilon_4 \right) \cdot dB}{t}$$

Before we evaluate (A5.1.7), we must discuss the meaning of the limit. Sending time t to infinity means that the short-term interest rate r_D reaches its stationary solution r^S associated with a stationary probability distribution and k reaches zero. By definition (A5.1.5a), S_1 then reaches the value $r^S/|r^S|$ which equals +1 for positive and -1 for negative values of r^S. Thus, the square of S_1 and S_1 to the power of four equals 1 in the limit. This is the reason why we could carry out the integration in (A5.1.6) explicitly. Plugging these values for S_1 into (A5.1.7), we see that the integrand in the second limit of (A5.1.7) depends only on stationary values. It can thus be integrated over the Brownian motion B so that its convergence properties depend on the behavior of B/t. B/t is N(0, 1/t) distributed and converges to a normal distribution with all moments becoming zero when t tends to infinity. As a consequence, the second limit in (A5.1.7) tends to zero and the first

---

[9] It will soon become clear why it is allowed to treat S_1 as a quasi-constant in carrying

limit converges to the integrand integrated over the whole stationary probability distribution:

$$(A5.1.8) \qquad \lambda = \int_{-\infty}^{\alpha_K - \delta - (1-z)\cdot\gamma\cdot\beta_K^2} \left(\varepsilon_1(r^S) - \frac{\varepsilon_2(r^S)^2}{2} \right) \cdot p(r^S) \cdot dr^S$$

Since we have derived the stationary density already in Appendix 3.7, we just state it here:

$$(A5.1.9) \qquad \begin{aligned} p(r^S) &= m \cdot (r^S - \alpha_K + \delta)^\omega \cdot (\beta_0 + \beta_1 \cdot (r^S - \alpha_K + \delta))^\xi \\ &\cdot \exp\left(\frac{\psi}{r^S - \alpha_K + \delta} + \frac{\zeta}{\beta_0 + \beta_1 \cdot (r^S - \alpha_K + \delta)} \right) \end{aligned}$$

with:

$$\omega = -2 + \frac{2 \cdot (\alpha_1 \cdot \beta_0 - 2 \cdot \alpha_0 \cdot \beta_1)}{\beta_0^3}$$

$$\xi = -2 + \frac{2 \cdot (\alpha_3 \cdot \beta_0^3 + \beta_1^2 \cdot (-\alpha_1 \cdot \beta_0 + 2 \cdot \alpha_0 \cdot \beta_1))}{\beta_0^3 \cdot \beta_1^2}$$

$$\psi = -\frac{2 \cdot \alpha_0 \cdot \beta_0}{\beta_0^3}$$

$$\zeta = \frac{2 \cdot \beta_0 \cdot (\alpha_3 \cdot \beta_0^3 - \beta_1 \cdot (\alpha_2 \cdot \beta_0^2 + \beta_1 \cdot (-\alpha_1 \cdot \beta_0 + \alpha_0 \cdot \beta_1)))}{\beta_0^3 \cdot \beta_1^2}$$

(A5.1.8) and (A5.1.9) together determine the top Lyapunov exponent. The integration cannot be carried out analytically. In order to show the uniqueness of the sign of the Lyapunov exponent, it would be sufficient if one could show that the integrand $\varepsilon_1(r^S)$ - $\varepsilon_2(r^S)^2/2$ had a unique sign. Unfortunately, the sign of this integrand changes within $(-\infty, \alpha_K - \delta - (1 - z)\gamma \beta_K^2)$ so that we are unable to prove a unique positive sign of the exponent that would imply instability of $k_1 = 0$. However, we can evaluate the integral (A5.1.8) numerically for a given set of parameters. We choose again: $\alpha_K = 0.075$, $\beta_K = 0.05$, $\delta = 0.015$, $\gamma = 5$ and $\rho = 0.1$. Additionally, we allow the tax rate and the public expenditure ratio to take on different values such that the fiscal policy constraints (3.23) and (3.28) are fulfilled. This yields Table

out this integration.

5.1 depicted after Proposition 5.1 in the chapter. The table shows that all top Lyapunov exponents are positive so that for our assumed parameter constellation $k_1 = 0$ is indeed an unstable equilibrium.

Appendix 5.2: Proof of Lemma 5.1:

Recalling condition 1) within Theorem 5.1 we get:

$$\varepsilon(|x|) \geq 1 - \frac{d_e(x)}{2}$$

Taking the equality (which naturally satisfies the inequality, too) and using the results prior to the statement of Lemma 5.1 gives:

$$\varepsilon(|x|) = 1 - \frac{1}{2} \cdot \left(\omega_0(\hat{x}) + \omega_1(\hat{x}) \cdot |x|^2 + O(|x|^4)\right)$$

$$\Rightarrow \varepsilon(z) = 1 - \frac{1}{2} \cdot \omega_0(\hat{x}) - \frac{1}{2} \cdot \omega_1(\hat{x}) \cdot z^2 - \frac{1}{2} \cdot O(z^4)$$

$$= 1 - \frac{1}{2} \cdot \omega_0(\hat{x}) - \frac{1}{2} \cdot \omega_1(\hat{x}) \cdot z^2 + O(z^4)$$

We use this result and plug it into condition 2) of Theorem 5.1. This yields the following calculations step by step:

$$\int_0^1 e^{-\int_y^1 \frac{\varepsilon(z)}{z} dz} \cdot \frac{dy}{y}$$

$$= \int_0^1 e^{-\int_y^1 \left(\frac{1-\frac{1}{2}\omega_0(\hat{x})}{z} - \frac{1}{2}\omega_0(\hat{x}) \cdot z + O(z^3)\right) dz} \cdot \frac{dy}{y}$$

$$= \int_0^1 e^{\left(1-\frac{1}{2}\omega_0(\hat{x})\right)\log(y) - \frac{1}{4}\omega_0(\hat{x}) \cdot y^2 + O(y^4) + c_1} \cdot \frac{dy}{y}$$

$$= \int_0^1 c_2 \cdot e^{-\frac{1}{4}\omega_0(\hat{x}) \cdot y^2 + O(y^4)} \cdot \frac{y^{1-\frac{1}{2}\omega_0(\hat{x})}}{y} \cdot dy$$

$$= \int_0^1 \frac{c_2 \cdot e^{-\frac{1}{4}\omega_0(\hat{x})\cdot y^2 + O(y^4)}}{y^{\frac{1}{2}\omega_0(\hat{x})}} \cdot dy$$

$$= \left[\frac{c_2 \cdot e^{-\frac{1}{4}\omega_0(\hat{x})\cdot y^2 + O(y^4)} \cdot y^{1-\frac{1}{2}\omega_0(\hat{x})}}{1 - \frac{1}{2}\cdot\omega_0(\hat{x})} \right]_0^1$$

$$- \int_0^1 \frac{c_2 \cdot e^{-\frac{1}{4}\omega_0(\hat{x})\cdot y^2 + O(y^4)} \cdot y^{1-\frac{1}{2}\omega_0(\hat{x})} \cdot (-\frac{1}{2}\cdot\omega_0(\hat{x})\cdot y + O(y^3))}{1 - \frac{1}{2}\cdot\omega_0(\hat{x})} \cdot dy$$

Note that c_1 denotes an integration constant, c_2 equals $\exp(c_1)$ and the last line results from integrating by parts.

In order to verify Lemma 5.1, we show that the first expression (i.e. the one in brackets) in the last line approaches infinity for $\omega_0(\hat{x}) \geq 2$. If $\omega_0(\hat{x}) = 2$ holds, then the denominator of the fraction within brackets becomes zero whereas the numerator stays finite. Thus, this term tends to infinity. When $\omega_0(\hat{x}) > 2$ is valid, then the denominator becomes negative. Additionally, the y-term in the numerator gets a negative power so that it tends to infinity at the lower boundary $y = 0$. Hence, the bracket approaches infinity at $y = 0$. This proves Lemma 5.1.

6 Public debt dynamics

6.1 Introduction

In this chapter, we will address the last economic question resulting from the chosen model framework: how does public indebtedness evolve and how does fiscal policy and financial market interaction influence this evolution? We will take 'public debt per output' (i.e. the debt ratio) as the appropriate measure for public indebtedness. The debt ratio is usually associated with the question whether a present stock of public debt is compatible with default-free future debt service which would guarantee intertemporal solvency of the government. This solvency question itself does, however, not stand in the foreground of this chapter. The reason is that we always assume that the tax rate and the public expenditure ratio are subject to those fiscal policy constraints developed in Chapter 3. These conditions were shown to fulfill the transversality condition, thereby ruling out Ponzi-game dynamics of public debt as pointed out by Obstfeld/Rogoff (1996, p. 717) [1]. Thus, the main purpose in this chapter is to analyze the model dynamics of the debt ratio, especially with regard to the underlying parameters and variables characterizing fiscal policy and financial market behavior.

The chapter is organized as follows: using the equilibrium short-term interest rate relation developed in Chapter 3, we will derive an equation characterizing the debt ratio. We then study some global properties of this public indebtedness measure. It is shown that the debt ratio's sign is chiefly determined by the short-term interest rate, whereas its magnitude is influenced by the capital output ratio and thus by the growth process. Moreover, we will show that convergence of the growth process to the lower-growth region is sufficient for stabilizing the public debt ratio. Since this reasoning does not help us to pin down the qualitative dynamics of public debt in the higher-growth region, we will derive the stochastic

---

[1] This argumentation need no longer hold in an overlapping generations model as Buiter/Kletzer (1997) discuss in a recent paper.

dynamics associated with the debt ratio and examine regions in the debt ratio's state space where the debt ratio remains bounded. Additionally, we study under which conditions the debt ratio dynamics is stabilized with high probability. For this purpose, we analyze the crucial role of the drift coefficient for the debt ratio dynamics. All these considerations, which are part of Section 2, make clear that the debt ratio will be pinned down at quite low levels as soon as either the capital per output process attains the lower-growth region or the interest rate becomes sufficiently low.

In Section 3, we compute and interpret the short and long run effects of short-term interest rates and fiscal policy on the debt ratio. These effects are not always unique and their sign and magnitude often depend on the level of the considered variables. This gives rise to the conjecture uttered in Chapter 1: there are nonlinear feedback effects at work between the different model variables that cannot be explained by models with linear dynamics and clear-cut causality structure. The chapter closes with a summary of the results.

6.2 Local and global behavior of the debt ratio

The first step is to determine the debt ratio. Recalling the equilibrium short-term interest rate equation (3.18) we get:

$$(3.18) \quad r_D = \alpha_K - \delta - \beta_K^2 \cdot \gamma \cdot \frac{K}{K+D}$$

We divide both the numerator and the denominator of the fraction on the right-hand side of (3.18) by Y. Substituting k and $\hat{d}$ for K/Y and D/Y, this equation can be solved for the debt ratio $\hat{d}$:

$$(6.1) \quad \hat{d} = \frac{r_D - \alpha_K + \delta + \beta_K^2 \cdot \gamma}{\alpha_K - \delta - r_D} \cdot k$$

Equation (6.1) shows that the evolution of the public debt ratio is determined solely by the evolution of two variables: the short-term interest rate r_D, whose dynamics were studied in Chapter 3, and the capital output ratio k studied in Chapter 5. Both variables were seen to yield no closed-form solutions in terms of the two independent variables, time and the Brownian motion. This implies that we will not get a closed-form solution for $\hat{d}$ either. However, we can derive some qualitative global results regarding the public debt ratio by using (6.1). By 'global results', we mean properties like the sign of $\hat{d}$, upper and lower bounds for $\hat{d}$ etc. Computing the dynamics of $\hat{d}$ by using (6.1), we can then also look for irregular points in the state space of $\hat{d}$. This would imply the existence of boundaries that may not be crossed by the debt ratio process $\hat{d}$. The study of the behavior of $\hat{d}$ at such irregular points or boundaries is what we call 'local behavior'. The global and local results together give us some impression about the dynamics of the debt ratio process.

Back to (6.1): since we have shown in Chapter 5 that k is always positive, the sign of $\hat{d}$ depends only on the fraction in (6.1). Assuming that the fiscal policy constraints (3.23), (3.27) and (3.28) hold, we know that the denominator of this fraction is always positive. Thus, the sign of the numerator determines the sign of $\hat{d}$. The numerator sign is positive for $r_D > \alpha_K - \delta - \beta_K^2 \cdot \gamma$, negative for $r_D < \alpha_K - \delta - \beta_K^2 \cdot \gamma$ and zero for $r_D = \alpha_K - \delta - \beta_K^2 \cdot \gamma$. This leads to the first proposition regarding global behavior of $\hat{d}$:

Proposition 6.1:

The debt ratio is positive for $r_D \in (\alpha_K - \delta - \beta_K^2 \cdot \gamma, \alpha_K - \delta - (1-z) \cdot \beta_K^2 \cdot \gamma)$ and negative for $r_D \in (-\infty, \alpha_K - \delta - \beta_K^2 \cdot \gamma)$.

<u>Proof:</u> Recalling that $r_D = \alpha_K - \delta - (1-z) \cdot \beta_K^2 \cdot \gamma$ is the upper boundary for the short-term interest rate process, the proposition is clear from the above discussion.

The economic reasoning behind Proposition 6.1 is straightforward: given that short-term interest rates are relatively high (i.e. $r_D > \alpha_K - \delta - \beta_K^2 \cdot \gamma$), the government bears a relatively high burden of interest payments which implies that a positive debt ratio is maintained. Conversely, low short-term interest rates imply low potential interest burdens so that the government may run budget surpluses and hence becomes a creditor vis-à-vis its own private sector.

Whereas the sign of the debt ratio depends only on the short-term interest rate, the magnitude of the debt ratio depends mainly and linearly on the capital output ratio and therefore growth rates. A high public debt ratio is hence attributable to high growth rates. This leads directly to the next question: are there upper and lower boundaries on the debt ratio? Assume for a moment that the capital output ratio is below 1 - z, i.e. in the lower-growth region. Then k will always be confined to this region and has a maximal value at $k_2 = 1 - z$, as Chapter 5 has shown. An upper boundary for the debt ratio with regard to k is then given as:

$$(6.2) \quad \hat{d} = \frac{r_D - \alpha_K + \delta + \beta_K^2 \cdot \gamma}{\alpha_K - \delta - r_D} \cdot (1 - z)$$

For which short-term interest rate values does $\hat{d}$ attain a maximum or minimum? In order to answer this question, we take the derivative of $\hat{d}$:

$$(6.3) \quad \frac{d(\hat{d})}{dr_D} = \frac{\beta_K^2 \cdot \gamma \cdot (1 - z)}{(\alpha_K - \delta - r_D)^2} > 0$$

Since the derivative (6.3) is always positive, the debt ratio grows monotonically in r_D. We can thus conclude that the debt ratio attains its maximum (minimum) at the right (left) boundary of the state space of r_D. Since the analysis of Chapter 3 showed that r_D always stays on the interval $(-\infty, \alpha_K - \delta - (1 - z) \cdot \gamma \cdot \beta_K^2)$, we can therefore state the second proposition:

Proposition 6.2:

The debt ratio attains its maximum at $r_D = \alpha_K - \delta - (1 - z) \cdot \gamma \cdot \beta_K^2$ and its minimum at $r_D = -\infty$ given that the economy is in the lower-growth

region. The maximum value is $\hat{d} = z$, the minimum value is $\hat{d} = -(1 - z) = -k_2$. Moreover, $\hat{d}$ is always bounded from below at -k.

Proof: obvious from the above discussion.

Proposition 6.2 states that, once the capital output ratio reaches the lower-growth region, public debt per output will always stay within the boundaries -(1 - z) and z. These boundaries are solely determined by the public expenditure ratio. A higher z means higher boundaries and vice versa. The model has thus the interesting feature that it is self-stabilizing with regard to public indebtedness once the lower-growth region is reached. An economic explanation could be the following: when growth rates settle down in the lower-growth region, this implies that overall output (or income) changes more slowly. Since output drives public expenditure, stochastic shocks affecting productivity and output do no longer cause such strong variations in public expenditure compared to the higher-growth regime. Less variation in public expenditure implies less variation in primary deficits. The consequence is that the public debt ratio does fluctuate less strongly than in the higher-growth regime. It is even bounded from above and below, as Proposition 6.2 shows. This stabilizing feature is mainly caused by the strict fiscal policy restrictions developed in Chapter 3. If these restrictions are not fulfilled, the growth process may either never reach the lower-growth region or leave it again having reached it once. The debt ratio needs not be bounded then. This leads to another key question: how does the debt ratio evolve in the higher-growth region (i.e. for $k > 1 - z$)? Since k explicitly depends on r_D (see (5.2b)), we must not ignore the influence of r_D when we want to take derivatives in (6.1) with respect to r_D in order to derive first-order conditions for global extreme values of the debt ratio. Unfortunately, we cannot determine k in terms of r_D since the corresponding stochastic differential equation of k, (5.2b), has no explicit closed-form solution [2]. Instead, we

---

[2] A possible way out of this dilemma could be the following: one postulates a specific functional form of k depending on r_D and substitutes it into the dynamics of k, i.e. (5.2b). Simultaneously, one calculates the dynamics of k applying Ito's Lemma to the postulated functional form of k. The parameter coefficients of the postulated functional form can then be obtained by comparing the two dynamics to each other and equalizing the parameters in front of the lowest order expressions of r_D. The problem with this approach is, however,

derive the dynamics of the debt per output ratio $\hat{d} = \dfrac{D}{Y}$ in form of a stochastic differential equation depending solely on $\hat{d}$ and r_D. We then examine the dependence of the debt ratio dynamics on the short-term interest rate r_D.

Since $\hat{d}$ is a C^∞-function of D and Y (i.e. infinitely often differentiable in D and Y) and since both variables follow stochastic differential equations given by (3.1) and (3.20), we use Ito's Lemma to calculate the differential of the debt ratio as follows:

$$(6.4) \quad \hat{D} = \frac{D}{Y} \Rightarrow d\hat{D} = \frac{dD}{Y} - \frac{D}{Y^2} \cdot dY + \frac{D}{Y^3} \cdot d\langle Y \rangle - \frac{1}{Y^2} \cdot d\langle D, Y \rangle$$

Plugging in (3.1) and (3.20) and making use of (6.1) in order to eliminate k, we finally obtain the debt ratio dynamics:

$$(6.5) \quad d(\hat{d}) = \left(\begin{array}{l} (r_D - \tau) \cdot \hat{d} + \left(z \cdot \alpha_K - \tau - \alpha_K \cdot \hat{d} \right) \cdot \dfrac{(\alpha_K - \delta - r_D) \cdot \hat{d}}{r_D - \alpha_K + \delta + \gamma \cdot \beta_K^2} \\[3mm] - \beta_K^2 \cdot (z - \hat{d}) \cdot \left(\dfrac{(\alpha_K - \delta - r_D) \cdot \hat{d}}{r_D - \alpha_K + \delta + \gamma \cdot \beta_K^2} \right)^2 \end{array} \right) \cdot dt$$

$$+ \beta_K \cdot \left(z - \hat{d} \right) \cdot \frac{(\alpha_K - \delta - r_D) \cdot \hat{d}}{r_D - \alpha_K + \delta + \gamma \cdot \beta_K^2} \cdot dB$$

In both the drift and diffusion term of (6.5), a certain fraction appears. This fraction equals k due to (6.1). It is important to keep this in mind since we will first examine what is happening to the debt ratio dynamics when the debt ratio attains a value of zero. The denominator of the fraction becomes zero but since the numerator becomes also zero, the whole fraction does not tend to infinity and we can replace the fraction by k. (6.5) looks then as follows:

---

that the computations involved get highly complicated. The reason for this is that one needs nonlinear specifications of k in terms of r_D when one focuses on functional forms that aim to yield good approximations. We thus refrain from this approach and postpone it to future work.

$$(6.6) \quad d(\hat{d})\big|_{\hat{d}=0} = \left(z \cdot \alpha_K - \tau - \beta_K^2 \cdot z \cdot k\right) \cdot k \cdot dt + \beta_K \cdot z \cdot k \cdot dB$$

The debt ratio dynamics do not reach a boundary, let alone a fixed point at $\hat{d} = 0$. This implies that the debt ratio 'is always free' to attain positive or negative values. As (6.1) shows, the respective sign depends solely on the short-term interest rate. From now on, we concentrate only on short-term interest rate values for which the debt ratio is different from zero.

In Proposition 6.2, we have already shown that the debt ratio has an upper boundary at $\hat{d} = z$ given that the capital output ratio is in the lower-growth region. But even if k is in the higher-growth region, $\hat{d} = z$ has a special meaning. From the dynamics (6.5), we recognize that $\hat{d} = z$ is an irregular point since the diffusion term vanishes. We thus get the locally deterministic dynamics of the debt ratio:

$$(6.7) \quad d(\hat{d})\big|_{\hat{d}=z} = \underbrace{\frac{(r_D - \tau) \cdot (r_D - \alpha_K + \delta + \gamma \cdot \beta_K^2) - \tau \cdot (\alpha_K - \delta - r_D)}{r_D - \alpha_K + \delta + \gamma \cdot \beta_K^2}}_{\text{drift at } \hat{d}=z} \cdot z \cdot dt$$

Depending on whether the drift in (6.7) is positive or negative, the debt ratio may be bounded below or above at $\hat{d} = z$. This yields the following proposition:

Proposition 6.3:

Let $r_{D,7}$ and $r_{D,9}$ denote the roots of the numerator of the drift in (6.7) and $r_{D,8}$ the root of the denominator. Then the drift in (6.7) is positive if $r_{D,9} < r_D$ holds and negative if $r_{D,8} < r_D < r_{D,9}$ holds.

Proof: see Appendix 6.1.

Proposition 6.3 implies that it depends on the short-term interest rate value whether the debt ratio at $\hat{d} = z$ is locally bounded from above or below. This result, while interesting in its own right, does not allow us to confine the debt ratio when k is in the higher-growth region. Yet, we can state a sufficient condition for $\hat{d} = z$ to become an upper local boundary if we represent the debt ratio dynamics in a different way. Replacing the interest rate dependency in the debt ratio dynamics (6.5) via (6.1), we get:

$$
(6.8) \quad d(\hat{d}) = \left(
\begin{array}{l}
\left(\alpha_K - \delta - \tau - \alpha_K \cdot k + \beta_K^2 \cdot k^2 - \beta_K^2 \cdot \gamma \cdot \dfrac{k}{k + \hat{d}} \right) \cdot \hat{d} \\
+ \left(z \cdot (\alpha_K - \beta_K^2 \cdot k) - \tau \right) \cdot k
\end{array}
\right) \cdot dt \\
+ (z - \hat{d}) \cdot \beta_K \cdot k \cdot dB
$$

with the drift of $\hat{d}$ at $\hat{d} = z$ being given as:

$$
(6.9) \quad \text{drift}(\hat{d}) = (\alpha_K - \delta - \tau) \cdot z - \beta_K^2 \cdot \gamma \cdot z \cdot \frac{k}{k + z} - \tau \cdot k
$$

The derivative of the drift with respect to k and the limits of the drift for k tending to zero and infinity at $\hat{d} = z$ can now be computed as follows:

$$
(6.10) \quad \frac{d(\text{drift}(\hat{d}))}{dk} = -\beta_K^2 \cdot \gamma \cdot \left(\frac{z}{k + z} \right)^2 - \tau < 0
$$

$$
(6.11) \quad \lim_{k \to 0} \left(\text{drift}(\hat{d}) \right) = (\alpha_K - \delta - \tau) \cdot z
$$

$$
(6.12) \quad \lim_{k \to \infty} \left(\text{drift}(\hat{d}) \right) = -\infty
$$

As we see from (6.10), the local drift of $\hat{d}$ at $\hat{d} = z$ is monotonically falling for rising values of k. In the limit, the drift tends to minus infinity for k tending to infinity. According to the mean value theorem, the drift of $\hat{d}$ at $\hat{d}$ = z can hence only have one root if its limit for $k \to 0$ is positive. This holds only if $\alpha_K - \delta - \tau$ is positive. If $\alpha_K - \delta - \tau$ is negative, however, then the sign of the drift of $\hat{d}$ at $\hat{d} = z$ will always be negative thus implying that the public debt per output ratio can never exceed $\hat{d} = z$ if it starts below this value. We now state a sufficient condition for $\hat{d} = z$ to be an upper boundary:

Proposition 6.4:

If $\tau \geq \alpha_K - \delta$ holds, then the debt ratio process $\hat{d}$ starting within $[0, z]$ is bounded from above at the boundary $\hat{d} = z$. If $\hat{d}$ starts with a value higher than z and reaches z, it will then always remain below z.

Proof: obvious from the above discussion.

Proposition 6.4. is somewhat sharper than Proposition 6.2. It states the condition which 'forces' the debt ratio into a region of low values once the debt ratio has sunk below the public expenditure ratio without k having to be in the lower-growth region. The debt ratio is from then on always 'trapped' in this region. Exploding debt ratios can then never happen. The economic message from Proposition 6.4 is that setting the tax rate equal to or higher than the net return on capital prevents the debt ratio from exceeding the expenditure ratio z given that its initial value is lower than z or that it falls below z in the course of time. The reason is that the government is able to raise sufficient taxes so that it needs not finance its deficit by further borrowing. Critical for this result to hold is certainly that in this model taxes are not levied on income streams and thus do not distort the investment-saving decision of the private sector directly. In the case of income taxes, it could happen that increasing tax rates lead to less capital accumulation and output. Although the level of public debt could be decreased by such a policy, the debt ratio could nonetheless rise owing to the loss of output.

We have to recall that the tax rate constraint (3.23) restricts the tax rate from reaching arbitrary high values. For Proposition 6.4 to become possible, the following condition has thus to be fulfilled:

$$(6.13) \quad \rho > \frac{1}{2} \cdot (\gamma - 1) \cdot \gamma \cdot \beta_K^2$$

The higher the elasticity of substitution γ, which is simultaneously a measure of risk aversion, the less likely can taxation be set so that the debt ratio is bounded from above. The less risk averse the representative household, the more leeway the government has to set a tax rate so that it meets its fiscal constraints.

The whole collection of propositions stated above implies that $\hat{d}$ does always move within one of the following two regions: $R_1 = (-k, z)$ or $R_2 = (z, \infty)$. Moreover, the propositions shed some light on how $\hat{d}$ behaves in R_1 and at the boundary $\hat{d} = z$. However, in light of empirical evidence that many countries face a debt ratio substantially higher than the public expenditure ratio, it is important to see what is happening when $\hat{d}$ is in the region R_2. From (6.1), we know that the debt ratio will become negative if r_D sinks below some critical value. But is there also something like a built-in stabilizing effect of the short-term interest rate when the short-term interest rate remains above this critical value? For this purpose, we now look at the dynamics (6.5), especially at the drift term, in the situation where $r_D \in \alpha_K - \delta - \beta_K^2 \cdot \gamma, \alpha_K - \delta - (1-z) \cdot \beta_K^2 \cdot \gamma$. The reason is that the drift represents the most important ingredient of a SDE since it can be interpreted as the time change of the diffusion process in absence of stochastic shocks. If the drift has a zero root, then the diffusion process described by the solution of the SDE becomes locally a martingale, meaning that it fluctuates driftless at the root. Moreover, if the drift is positive left from a zero root and negative right from it, then the diffusion process has always the tendency to return to this root unless very big shocks appear that neutralize the effect of the drift. If we are able to show that the drift in (6.5) is sufficiently negative for reasonable ranges of $\hat{d}$ on the presumed range of r_D and additionally possesses such a root, then we can conclude that $\hat{d}$ will in all likelihood finally 'settle down' nearby the root rather than grow all the time. In turn, this feature would give rise to an automatic stabilization property of the interest rates with regard to the public debt dynamics. The drift of (6.5) can be written as:

(6.14) $\quad \text{drift}(\hat{d}) = \left(f(r_D) - g(r_D) \cdot \hat{d} + h(r_D) \cdot \hat{d}^2 \right) \cdot \hat{d}$

with:

$$f(r_D) = \frac{r_D^2 - r_D \cdot \left((1+z) \cdot \alpha_K - \delta - \gamma \cdot \beta_K^2\right) + z \cdot \alpha_K \cdot (\alpha_K - \delta) - \tau \cdot \gamma \cdot \beta_K^2}{r_D - \alpha_K + \delta + \gamma \cdot \beta_K^2}$$

$$g(r_D) = \frac{\alpha_K \cdot (\alpha_K - \delta - r_D)}{r_D - \alpha_K + \delta + \gamma \cdot \beta_K^2} + \beta_K^2 \cdot z \cdot \left(\frac{\alpha_K - \delta - r_D}{r_D - \alpha_K + \delta + \gamma \cdot \beta_K^2}\right)^2 > 0$$

$$h(r_D) = \beta_K^2 \cdot \left(\frac{\alpha_K - \delta - r_D}{r_D - \alpha_K + \delta + \gamma \cdot \beta_K^2}\right)^2 > 0$$

It is notable that the drift's sign depends solely on the sign of the bracket within (6.14). This bracket has the functional form of a parabola in $\hat{d}$. Due to the signs of the auxiliary functions g and h, we know that the parabola's apex is the global minimum of the bracket. The root of the drift left to the minimum is the one we are looking for because the diffusion process will stay in its neighborhood with high probability as argued above. Computing the minimum ($\hat{d}_{min}$) and the roots ($\hat{d}_{1/2}$) of the bracket, we get:

$$(6.15) \quad \hat{d}_{min} = \frac{1}{2} \cdot \left(\frac{\alpha_K \cdot (r_D - \alpha_K + \delta + \gamma \cdot \beta_K^2)}{\beta_K^2 \cdot (\alpha_K - \delta - r_D)} + z\right) > 0$$

$$(6.16) \quad \hat{d}_{1/2} = \hat{d}_{min} \mp \underbrace{\sqrt{\hat{d}_{min}^2 - \frac{f(r_D)}{h(r_D)}}}_{\text{discriminant}}$$

From (6.16), we can deduce that the critical condition for negative drift values is that both roots exist because the drift is only negative between these roots. Left to the smaller and right to the bigger root, the drift is positive. Two roots exist if the discriminant in (6.16) is strictly positive. Otherwise, no roots exists or, as a special case, just one root exists at which the drift is zero. In these cases, the drift is always positive. A positive drift, however, implies steadily growing debt ratios in average, at least as long as r_D stays within $(\alpha_K - \delta - \beta_K^2 \cdot \gamma, \alpha_K - \delta - (1-z) \cdot \beta_K^2 \cdot \gamma)$. No stabilization of the economy's fiscal stance happens then. Making use of (6.15) as well as of the equations for f(r_D) and g(r_D), the discriminant can be written as:

(6.17)

$$\hat{d}_{min}{}^2 - \frac{f(r_D)}{h(r_D)} \equiv \left(\frac{\alpha_K \cdot (r_D - \alpha_K + \delta + \gamma \cdot \beta_K^2)}{\beta_K^2 \cdot (\alpha_K - \delta - r_D)} + z \right)^2 - \frac{r_D - \alpha_K + \delta + \gamma \cdot \beta_K^2}{\beta_K^2 \cdot (\alpha_K - \delta - r_D)^2}$$
$$\cdot 4 \cdot (r_D^2 - r_D \cdot ((1+z) \cdot \alpha_K - \delta - \gamma \cdot \beta_K^2) + z \cdot \alpha_K \cdot (\alpha_K - \delta) - \tau \cdot \gamma \cdot \beta_K^2)$$

The non-negativity of this discriminant implies the condition:

(6.18) $\hat{d}_{min}{}^2 - \dfrac{f(r_D)}{h(r_D)} > 0$

We can now state the following proposition:

Proposition 6.5:

If inequality (6.18) is valid for all $r_D \in (\alpha_K - \delta - \beta_K^2 \cdot \gamma, \alpha_K - \delta - (1-z) \cdot \beta_K^2 \cdot \gamma)$, then the drift of the debt ratio dynamics is negative for $\hat{d} < \hat{d}_2$. The lower the initial debt ratio is compared to $\hat{d} < \hat{d}_2$, the higher is the probability that $\hat{d}$ remains permanently in the neighborhood of $\hat{d}_1$.

Proof: obvious from the above discussion.

Proposition 6.5 is thus a stabilization statement concerning public indebtedness.

In principle, we could now analytically derive the parameter conditions that guarantee inequality (6.18). This, however, would yield complicated conditions that lend themselves not to economic interpretations. We therefore illustrate the rationale behind our argumentation with a numerical example. Taking the same values for the model parameters as in Chapter 3 we plot condition (6.18) over the range of all feasible tax rates and short-term interest rates.

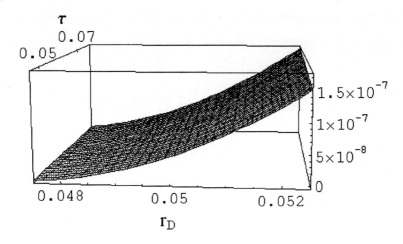

Figure 6.1: Plot of condition (6.18).

Figure 6.1 shows that condition (6.18) is always fulfilled. We can now additionally plot the drift function which yields Figure 6.2.

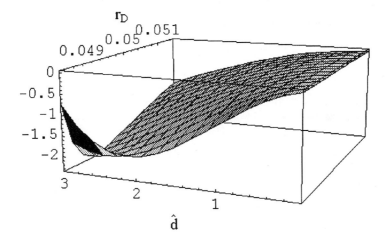

Figure 6.2: Plot of the drift function.

We see that the drift is indeed smaller than zero for all reasonable debt ratio values. Thus, the debt ratio dynamics will on average ensure the debt ratio to fall so that the fiscal stance of the public sector is stabilized. As (6.14) suggests, however, the drift can become positive thus implying an explosion of the debt ratio with a high probability given that the short-term interest rate does not sink below the level of $r_D = \alpha_K - \delta - \beta_K^2 \cdot \gamma$ [3]. However, this is only feasible for debt ratio values far beyond those observed in reality [4].

6.3 Short and long run effects of fiscal policy and interest rates on the debt ratio

Having examined some local and global properties of the debt ratio dynamics in the last section, we now look at the effects τ, z and r_D may have on the debt ratio in the short and long run. This means that we will analyze how infinitesimal changes of τ, z and r_D immediately (short run) and finally (when time meets infinity, i.e. long run) affect the debt ratio.

6.3.1 Short run effects

Taking the short run perspective first, we have to calculate the influence of τ, z and r_D on the drift and diffusion term of the stochastic dynamics (6.5). Doing so delivers the following results:

(6.19a)
$$\frac{\partial(\text{drift}(\hat{d}))}{\partial r_D} = \frac{\left(\left(\alpha_K + 2\cdot\beta_K^2\cdot\hat{d}\right)\cdot\left(r_D - \alpha_K + \delta\right) + \gamma\cdot\beta_K^2\cdot\alpha_K\right)\cdot\left(\hat{d} - z\right)\cdot\hat{d}\cdot\gamma\cdot\beta_K^2}{\left(r_D - \alpha_K + \delta + \gamma\cdot\beta_K^2\right)^3}$$
$$+\hat{d} + \frac{\tau\cdot\hat{d}\cdot\gamma\cdot\beta_K^2}{\left(r_D - \alpha_K + \delta + \gamma\cdot\beta_K^2\right)^2}$$

(6.19b) $$\frac{\partial(\text{diffusion}(\hat{d}))}{\partial r_D} = \frac{\left(\hat{d} - z\right)\cdot\gamma\cdot\beta_K^3\cdot\hat{d}}{\left(r_D - \alpha_K + \delta + \gamma\cdot\beta_K^2\right)^2}$$

---

[3] Note that we have shown in Proposition 6.1 that for values of r_D smaller than $r_D = \alpha_K - \delta - \beta_K^2\cdot\gamma$, the debt ratio becomes negative, banning the danger of an exploding debt ratio.

[4] For our parameter constellation, the debt ratio would have to exceed 300% by far in order to yield explosive debt ratio paths. Additionally, this explosion could only happen for short-term interest rates always remaining higher than $r_D = \alpha_K - \delta - \beta_K^2\cdot\gamma$.

$$(6.20a) \quad \frac{\partial(\text{drift}(\hat{d}))}{\partial \tau} = -\frac{\gamma \cdot \beta_K^2}{r_D - \alpha_K + \delta + \gamma \cdot \beta_K^2} \cdot \hat{d} < 0$$

$$(6.20b) \quad \frac{\partial(\text{diffusion}(\hat{d}))}{\partial \tau} = 0$$

$$(6.21a) \quad \frac{\partial(\text{drift}(\hat{d}))}{\partial z} = \left(\alpha_K - \beta_K^2 \cdot \underbrace{\frac{(\alpha_K - \delta - r_D) \cdot \hat{d}}{r_D - \alpha_K + \delta + \gamma \cdot \beta_K^2}}_{k} \right) \cdot \underbrace{\frac{(\alpha_K - \delta - r_D) \cdot \hat{d}}{r_D - \alpha_K + \delta + \gamma \cdot \beta_K^2}}_{k}$$

$$(6.21b) \quad \frac{\partial(\text{diffusion}(\hat{d}))}{\partial z} = \frac{(\alpha_K - \delta - r_D) \cdot \beta_K \cdot \hat{d}}{r_D - \alpha_K + \delta + \gamma \cdot \beta_K^2} > 0$$

In view of the empirical evidence that in almost any country the public debt ratio is positive, we will for the further analysis assume that the short-term interest rate remains bigger than $r_D = \alpha_K - \delta - \beta_K^2 \cdot \gamma$ since this guarantees positive debt ratio values (see Proposition 6.1). Under this assumption, the signs of the effects (6.20a) and (6.21b) become clear.

We will now focus first on the role the short-term interest rate plays for the debt ratio in the short run. (6.19b) shows that an increase in r_D enhances the diffusion term and hence volatility of $\hat{d}$ if and only if $\hat{d}$ is bigger than the public expenditure ratio z. This effect can be explained by the same mechanism as in the last chapter: increasing short-term interest rates lead to higher opportunity costs of capital and render government bonds more attractive for investors. As a result, the proportion of available investment resources which is invested in capital sinks. Simultaneously, rising short-term interest rates depress consumption. For given private wealth, more resources become available for investment purposes. In terms of capital accumulation, this positive effect may outweigh the direct portfolio reshuffling effect. As a consequence, an increase in r_D may either improve or worsen capital accumulation and income generation. Income, in turn, drives government expenditure proportionally. Since the source of volatility of public debt lies in the volatility of public expenditure (see debt accumulation equation (3.20)), we can conclude that an increase in capital via increasing r_D leads to higher volatility of the public debt ratio. Accordingly, if the second effect on capital accumulation due to a rise in r_D overcompensates the portfolio reshuffling effect, the volatility of the public debt ratio sinks.

The influence of r_D on the drift of $\hat{d}$ is quite complicated since the sign of (6.19a) is not unique. In most cases, it will be positive. For small values of $\hat{d}$ and r_D, it is conceivable that the sign becomes negative. As in the just discussed case of debt ratio volatility, the two contrary effects on capital accumulation and hence on government expenditure are also at work as regards the drift of the public debt ratio. An increase in r_D, however, additionally enhances the drift of the interest burden of old debt and thereby increases the drift of debt accumulation and debt ratio. This interest burden effect is the smaller the lower $\hat{d}$ and r_D. Ultimately, the consumption-induced reduction in the drift of $\hat{d}$ may overcompensate the sum of the portfolio reshuffling and interest burden effect.

Turning to the short run effect of the tax rate on $\hat{d}$, we see from (6.20a-b) that an increase in τ does not change the volatility of $\hat{d}$ but diminishes its drift. The reason for both effects is clear: the government budget constraint (3.10) shows that the tax rate only affects the drift of public debt but not the diffusion. Had we allowed taxation to be also a locally stochastic process (for example, like Eaton (1981)), we would have ended up with a non-vanishing effect of the tax rate on the volatility of the public debt ratio. In the short run, a tax rate increase leads to the drift effect of more tax revenues since the tax base (i.e. private wealth) does not react on tax rate changes immediately. As a consequence, the drift of the debt and the debt ratio decreases [5].

---

[5] It is noteworthy that this negative short run effect on the drift of $\hat{d}$ may also exist in the medium run although tax revenues then get smaller compared to the short run since higher tax rates harm wealth accumulation. Simultaneously, however, less wealth implies less resources for capital accumulation which reduces government expenditure. If this decreasing effect on government expenditure is stronger than the loss in tax revenues than the primary deficit improves. This slows down debt accumulation so that the negative sign of the drift effect may remain even in the medium run.

Regarding the short run influence of the public expenditure ratio z, (6.21b) tells us that rising z implies higher volatility of the debt ratio. This is easily understandable: higher values of z imply higher volatility of government expenditure, hence higher volatility of primary deficits and finally higher volatility of the debt ratio. The drift effect of rising z on the debt ratio is similar to the one on the capital output ratio derived in Chapter 5. If the capital output ratio exceeds the value α_K/β_K^2 then an increase in z will diminish the drift of $\hat{d}$ and vice versa (the reason for this effect was already discussed in some detail in the last chapter so that we will remain brief in our explanation). In a nutshell, risk averse households appreciate higher values of z in times of quite negative productivity shocks since the government then confiscates relatively less resources for own spending compared to situations where z is set to lower values. This dampening effect may stimulate or at least harm capital and wealth accumulation less strongly. The tax base and hence tax revenues are not reduced less. Consequently, the pressure on deficits and thus debt is lowered which explains the negative effect of rising z on the drift of $\hat{d}$ in cases where k exceeds α_K/β_K^2.

6.3.2 Long run effects

In Chapter 3 and 5 we already discussed long run effects of fiscal policy on the short-term interest rate and the capital output ratio. We did this by either explicitly showing or implicitly assuming that a stationary probability distribution of the stochastic processes at stake does exist and will be attained ultimately. Then we calculated this distribution as the solution of a stationary Fokker-Planck equation and computed the respective derivatives. Applying this procedure here, we face the following problem: the debt ratio process does not possess fixed upper and lower boundaries as the short-term interest rate and capital output ratio process did. Without such boundaries, which both have to be non-attainable, there is hardly a chance that a stationary probability distribution exists. Without such a distribution, any long run analysis regarding the influence of model parameters is impossible. Nonetheless, there is a way out of the dilemma. As Proposition 6.2 shows, there is a variable lower boundary of $\hat{d}$ at -k. Assuming that k finally gets trapped in the interval $(0,\ 1-z)$ and that r_D is eventually bigger than $r_D = \alpha_K - \delta - \beta_K^2 \cdot \gamma$, we can then conclude that the debt ratio is confined to the interval $(0,\ z)$ (see Proposition 6.1). This assumption together with the Skorohod (1989) theorem cited in Proposition 3.6 enables us to calculate a stationary probability distribution associated with $\hat{d}$, albeit we have to assume additionally that the long run dynamics of $\hat{d}$ is not influenced by the dynamics of r_D as already argued in the last chapter. This implies that we have to treat r_D as a parameter only since otherwise the stationary version of the Fokker-Planck equation would not be easily integrable. The stationary probability density for $\hat{d}$ can then be shown to be given as:

(6.22)

$$p(\hat{d}) = \frac{m \cdot a_2^2}{\beta_K^2 \cdot \hat{d}^6} \cdot \left(\frac{\hat{d}}{z-\hat{d}}\right)^{\frac{3 a_1 a_2^2}{\beta_K^2 z^4} + \frac{\alpha_K a_2}{\beta_K^2 z^3} \frac{1}{z^2}+2} \cdot \exp\left(\frac{a_1 \cdot a_2^2 \cdot \left(z^2 + 3 \cdot \hat{d} \cdot z - 6 \cdot \hat{d}^2\right)}{2 \cdot \beta_K^2 \cdot \hat{d}^2 \cdot (\hat{d}-z) \cdot z^3} + \frac{2 \cdot \beta_K^2 \cdot \hat{d} \cdot z - a_2 \cdot \alpha_K \cdot (2 \cdot \hat{d}+z)}{2 \cdot \beta_K^2 \cdot \hat{d}^2 \cdot z^2} \right)$$

with:

$$a_1 = \frac{r_D \cdot \left(r_D - \alpha_K + \delta + \gamma \cdot \beta_K^2\right) - \tau \cdot \gamma \cdot \beta_K^2}{r_D - \alpha_K + \delta + \gamma \cdot \beta_K^2} = r_D - \frac{\tau \cdot \gamma \cdot \beta_K^2}{r_D - \alpha_K + \delta + \gamma \cdot \beta_K^2}$$

$$a_2 = \frac{r_D - \alpha_K + \delta + \gamma \cdot \beta_K^2}{\alpha_K - \delta - r_D} > 0$$

The integration constant m in (6.22) has to be determined in the same way as in the long run analysis of Chapter 3 and 5. Neglecting the influence of the tax rate τ and the public expenditure ratio z on m, we calculate the following derivatives:

(6.23)

$$\frac{dp(\hat{d})}{dr_D} = \begin{pmatrix} \ln\left(\frac{\hat{d}}{z-\hat{d}}\right)\cdot\left(\frac{3\cdot a_2^2}{\beta_K^2\cdot z^4}\cdot\frac{da_1}{dr_D} + \frac{6\cdot a_1\cdot a_2}{\beta_K^2\cdot z^4}\cdot\frac{da_2}{dr_D} + \frac{\alpha_K}{\beta_K^2\cdot z^3}\cdot\frac{da_2}{dr_D}\right) \\ + \frac{6\cdot\hat{d}^2 - 3\cdot\hat{d}\cdot z - z^2}{2\cdot\beta_K^2\cdot\hat{d}^2\cdot(z-\hat{d})\cdot z^3}\cdot a_2\cdot\left(a_2\cdot\frac{da_1}{dr_D} + 2\cdot a_1\cdot\frac{da_2}{dr_D}\right) \\ + \frac{2}{a_2}\cdot\frac{da_2}{dr_D} - \frac{\alpha_K\cdot(2\cdot\hat{d}+z)}{2\cdot\beta_K^2\cdot\hat{d}^2\cdot z^2}\cdot\frac{da_2}{dr_D} \end{pmatrix}\cdot p(\hat{d})$$

(6.24)

$$\frac{dp(\hat{d})}{d\tau} = -\left(\ln\left(\frac{\hat{d}}{z-\hat{d}}\right) + \frac{z\cdot(6\cdot\hat{d}^2 - 3\cdot z\cdot\hat{d} - z^2)}{6\cdot\hat{d}^2\cdot(z-\hat{d})}\right)\cdot\frac{3\cdot a_2^2}{\beta_K^2\cdot z^4}\cdot\frac{\gamma\cdot\beta_K^2\cdot p(\hat{d})}{r_D - \alpha_K + \delta + \gamma\cdot\beta_K^2}$$

$$< 0 \Leftrightarrow \hat{d} > 0.6346\cdot z$$

(6.25)

$$\frac{dp(\hat{d})}{dz} = \begin{pmatrix} \ln\left(\frac{\hat{d}}{z-\hat{d}}\right)\cdot\left(-\frac{12\cdot a_1\cdot a_2^2}{\beta_K^2\cdot z^5} - \frac{3\cdot\alpha_K\cdot a_2}{\beta_K^2\cdot z^4} + \frac{2}{z^3}\right) + \frac{a_2\cdot\alpha_K\cdot(4\cdot\hat{d}+z)}{2\cdot\beta_K^2\cdot\hat{d}^2\cdot z} \\ + \frac{(2\cdot z+3\cdot\hat{d})\cdot(\hat{d}-z)\cdot z - (z^2+3\cdot\hat{d}\cdot z - 6\cdot\hat{d}^2)\cdot(3\cdot\hat{d}-4\cdot z)}{(2\cdot\beta_K^2\cdot\hat{d}^2\cdot(\hat{d}-z)\cdot z^3)^2} \\ \cdot 2\cdot\beta_K^2\cdot\hat{d}^2\cdot a_1\cdot a_2^2\cdot z^2 - \frac{\frac{3\cdot a_1\cdot a_2^2}{\beta_K^2\cdot z^4} + \frac{\alpha_K\cdot a_2}{\beta_K^2\cdot z^3} - \frac{1}{z^2} + 2}{z-\hat{d}} - \frac{1}{\hat{d}\cdot z^2} \end{pmatrix}\cdot p(\hat{d})$$

(6.24) shows that an increase in the tax rate raises the probability of $\hat{d}$ if and only if $\hat{d}$ is smaller than some critical value. This critical value is given by 0.6346 times z which is the root of the bracket in (6.24). Debt ratios below (above) this value gain (loose) probability mass in the long run when the tax rate rises and vice versa. This does not mean that high debt ratios cannot occur. In fact, they can but the respective probability decreases with increasing τ. In order to understand this effect, it is necessary to recall all relevant economic mechanisms determining public debt. Ceteris paribus, a higher tax rate increases tax revenues. In the long run, however, rising tax rates harm wealth accumulation (3.21) and the tax base will decline, thereby questioning the positive effect of tax rate increases on tax revenues. On the other hand, a tax rate increase initially improves the budget deficit and reduces the debt burden. This lowers the short-term interest rate. Hence, investment in capital becomes more attractive, inducing a positive effect on capital accumulation, output and finally on government expenditure. Although higher government spending may again deteriorate public deficits and public debt, higher growth helps keeping the debt ratio down. In the long run, (6.24) tells us that the debt ratio decreasing effects dominate the debt ratio increasing effects.

Unfortunately, the derivatives in (6.23) and (6.25) remain inconclusive. In order to get an idea, we calculate the brackets of (6.23) and (6.25) for our usual set of parameter values with $\tau = 7\%$ and $z = 40\%$. Subsequently, we plot the results for both brackets over the assumed range of the short-term interest rate and the debt output ratio.

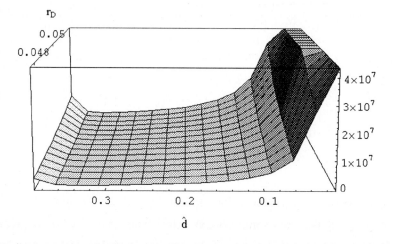

Figure 6.3: Sign of the interest rate effect on the debt ratios stationary probability.

Figure 6.3 shows that the bracket of (6.23) is always positive for the considered set of parameters and the value range of r_D and $\hat{d}$. This implies that increasing short-term interest rates raise the probability of debt ratios with values between (0, z) in the long run. Conversely, falling interest rates decrease this probability. This confirms earlier investigations which led us to the conclusion that rising interest rates may stabilize the public debt ratio given that the debt ratio is not extraordinarily high.

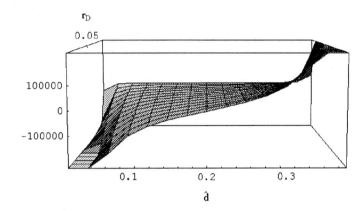

Figure 6.4: Sign of the government expenditure ratio effect on the debt ratios stationary probability.

Looking on Figure 6.4, the bracket of (6.25) is seen to be positive only from a certain level of $\hat{d}$ on. For smaller debt ratios, the bracket is negative. Additionally, a lower interest rate requires a higher debt ratio in order to guarantee a positive sign of rising z on (6.25). Thus, rising public expenditure ratios increase the probability of high debt ratios and diminish the probability of low debt ratios to be reached in the long run. Low short-term interest rates tend to amplify, high interest rates tend to smooth this effect. The explanation is clear-cut: higher expenditure ratios tend to worsen primary deficits and impair public indebtedness. Simultaneously present high short-term interest rates amplify the effect on indebtedness since they impose heavier burdens of interest payments. In the end, higher debt ratios become therefore more likely, lower more unlikely.

The results regarding the long run have to be viewed skeptically: the stationary probability density (6.22) could only be derived by assuming the short-term interest rate to be a constant. Moreover, we cannot prove that the debt ratio will indeed 'settle down' on the interval (0, z). Finally, the effects of the tax rate and the expenditure ratio do not only influence the probability density (6.22) directly but also indirectly through the influence on r_D. A mathematically water-proof analysis, however, can only be made numerically using a 'correct' set of parameter values. This is not at hand presently.

6.4 Short summary

The equilibrium condition for the short-term interest rate has revealed that the debt ratio is critically determined by the short-term interest rate together with the capital output ratio. Debt dynamics are therefore driven by the interest rate and growth dynamics. The level of the short-term interest rate determines the sign of the debt ratio, the capital output ratio mainly influences the magnitude of the public debt ratio. On average, high debt levels are only compatible with high growth rates, but the question whether debt ratios are stabilized (i.e. sink) is chiefly linked to the question whether interest rates sink below a critical level or not. Moreover, we saw that there are two situations in which the debt ratio cannot exceed an upper boundary equal to the public expenditure ratio z: if the economy is in the lower-growth regime or if the tax rate exceeds the net return on capital. If the debt ratio starts with higher values than z, we were able to show that under certain plausible parameter constellations and initial conditions the debt ratio will finally converge to a region of quite low values, possibly even negative ones.

In the last part of the chapter, we examined short and long run effects of the interest rate and the fiscal policy parameters on the debt ratio dynamics. We found out that increasing short-term interest rates may have varying short and long run effects on the debt ratio depending on whether primary deficits are improved by possible crowding-in effects on capital accumulation and growth and whether such effects compensate fully or only partially for rising interest payments. Rising tax rates were seen to lower debt ratios in the short run and to lead to higher probabilities of low debt ratio levels in the long run. Finally, higher public expenditure ratios were seen to yield higher debt ratios in the short run only if the capital output ratio is sufficiently low. The reason for this effect lies mainly in the fact that relatively high levels of public expenditure ratios 'dampen' big negative productivity shocks. This may stimulate capital accumulation and growth. Since the whole effect on the debt ratio holds only for high capital output ratios, the expansive effect on the tax base is bigger than the expansive effect on the public expenditure base. This improves the primary balance. As a result, the stock of public debt decreases or at least grows less strongly than output.

In a nutshell, the conventional wisdom that high debt ratios go together with high interest rates is confirmed. But the analysis has clearly shown that it is the interest rate dynamics that mainly drives the debt dynamics. For stable public debt ratios to occur, it is sufficient that either the interest rate dynamics prompt the growth process to converge to a lower-growth region or the interest rate itself settles down at a sufficiently low level. Financial market behavior is hence of critical importance when one wants to understand the dynamic implications of economic growth and public indebtedness.

Appendix 6.1: Proof of Proposition 6.3

Recalling (6.7), we can write the drift as a function $f(r_D)$:

$$(A6.1.1) \qquad f(r_D) = \frac{r_D^2 - r_D \cdot (\alpha_K - \delta - \gamma \cdot \beta_K^2) - \tau \cdot \gamma \cdot \beta_K^2}{r_D - \alpha_K + \delta + \gamma \cdot \beta_K^2}$$

We have to distinguish two cases: 1) the denominator of $f(r_D)$ is positive or 2) the denominator of $f(r_D)$ is negative. Obviously, the drift function is always positive when both the numerator and the denominator share the same sign. Thus, we need to gain some insight as regards the sign of the numerator. For this purpose we calculate its roots:

$$(A6.1.2) \qquad \begin{aligned} r_{D,9} &= \frac{1}{2} \cdot \left(\alpha_K - \delta - \gamma \cdot \beta_K^2 + \sqrt{(\alpha_K - \delta - \gamma \cdot \beta_K^2)^2 + 4 \cdot \tau \cdot \gamma \cdot \beta_K^2} \right) \\ r_{D,7} &= \frac{1}{2} \cdot \left(\alpha_K - \delta - \gamma \cdot \beta_K^2 - \sqrt{(\alpha_K - \delta - \gamma \cdot \beta_K^2)^2 + 4 \cdot \tau \cdot \gamma \cdot \beta_K^2} \right) \end{aligned}$$

The ranking of the roots is $r_{D,7} < 0 < r_{D,9}$. Because the numerator of $f(r_D)$ is a parabola in r_D, we can easily check that the numerator is negative for $r_D \in (r_{D,7}, r_{D,9})$, zero at the roots and positive elsewhere. Since the root of the

228

denominator of $f(r_D)$, $r_{D,8} = \alpha_K - \delta - \gamma \cdot \beta_K^2$, lies between the two roots of (A6.1.2), we can distinguish the following four cases, at least in principle:

1. If $r_D < r_{D,7}$ then $f(r_D)$ (i.e. the drift of (6.7)) is negative.

2. If $r_{D,7} < r_D < r_{D,8}$ then $f(r_D)$ (i.e. the drift of (6.7)) is positive.

3. If $r_{D,8} < r_D < r_{D,9}$ then $f(r_D)$ (i.e. the drift of (6.7)) is negative.

4. If $r_{D,9} < r_D$ then $f(r_D)$ (i.e. the drift of (6.7)) is positive.

However, we must not forget that values for r_D smaller than $r_{D,8}$ are not allowed for a debt ratio of z and positive capital output ratio k (see (6.1)). The first two cases thus cancel out and Proposition 6.3 is proved.

7 Summary, conclusions and outlook on future research

7.1 Summary of the main results

In this thesis, we have studied the interaction of fiscal policy and financial market behavior in a dynamic general equilibrium model of a real, closed economy. Output was produced via a linear production function with capital as sole input. The private sector was introduced as a representative household solving its intertemporal consumption and saving/investment problem subject to its dynamic budget constraint. The structure of the financial market was characterized by the exogenously given types of assets: capital, short-term government bonds, private sector bonds of free maturity. The public sector was described by exogenously given rules regarding taxation and public spending. Resulting fiscal deficits drive public debt. Public debt appears only in form of short-term government bonds. In case public debt happens to be negative, this is equivalent to the government being in a creditor position relative to the private sector.

In Chapter 2, the model setting is deterministic. It serves as a benchmark against which to compare the results in all subsequent chapters. The main results obtained are:

- In equilibrium, the rates of return are equalized between all assets and constant. The term structure of interest rates is flat.

- The asset returns are independent of fiscal policy.

- The accumulation dynamics of private capital, public debt and private wealth are linear and can be solved explicitly.

- Optimality of the household's maximization problem requires an upper ceiling on the tax rate. This ceiling depends on preference and technology parameters only.

- A strong one-to-one relationship between the tax rate and the government expenditure ratio is necessary to prevent the stock of capital from approaching zero. Hence there is only one degree of freedom for fiscal policy, and even that is constrained by the preceding constraint on the tax rate.

- Additionally, initial public debt has to be either zero or even negative to guarantee viability, i.e. the government must be in a creditor position relative to the private sector.

- The growth rate is time-dependent, accelerates through time and attains a steady-state in the long run.

- The time path of growth rates depends negatively on tax rates and public expenditure ratios and positively on the marginal product of capital. Only if the tax rate is sufficiently smaller than the equilibrium asset returns, growth will be always positive.

- The time path of growth depends negatively on the initial capital stock. The conclusion is that an initially poorer economy faces higher growth rates than initially wealthier economies. This feature resembles the convergence property of the neoclassical growth model.

- The initial creditor position of the government relative to the private sector will be maintained all the time. Although the government runs primary deficits, they will be more than offset by interest earnings resulting from the net creditor position. As a consequence, the creditor position relative to output increases over time and converges against a steady-state value.

In Chapter 3, we develop the stochastic version of the benchmark model of Chapter 2 by introducing technological risk in the production function. The consequences are:

- the equilibrium dynamics of capital and debt accumulation cease to be linear. Technically speaking, the reduced form of the model consists of a system of two interwoven nonlinear stochastic differential equations that can not be solved explicitly.

- The short-term interest rate dynamics can be represented by an autonomous, nonlinear stochastic differential equation. Short-term interest rates float all the time in a nonlinear fashion.

- Interest rate dynamics are influenced by fiscal policy.

- As in the benchmark model, there is an upper ceiling on the tax rate to ensure optimality of the household's maximization problem.

- Additionally, the interest rate dynamics together with the constraint to prevent the capital stock from approaching zero imposes a lower and an upper ceiling on the government expenditure ratio. Subject to the three constraints, fiscal policy in the stochastic setting retains its two degrees of freedom.

- The fiscal policy restrictions imply that the short-term interest rate moves on a bounded interval containing positive and negative values. Furthermore, it could be shown that the short-term interest rate dynamics, though not possessing a fixed point at which it would come to rest, tends to a stochastic steady-state.

- The stochastic steady-state is characterized by a stationary (i.e. time-independent) probability distribution associated with the short-term interest rate. This distribution can be used to compute long run effects of fiscal policy and to compare them with the respective short run effects derived directly from the dynamics of the short-term interest rate.

- Rising tax rates lead to decreasing short-term interest rates in the short run and higher probability for lower short-term interest rates in the long run. The partial negative effect of increasing primary surpluses on interest rates is clearly dominating. The short run effect of a rising government expenditure ratio was seen to depend on the interest rate level, while the

long run effect tended to increase the probability of higher short-term
interest rates.

Chapter 4 is devoted to the analysis of the term structure of interest rates:

- Using the short-term interest rate dynamics, we derive a partial differential
  equation (PDE) whose solution describes the price of private bonds. With
  this solution, one can determine the term structure of interest rates.

- Since this PDE cannot be solved in closed-form, we use a special
  approximation scheme to derive an approximate solution. Using this
  solution, we are able to characterize the term structure and plot the yield
  curve.

- We develop the parameter constellations that must prevail for the four
  most characteristic term structure relations (flat, normal, hump-shaped
  and inverse) to come out.

- Given technology and household parameters, the specific choice of fiscal
  policy parameters determines the term structure. Infinitesimal changes in
  the tax rate and in the government expenditure ratio may imply the
  transition from one term structure relation to another. It is also possible to
  synchronize changes in the tax rate and the government expenditure such
  that the term structure remains invariant.

- The main transmission mechanism through which fiscal policy influences
  the shape of the yield curve is the impact on the dynamic composition of
  primary deficits. The changed primary deficit dynamics lead to altered
  expected short-term interest dynamics in the future which are reflected in
  the different yield curve shapes.

In Chapter 5, we study the effect of fiscal policy on the growth dynamics:

- Economic growth is driven by the evolution of the capital output ratio.

- Given the parameter constraints on fiscal policy, the capital output ratio is
  always positive and moving either in a lower-growth or higher-growth

area. These areas have to be understood in terms of expected growth rates. Occasional growth rates may well be high in the lower-growth area. On average, however, growth rates should be significantly lower in the lower-growth area.

- The stochastic evolution of the economy can lead the growth path from the higher-growth area to the lower-growth area. Once the lower-growth region is reached, however, it can never be left again. The economy is then trapped in a low-growth environment.

- The short and long run growth effects of changes in the tax rate, the government expenditure ratio and the short-term interest rate dynamics point in the same direction.

- An increase in the tax rate tends to increase the capital output ratio and growth. The dominating effect thereby is that increasing tax rates lower consumption and leave more resources for investment. Although rising tax rates cause higher tax outlays, this effect is outweighed by the consumption effect.

- The effect of an increase in the government expenditure ratio on economic growth is level-dependent. Contrary to conventional wisdom (public expenditure is per se unproductive), an increase in the government expenditure ratio may stimulate growth in case the capital accumulation dampening effect caused by the government expenditure ratio in times of negative productivity shocks is dominating.

- An increasing short-term interest rate enhances the capital output ratio and growth if the short-term interest rate is sufficiently small and vice versa. Accordingly, crowding-in as well as crowding-out effects are possible. Two different effects are responsible for this phenomenon: on the one hand, rising short-term interest rates impair capital accumulation through portfolio reshuffling in favor of bonds. On the other hand, consumption is decreased so that more resources are available for investment. The sign of the ultimate effect depends on whether the portfolio or the consumption effect prevails.

In Chapter 6, we analyze the dynamics of the debt ratio:

- Contrary to the deterministic model, public indebtedness is clearly compatible with viability of the economy.

- The sign of the debt ratio is determined by the short-term interest rate dynamics, whereas its magnitude is also depending on the capital output ratio.

- High debt ratios go hand in hand with high growth rates. Short-term interest rates being equal, sinking growth rates lead on average to lower debt ratios.

- A rise in the tax rate leads to lower debt ratios in the short and long run. It diminishes debt accumulation and simultaneously increases capital accumulation and thus output. As a consequence, debt per output sinks.

- Rising government expenditure ratio has the same effect as on the capital output ratio. It usually increases the debt ratio, but if the capital output ratio is high enough, then it decreases the debt ratio. The reason is that then an increase in government expenditure ratio enhances growth and output so that the debt ratio sinks even though debt per se may rise.

- The debt ratio will ultimately be stabilized if the short-term interest rate eventually 'settles down' below some critical value.

- If the capital output ratio is in the lower-growth region or if the tax rate exceeds the instantaneously expected return on capital, then the debt ratio cannot exceed the government expenditure ratio once it is below.

- Even if the initial debt ratio is higher than the government expenditure ratio, the debt ratio will yet attain a comparably low level given that its initial starting value is not very high.

7.2 Assessment of the model results

The results of the thesis allow for conclusions that can be divided in two broad categories: first, the theoretical setting presented provides a first and valuable step to bridge the gap between traditional macroeconomic and traditional finance models; second, the introduction of risk allows for a deeper understanding of the effects of fiscal policy on public debt and economic growth via endogenous financial market reactions.

7.2.1 A first step to close the gap between macroeconomics and finance literature

The whole analysis carried out in this work has clearly shown the qualitative differences between a deterministic and stochastic setting of financial markets in a dynamic macromodel. The deterministic setting produced highly unrealistic features like strict equality of asset returns on financial markets and an always flat term structure.

These shortcomings vanish in the stochastic model version. Short-term interest rates are now subject to nonlinear stochastic dynamics never found before in finance literature but recently called for by leading researchers (for example, Ait-Sahalia (1995)). Additionally, the interest rate dynamics reflect the influence of fiscal policy. In traditional finance models, one would have to assume an ad-hoc dependency of model parameters on fiscal policy if one were convinced that fiscal policy is of importance for the respective dynamics. Moreover, our interest rate dynamics reveal a mean-reverting property in that the short-term interest rate will 'settle down' with high probability around the smallest root of the dynamics' drift term. Such mean-reverting behavior is standard among the mathematical finance models dealing with short-term interest rate dynamics. Whereas this property is introduced in an ad-hoc way in these models out of the desire to better explain observed market data, our analysis has clearly shown that this property can be derived from a general equilibrium, macroeconomic model setting. This is a very promising outcome since it shows that specific stylized facts on financial markets can be well reproduced by dynamic macroeconomic models. Thus, macroeconomic models with integrated stochastic financial markets may be able to uncover the economic nature of dynamic links affecting financial markets which are probably perceived by finance researchers, but which they cannot explain and thus not properly account for in their traditional way to introduce arbitrary factor dynamics. Using misspecified factor dynamics, however, can ultimately yield wrong results in asset pricing models, especially when the economic environment, in which the factors move, is not properly taken into account.

Considering our term structure model, it has the potential to deliver all term structures frequently found in empirical work. Furthermore, it allows to explain the influence of fiscal policy on the term structure not only qualitatively, but also quantitatively. When the yield curve changes only in level without altering its dependency regarding time to maturity (thereby conserving its term structure), then this can be explained by the evolution of the short-term interest rate dynamics only. If, however, the term structure changes, then this is explained by a change in the respective model parameters, for example by a change in fiscal policy. Although we have presently not estimated our model using the U.S. data for 1980 presented in Appendix 1.2, we think the model has the potential to deliver a plausible economic story for the observed yield curves in 1980. In this respect, it also outperforms usual term structure models from mathematical finance since they can account for but not identify the economic background behind observed yield curve changes. In view of many finance models employing more than one factor to sufficiently explain the term structure, our model has probably not enough factors to do this job equally well. However, it is no conceptual problem to extend it towards more factors. If, for example, a nominal economic setting is chosen and the money supply dynamics could be shown to interact with the (then nominal) short-term interest rate, maybe even influencing the diffusion term of the interest rate dynamics, then we will obtain a two-factor model with stochastic volatility in the interest rates. If such more advanced macroeconomic models with stochastic financial market setting can be successfully estimated, then the resulting term structure models could result in extremely useful practical applications (for example, for fund managers who want to immunize their bond portfolio against possible sudden changes in fiscal and/or monetary policy). Thus, future use of finance models rooting in macroeconomic dynamics seems to be a promising yet absolutely unexplored working field.

7.2.2 Fiscal policy, growth and endogenous financial market reactions

In terms of economic growth and public debt, the deterministic model setting leads to quite disappointing outcomes in view of empirical evidence. Public debt and debt ratios are negative for all time when fiscal policy is to achieve viability. Growth rates can change their signs at most once. Once positive, they will continue to be so all the time. Moreover, they will always accelerate.

The main reason for these unspectacular and simultaneously unsatisfactory results is that asset prices do not react to fiscal policy and do not move over time. Prices do hence not fulfill their most precious task: acting as signals for market participants thereby transmitting information about the scarcity of economic resources so that these resources are used in the most efficient way. This shortcoming is overcome in the stochastic setting of financial markets, at least partially. Prices reflect fiscal policy influence and evolve dynamically. The most important price, i.e. the short-term interest rate, shows nonlinear feedback effects on the stocks of capital and debt (see (3.18)) thereby reacting on signals as regards scarcity of resources (i.e. the magnitude of both stocks). However, asset prices do not fully internalize the possible scarcity of capital due to the constant expected marginal product of capital feature of the production function. Thus, fiscal policy still bears some responsibility as regards viability of the economy, but, contrary to the deterministic setting, retains its original degree of freedom. Since prices in the stochastic model version come much closer to the function they are granted by economists, economic variables face much more pleasant properties in this framework. Growth dynamics allow for positive and negative growth rates, with negative ones occurring not very often. Growth dynamics could be seen to have a long run tendency to a region of lower-growth if certain parameter conditions hold. This is a feature many economists will agree upon. Moreover, fiscal policy and especially interest rate dynamics play a very important role for the question whether the long run growth tendency applies or not. The qualitative effects on public debt dynamics also show far more realistic outcomes than in the deterministic model. Initial public debt has not to be negative to assure viability and the debt ratio does not monotonically have to either decrease or increase all the time. It is free to fluctuate, but simultaneously distinguishes itself from ordinary driftless stochastic processes by a drift that reflects the influence of financial markets. As the analysis of the debt ratio dynamics has shown, it is sufficient for fiscal stabilization that the short-term interest rate attains a sufficiently low level.

If the model was a good description of reality, this would imply that debt stabilization need not be explicitly forced (as in the Maastricht Treaty, for example), but could be guaranteed (as a by-product, so to say) by setting the fiscal policy parameters in a way compatible with low interest rates. Financial markets would then assure fiscal stability. This argumentation, of course, assumes governments that acknowledge their historic debt burdens. It does not automatically imply that the deficit and debt criteria in the Maastricht Treaty are wrong, even if our model was a fairly good description of reality. The reason is that a government, though debt would be stabilized in the long run due to the resulting dynamics, could deliberately decide to threaten with debt default. This possibility is not part of our model, hence we do and can not reject the stability criteria on the basis of the model outcome. Yet, the debt dynamics clarify that there are important inherent feedback mechanisms between fiscal policy and financial markets in a risky setting that should be further explored in future theoretical work to widen understanding. This work needs to be accompanied by empirical research, since this is the only way to discover whether the theoretical links are of significant magnitude in reality.

7.3 Outlook on future research

We divide our suggestions for future research in two parts: (i) suggestions for empirical applications; (ii) suggestions regarding the extension of the theoretical framework:

7.3.1 Suggestions for empirical applications

The model at hand should be either calibrated or estimated in future work. It is conceivable to use as the data basis either financial market data in order to estimate the interest rate dynamics or data of macroeconomic variables whose dynamics could then be jointly calibrated or estimated. The reason for such a procedure is clear: if we had reliable numerical values for the seven different model parameters, then we would be easily able to calculate all the theorems necessary to understand the qualitative dynamic features of the fiscal and financial market variables more completely. Moreover, it would then be easily possible to carry out sensitivity analysis with regard to changes of any arbitrary parameter and interpret the outcomes economically. Not calibrating or estimating means that we would have to do all the necessary calculations for either a vast set of possible or a small set of totally arbitrary parameter value combinations. The first choice is prohibitively expensive in terms of time and equipment [1]. For the second choice, we cannot assure not to move in empirical nirvana. Both choices are unsatisfactory, hence empirical work has to be done.

Possible ways to go as regards estimating and calibrating are the following: we could, for example, imagine to do Monte Carlo simulations for a special variable. One first discretizes the stochastic dynamics according to some well-known scheme, then 'draws' a set of standard normally distributed random variables (one value for any time point in the discretization scheme and one set for any time path we want to compute) and finally calculates the whole time path of the discretized dynamics for any possible set of parameter

---

[1] We should not withhold the fact, however, that also calibrating or estimating can be expected to be computationally demanding.

and random variable values. Subsequently, one picks those set of parameter values that matches best some pre-specified statistical moments of the computed time paths to the empirical moments of the observed time series. We could also estimate the model, either via simultaneous regressions using the different assumed model relationships (like the output equation, the taxation equation and the government expenditure equation) or by using the SDE driving the short-term interest rate and then applying the General Method of Moments (GMM) proposed by Hansen/Scheinkman (1995), the Efficient Method of Moments (EMM) proposed by Gallant/Tauchen (1996) or some other usual estimation procedure like maximum likelihood (Lo (1988)). As we can see, there are plenty of possibilities to be pursued when one wants to pin down the model parameters numerically. Econometric research strongly progresses in this direction and since computational power and intelligent software advances in similar pace, we suppose that future economic work in this direction will also grow.

7.3.2 Suggestions for theoretical extensions

The model structure should be expanded towards a more satisfying and detailed description of taxation and expenditure policy. Doing so could yield interesting new insights regarding the influence of different policy instruments on the term structure of interest rates within a risky environment of financial markets. Additionally, it would certainly be worth studying the fiscal variable dynamics in a more realistic setting of different taxation instruments and rules as well as for economically more plausible and accepted ways to model the motivation of government expenditure.

This leads directly to another interesting model expansion: the endogenization of fiscal policy. This seems to be the most interesting avenue for future research: first, one could overcome the necessity to choose ad-hoc behavioral policy rules exogenously. Second, one could then carry out a detailed welfare analysis of public policy in this stochastic environment. Third, a politico-economical foundation of public policy could be introduced according to the lines of literature mentioned in Section 1.2.2. This could lead to a possibly much closer description of real political processes and their interaction with the dynamic evolution of the economy. Fourth, one could examine the possibility of government default on its debt. Doing so would require to specify explicitly the strategic context of interaction between private households and the government which could yield surprising effects on the term structure, especially if the government was assumed to pursue some debt management goal and/or to have public choice elements within its target function.

An additional model refinement could encompass the extension into a nominal setting of the model economy. Monetary policy could be specified by either an exogenously given money supply rule or by introducing a central bank as an explicit strategic actor (for example, along the lines of Tabellini (1986)). This would enable us to scrutinize the influence of monetary policy on the term structure of interest rates and to examine how the interplay of monetary and fiscal policy influences debt dynamics, inflation, interest rates and economic growth. However, first steps in this direction show that the market equilibrium conditions already become highly nonlinear. It thus calls for the prudent use of advanced approximation methods. Nonetheless, this direction should not be viewed too skeptically for such approximation methods are at hand in the meantime and are gaining acceptance among theoretical economists (Judd (1998)).

An extension to a small open economy or even a two-country world seems highly interesting particularly in view of increasingly integrated financial markets. This would enable to study effects of asymmetric fiscal policy changes on term structures and exchange rates (real or nominal depending whether we stick to a real version or not) in a world of risk and nonlinearity. Moreover, one could introduce incomplete financial markets in such a setting (for an idea how to model this, in principle, see Devereux/Saito (1997)) and analyze whether and how the dynamic evolution of national public debt is synchronized by financial markets especially in terms of the degree of integration and incompleteness of these markets.

General appendix 1: Brownian motion and stochastic integration

In this general appendix, we want to present a brief introduction to the mathematical concept of 'Brownian motion' and to the idea how to build stochastic integrals a lá Ito with respect to Brownian motions. The reason for doing so is that these concepts are the base for those methods frequently used in the work at hand. Since there is a vast and excellent literature on these topics ranging from rigorous mathematical treatments (see, for example, Karatzas/Shreve (1991) or Todorovic (1992)) to more applications-oriented discussions of the subject (see, for example, Arnold (1973), Schuss (1980) or Gardiner (1983)), we briefly and only heuristically discuss them. As a consequence, reading this general appendix as well as the following ones is meant to help the reader gain some feeling for the concepts but cannot provide a complete understanding of the subject.

1.1 Brownian motion

Brownian motion (synonymously also known as Wiener process) is the title of an (in practical applications very commonly used) stochastic process named after the Scottish botanist Robert Brown. In 1827 he suspended small pollen grains in water and observed the motion of it. He found the motion to be very irregular, like being driven by a stochastic process. Almost 80 years later, in 1905, no minor than Albert Einstein came up with a mathematical theory that explained the motion of the particles. He explained the motion of the pollen as being triggered by crashes with water molecules whose movement were explained by the molecular-kinetic theory of heat. Einstein and also the Polish physicist Smoluchowski thus fathered the mathematical foundation of Brownian motion. Later on in the century, the Austrian-American cyberneticist Norbert Wiener advanced both the theoretical understanding as well as practical applications of Brownian motions and related stochastic concepts so far that today the process bears his name.

244

The idea behind Brownian motion can be heuristically described as follows: at any increment of time, a particle may move either 'a bit upward' with probability p or 'a bit downward' with probability 1 - p. The distribution of the displacement of the particle at arbitrary time t can be shown to be binomial. When the time increments and the magnitudes of upward or downward moves tend to zero in an appropriate way, one can apply the limit theorem of DeMoivre-Laplace and ends up with Brownian motion.

The exact definition of a Brownian motion (or Wiener process) is as follows:

Definition A.1.1:

A Brownian motion B(t) is a stochastic process with the following properties:

1. **Sample paths of B(t) are continuous with probability one.**

2. **Without loss of generality B(0) = 0.**

3. **The increment B(t+τ) - B(t) is normally distributed with expectation value of zero and variance τ, i.e. B(t) - B(0) $\approx$ N(0, t) = N(0, 1) $\sqrt{t}$, where '$\approx$' means: 'is distributed as'. Moreover, increments on non-overlapping time intervals are independently distributed.**

Especially feature 1) and 3) are remarkable. Feature 1) means that almost any path of a Brownian motion has no discontinuities like jumps, although at any point in time the process can make an instantaneous upward or downward movement. 'Almost any' means that there are also paths with jumps (some among infinitely many), but they occur with probability zero. Feature 3) means that any increment of a Brownian motion is distributed as the product between a standard normal distribution and the square root of the increment size (i.e. time t). This property has a very interesting consequence: it means that Brownian motions are processes of infinite variation implying that the differential quotient does not exist. This can be seen as follows: consider $\dot{B}(t)$ as the formal derivative of a Brownian motion with respect to time t.

Making use of 3) together with the definition of how to carry out differentiation we can write this as follows:

$$(A.1.1)\ \dot{B}(t) = \lim_{\tau \to 0}\frac{B(t+\tau)-B(t)}{\tau} = \lim_{\tau \to 0}\frac{\varepsilon \cdot \sqrt{\tau}}{\tau} = \lim_{\tau \to 0}\frac{\varepsilon}{\sqrt{\tau}} \to \infty,\quad \varepsilon \approx N(0,1)$$

(A.1.1) has important consequences: the notion of a Riemann integral is no longer straightforwardly applicable to integrals where Brownian motions act as integrators. The reason is that the integrators in the Riemann integral have to be processes of bounded variation. However, this does no longer hold for Brownian motions, as (A.1.1) shows. Thus, the way how integration with respect to Brownian motions has to be carried out calls for a different integral notion: the stochastic Ito integral.

1.2 Stochastic integration: The Ito integral

The problem discussed above can also be illustrated by considering the following integral and its approximation as a sum over the partition {0, t/n, 2 t/n, ..., (n-1) t/n, t}:

$$(A.1.2)\qquad \int_0^t B(t)\cdot dB(t) \cong \sum_{i=1}^n B\left(\frac{i}{n}\cdot t\right)\cdot\left(B\left(\frac{i+1}{n}\cdot t\right)-B\left(\frac{i}{n}\cdot t\right)\right)$$

Note, that if n tends to infinity the sum will converge to the integral in the Riemann sense. If we integrate the left side of (A.1.2) according to the usual rules and take the expectations, then we end up:

$$\int_0^t B(t)\cdot dB(t) = \frac{1}{2}\cdot B(t)^2$$

$$(A.1.3) \Rightarrow E\left[\int_0^t B(t)\cdot dB(t)\right] = \frac{1}{2}\cdot E[B(t)^2] = \frac{1}{2}\cdot Var[B(t)] + \frac{1}{2}\cdot\{E[B(t)]\}^2$$

$$= \frac{1}{2}\cdot Var[B(t)] = \frac{1}{2}\cdot t$$

246

The expectation equals hence t/2 and so far nothing seems to be wrong. But if we now consider the right-hand side of (A.1.2) and take expectations here, then we get [1]:

$$(A.1.4) \qquad E\left[\sum_{i=1}^{n} B\left(\frac{i}{n}\cdot t\right)\cdot\left(B\left(\frac{i+1}{n}\cdot t\right)-B\left(\frac{i}{n}\cdot t\right)\right)\right]=$$

$$(A.1.4) \qquad \sum_{i=1}^{n} E\left[\left(B\left(\frac{i}{n}\cdot t\right)-B(0)\right)\cdot\left(B\left(\frac{i+1}{n}\cdot t\right)-B\left(\frac{i}{n}\cdot t\right)\right)\right]=0$$

The fact that the middle term in the second line of (A.1.4) is zero stems from property 3) of Brownian motions, namely that increments of Brownian motions on non-overlapping time intervals are independently distributed. This result is somewhat surprising because it stands in sharp contrast to the outcome of (A.1.3)! However, the difference only emerged because we pretended that integral (A.1.2) could be evaluated according to the classical rules of calculus. But this is not correct for processes with infinite variation like Brownian motions. The Japanese mathematician Kyoshi Ito was the first to realize this. In his work during the 1940s, he rigorously defined a stochastic integral with respect to Brownian motion and finally came up with the following lemma:

Lemma A.1.1:

Let f be an at least twice continuously differentiable function. Then the following holds:

$$(A.1.5) \qquad f(B(t)) = f(0) + \int f'(B(t))\cdot dB(t) + \frac{1}{2}\cdot\int f''(B(t))\cdot dt$$

The first integral in (A.1.5) is a stochastic integral in the meaning of Ito, the second is Riemannian. The lemma is known as Ito's Lemma for Brownian motions. It serves as an integration or differentiation rule for smooth

---

[1] The right-hand side in the first line of (A.1.4) results from the fact that B(0) = 0.

functions of Brownian motions. Using Ito's Lemma in order to calculate the integral in (A.1.2) yields now:

$$\int f'(B(t)) \cdot dB(t) = f(B(t)) - f(0) - \frac{1}{2} \cdot \int f''(B(t)) \cdot dt$$

(A.1.6)
$$\Rightarrow \int B(t) \cdot dB(t) = \frac{1}{2} \cdot B(t)^2 - 0 - \frac{1}{2} \cdot \int 1 \cdot dt = \frac{1}{2} \cdot B(t)^2 - \frac{1}{2} \cdot t$$

$$\Rightarrow E\left[\int B(t) \cdot dB(t)\right] = \frac{1}{2} \cdot E\left[B(t)^2\right] - \frac{1}{2} \cdot t = \frac{1}{2} \cdot t - \frac{1}{2} \cdot t = 0$$

We see that the result of (A.1.6) is indeed no longer in contrast with the outcome of (A.1.4). The reason for the equality is that Ito has constructed his integral by constructing a sum like in (A.1.2). This means that he interpreted his integral as a sum where the integrand is evaluated at the left interval boundary of each summation term. In contrast to Ito, the Russian mathematician Stratonovich interpreted the integral in (A.1.2) as follows:

(A.1.7)
$$\int_o^t B(t) \cdot dB(t) \cong \sum_{i=1}^{n} B\left(\frac{i+0.5}{n} \cdot t\right) \cdot \left(B\left(\frac{i+1}{n} \cdot t\right) - B\left(\frac{i}{n} \cdot t\right) \right)$$

which means that he evaluates the integrand at the middle point between both interval boundaries of each summation term. Evaluating the expectation of this sum yields:

$$E\left[\sum_{i=1}^{n} B\left(\frac{i+0.5}{n} \cdot t\right) \cdot \left(B\left(\frac{i+1}{n} \cdot t\right) - B\left(\frac{i}{n} \cdot t\right) \right) \right] =$$

$$E\left[\sum_{i=1}^{n} \left(B\left(\frac{i+0.5}{n} \cdot t\right) - B\left(\frac{i}{n} \cdot t\right) \right)^2 \right]$$

(A.1.8)
$$+ E\left[\sum_{i=1}^{n} \frac{\left(B\left(\frac{i+0.5}{n} \cdot t\right) - B(0) \right)}{\cdot \left(B\left(\frac{i+1}{n} \cdot t\right) - B\left(\frac{i+0.5}{n} \cdot t\right) \right)} \right]$$

$$+ E\left[\sum_{i=1}^{n} \left(B\left(\frac{i}{n} \cdot t\right) - B(0) \right) \cdot \left(B\left(\frac{i+0.5}{n} \cdot t\right) - B\left(\frac{i}{n} \cdot t\right) \right) \right]$$

$$(A.1.8) \qquad = E\left[\sum_{i=1}^{n}\left(B\left(\frac{i+0.5}{n}\cdot t\right)-B\left(\frac{i}{n}\cdot t\right)\right)^{2}\right]=E\left[\frac{1}{2}\cdot B(t)^{2}\right]=\frac{1}{2}\cdot t$$

We see that Stratonovich's integration concept yields the same result as 'naively' applying the classical calculus to integral (A.1.2). Now, we can see what is so problematic about building a stochastic integral: in contrast to the Riemann integral, it really matters at which point of the partition interval the integrand is evaluated before the sum is calculated and then sent to the limit thus tending to the integral.

The question appears: why should we not just use Stratonovich's interpretation of a stochastic integral with the advantage that the integration and differentiation rules from classical calculus still apply? The reason is that Stratonovich's interpretation has an essential disadvantage: the integrand is not adapted to the filtration (i.e. the whole 'story' of past and current values) of the Brownian motion, but 'anticipates' it. What does this mean? Assume, for example, that we consider a stochastic integral where the integrand characterizes an asset trading strategy of an investor and the Brownian motion as integrator may denote the price process of this asset. Then, the stochastic integral denotes the accumulated gains or, respectively, losses the investor makes or suffers using the trading strategy. It is now economically straightforward that the trading strategy may depend on the Brownian motion in a functional way. When we think of the whole price process (i.e. the filtration of $B(t)$) as the information in our economic setting, however, then the holding of the efficient market hypothesis implies that trading strategies must not be based on the knowledge of future values of the price process, but are based on past and current information of prices. However, the use of the Stratonovich integral implies that trading strategies are based on the knowledge of future prices (i.e. future filtrations of $B(t)$) and thus anticipate the future. This clearly violates the efficient market hypothesis. In contrast, taking the Ito integral implies that trading strategies are adapted to the filtration of $B(t)$ and are thus economically more useful. This is the reason why Ito integrals are used in economic applications.

General appendix 2: Stochastic differential equations and diffusion processes

In this appendix, we want to briefly introduce the notion of stochastic differential equations (SDEs) and their representation as diffusion processes. We state sufficient conditions for existence and uniqueness of solutions of stochastic differential equations and an extension of Ito's Lemma to smooth functions of semimartingales (i.e. solutions of SDEs). Moreover, we show for some simple examples how to explicitly calculate solutions of SDEs. Then, we highlight the link between diffusion processes and stochastic differential equations and state some results that help characterize boundary behavior of diffusion processes. We restrict ourselves to some main essentials since there is a huge expert literature on both fields: regarding SDEs, see, for example, Arnold (1973), Karatzas/Shreve (1991), Øksendal (1991) or Durrett (1996). Diffusion processes are dealt with in, for example Stroock/Varadhan (1979), Karlin/Taylor (1981, Chapter 15), Pinsky (1995) or Durrett (1996, Chapter 6).

2.1 Stochastic differential equations

We will here only consider scalar (i.e. one-dimensional) SDEs, although the results also hold in a quite similar way for vector SDEs. The first theorem deals with sufficient conditions for a solution to be existing and unique:

Theorem A.2.1:

Given the following SDE:

(A.2.1) $\qquad dx = \mu(x,t) \cdot dt + \sigma(x,t) \cdot dB$

The following two conditions are sufficient for this SDE to have a unique solution:

250

$$
\text{(A.2.2)} \quad
\begin{aligned}
&\text{i)} \quad \left|\mu(x,t)\right| + \left|\sigma(x,t)\right| \leq C\cdot\left(1+\left|x\right|\right) \\
&\text{ii)} \quad \left|\mu(x,t)-\mu(y,t)\right| + \left|\sigma(x,t)-\sigma(y,t)\right| \leq D\cdot\left|x-y\right|
\end{aligned}
$$

where C and D are some constants.

Condition i) is referred to as the 'growth condition' and condition ii) is known as the 'Lipschitz condition'. The growth condition ensures that no explosion happens and the Lipschitz condition guarantees uniqueness of the solution (for an example, see Øksendal (1991, p. 49)). These conditions are only sufficient but not necessary so that solutions of SDEs can also exist and be unique if these conditions fail [1]. As a consequence, linear SDEs have always a unique solution. If the growth and Lipschitz condition cannot be shown to hold, then we have to turn to more advanced tools to study the qualitative behavior of SDEs. This is done later on when we talk about diffusion processes.

In the following, we will deal with scalar SDEs which are autonomous with respect to time:

$$
\text{(A.2.3)} \quad dx = \underbrace{\mu(x)\cdot dt}_{\text{drift}} + \underbrace{\sigma(x)\cdot dB}_{\text{diffusion}}
$$

This is no loss of generality, because if we face a scalar, time-dependent SDE like (A.2.1), then we can eliminate time by introducing it explicitly as another state variable. Doing so leads to an increase in the dimension (i.e. from dimension 1 to 2 and, thus, from a scalar to a vector SDE) but the resulting vector SDE is autonomous with respect to other than state variables. Since all the results hold for vector SDE's in a similar fashion, we constrain ourselves to the scalar case, mainly for ease of exposition.

The first idea when looking at (A.2.3) is to ask: why can't we just divide (A.2.3) by dt so that we get:

---

[1] Note, that the SDE (3.24a-b) describing the short-term interest rate violates these conditions on $[-\infty,\infty]$. If, however, the fiscal constraints (3.23), (3.27) and (3.28) hold, then we are able to show that the short-term interest rate is confined to the interval I_1. On

(A.2.3*) $\dot{x} = \mu(x) + \sigma(x) \cdot \dot{B}$

where $\dot{B}$ denotes the formal time derivative of B. Then, one could try to carry out variable separation and simply integrate the equation as usual. However, doing so would overlook the whole discussion in the last appendix: since we have learned there that B depends on $\sqrt{t}$, we know that the time derivative depends on $1/\sqrt{t}$ which tends to infinity when t tends to zero. $\dot{B}$ is hence not a well-defined mathematical object so that one has to turn to stochastic calculus to give (A.2.3) a senseful interpretation. Extending Ito's integral notion to an integral with respect to a semimartingale like we get the following general version of Ito's Lemma:

Lemma A.2.1:

Let f be an at least twice continuously differentiable function of a semimartingale x (for an exact definition of this property, see Durrett (1996, pp. 70)) given by the SDE (A.2.3). Then the following holds:

(A.2.4)

$$f(x) = f(x_0) + \int f'(x) \cdot \mu(x) \cdot dt + \int f'(x) \cdot \sigma(x) \cdot dB(t) + \frac{1}{2} \cdot \int f''(x) \cdot d\langle x \rangle$$

$$= f(x_0) + \int f'(x) \cdot \mu(x) \cdot dt + \int f'(x) \cdot \sigma(x) \cdot dB(t) + \frac{1}{2} \cdot \int f''(x) \cdot \sigma(x)^2 \cdot dt$$

$$= f(x_0) + \int \left(f'(x) \cdot \mu(x) + \frac{1}{2} \cdot f''(x) \cdot \sigma(x)^2 \right) \cdot dt + \int f'(x) \cdot \sigma(x) \cdot dB(t)$$

The integral over dB is a stochastic integral in the meaning of Ito. In deriving the last line, one has to take into account that '$\langle x \rangle$' denotes the quadratic variation of the process x. The differential of this quadratic variation, $d\langle x \rangle$ equals $\sigma(x)^2$ times dt.

---

this interval, both conditions can be shown to hold locally, thus guaranteeing existence and uniqueness of a solution of (3.24a-b).

(A.2.4) is the celebrated Ito Lemma for semimartingales. It serves as an integration or differentiation rule for smooth functions of semimartingales. Since most of the stochastic dynamics in economic models can be described as semimartingales in form of an SDE like (A.2.3), (A.2.4) is an extremely valuable tool. In order to illustrate this, let us consider the following example:

(A.2.5)
$$dx = \mu \cdot x \cdot dt + \sigma \cdot x \cdot dB \Rightarrow \frac{dx}{x} = \mu \cdot dt + \sigma \cdot dB$$

(A.2.5) is, for example, the description of the stock price dynamics Black/Scholes (1973) used in their well-known derivation of option prices. Integrating this equation, we note that the natural logarithm of x will be involved. Calculating its derivative according to Ito's Lemma (A.2.4) in differential form, we get:

$$f(x) \equiv \ln x$$

$$\Rightarrow df(x) \equiv d\ln x = \frac{dx}{x} - \frac{1}{2} \cdot \frac{d\langle x \rangle}{x^2}$$

(A.2.6)
$$\Rightarrow d\ln x = \frac{dx}{x} - \frac{1}{2} \cdot \frac{\sigma^2 \cdot x^2}{x^2} \cdot dt = \frac{dx}{x} - \frac{1}{2} \cdot \sigma^2 \cdot dt$$

$$\Rightarrow \frac{dx}{x} = d\ln x + \frac{1}{2} \cdot \sigma^2 \cdot dt$$

Now, we can equate (A.2.5) and (A.2.6) which yields after some steps:

$$d\ln x + \frac{1}{2} \cdot \sigma^2 \cdot dt = \mu \cdot dt + \sigma \cdot dB$$

$$\Rightarrow d\ln x = \left(\mu - \frac{1}{2} \cdot \sigma^2 \right) \cdot dt + \sigma \cdot dB$$

(A.2.7)
$$\Rightarrow \ln x = \ln x_0 + \left(\mu - \frac{1}{2} \cdot \sigma^2 \right) \cdot t + \sigma \cdot B$$

$$\Rightarrow x = \hat{x}_0 \cdot e^{\left(\mu - \frac{1}{2} \cdot \sigma^2 \right) \cdot t + \sigma \cdot B}$$

(A.2.7) shows clearly where the difference would lie if we had naively applied usual deterministic integration techniques to (A.2.5): the term '1/2

σ^{2}' in front of time t in the argument of the exponent would have missed. Thus, Ito's Lemma is the only consistent tool to determine stochastic Ito integrals whether the integrators be Brownian motions or, more general, semimartingales.

Finally, we want to show, using a more difficult example, how to proceed when we are interested in trying to calculate a solution to a SDE like (A.2.3). We take the following example (see Kloeden/Platen (1992, pp. 124), but without calculations):

(A.2.8) $\qquad dx = -(\alpha + \beta^2 \cdot x) \cdot (1 - x^2) \cdot dt + \beta \cdot (1 - x^2) \cdot dB$

Here, it is not possible to separate x from one side of the equation as before. We thus have to take a different way. The trick is to find a variable transformation $y = g(x)$ so that y becomes a local martingale [2]. Local martingale means that a stochastic process can be described by an SDE like (A.2.3) but has a vanishing drift term. Looking on Ito's Lemma (A.2.4), for $y = g(x)$ to become a local martingale, the following condition must hold:

(A.2.9)
$$g'(x) \cdot \mu(x) + \frac{1}{2} \cdot g''(x) \cdot \sigma(x)^2 = 0$$
$$\Rightarrow y \equiv g(x) = \int \exp\left(-2 \cdot \int \frac{\mu(x)}{\sigma(x)^2} \cdot dx\right) \cdot dx$$

Calculating y using the data of (A.2.8), we obtain:

(A.2.10)
$$y = \int \exp\left(-2 \cdot \int \frac{-(\alpha + \beta^2 \cdot x)}{\beta^2 \cdot (1 - x^2)} \cdot dx\right) \cdot dx$$
$$\Rightarrow y = \int \exp\left(\frac{(\alpha - \beta^2) \cdot \log(x+1)}{\beta^2} - \frac{(\alpha + \beta^2) \cdot \log(x-1)}{\beta^2}\right) \cdot dx$$

---

[2] The local martingale property is pretty much the same as the martingale property except that expectation may only hold locally not necessarily globally because a local martingale need not be integrable. A stochastic process which is a martingale is thus also a local martingale but the other way round may not hold. For an exact definition, see Durrett (1996, pp.37 and pp. 113).

$$\Rightarrow y = \int \left((x+1)^{\frac{\alpha-\beta^2}{\beta^2}} \cdot (x-1)^{-\frac{\alpha+\beta^2}{\beta^2}} \right) \cdot dx$$

(A.2.10)

$$\Rightarrow y = -\frac{\beta^2}{2 \cdot \alpha} \cdot \left(\frac{x+1}{x-1} \right)^{\frac{\alpha}{\beta^2}} = g(x)$$

If we apply Ito's Lemma to $y = g(x)$, we get the following dynamics for y:

(A.2.11)
$$dy = -\beta \cdot \left(\frac{x+1}{x-1} \right)^{\frac{\alpha}{\beta^2}} \cdot dB$$

$$\Rightarrow dy = \frac{2 \cdot \alpha}{\beta} \cdot y \cdot dB$$

Note that the step from the first to the second line resulted by the use of (A.2.10). (A.2.11) shows that y is indeed a local martingale for it has no drift. It is now easy to solve (A.2.11) by again using Ito's Lemma as in the example before:

(A.2.12)
$$\frac{dy}{y} = \frac{2 \cdot \alpha}{\beta} \cdot dB$$

$$\Rightarrow y = c \cdot e^{-\frac{2 \cdot \alpha^2}{\beta^2} \cdot t + \frac{2 \cdot \alpha}{\beta} \cdot B}$$

and together with (A.2.10) this yields finally:

$$-\frac{\beta^2}{2 \cdot \alpha} \cdot \left(\frac{x+1}{x-1} \right)^{\frac{\alpha}{\beta^2}} = c \cdot e^{-\frac{2 \cdot \alpha^2}{\beta^2} \cdot t + \frac{2 \cdot \alpha}{\beta} \cdot B}$$

(A.2.13)
$$\Rightarrow x = -\frac{1 + \left(-\frac{2 \cdot \alpha \cdot c}{\beta^2} \right)^{\frac{\beta^2}{\alpha}} \cdot e^{-2 \cdot \alpha \cdot t + 2 \cdot \beta \cdot B}}{1 - \left(-\frac{2 \cdot \alpha \cdot c}{\beta^2} \right)^{\frac{\beta^2}{\alpha}} \cdot e^{-2 \cdot \alpha \cdot t + 2 \cdot \beta \cdot B}} \qquad \Rightarrow x_0 = -\frac{1 + \left(-\frac{2 \cdot \alpha \cdot c}{\beta^2} \right)^{\frac{\beta^2}{\alpha}}}{1 - \left(-\frac{2 \cdot \alpha \cdot c}{\beta^2} \right)^{\frac{\beta^2}{\alpha}}}$$

$$\Rightarrow x = \frac{x_0 - 1 + (x_0 + 1) \cdot e^{-2 \cdot \alpha \cdot t + 2 \cdot \beta \cdot B}}{1 - x_0 + (x_0 + 1) \cdot e^{-2 \cdot \alpha \cdot t + 2 \cdot \beta \cdot B}}$$

Thus, the quite complicated SDE (A.2.8) yields a not very complicated solution (A.2.13). The key in explicitly solving SDEs is not to find the local martingale (A.2.10) but to get a local martingale that is easy enough to be explicitly solvable. This was here the case as (A.2.11) showed. In most of the SDEs one meets in interesting examples this is, however, not necessarily the case. According to the so-called 'time change theorem' (mentioned, for example, in Durret (1996)), one can prove that any local martingale is expressible as a Brownian motion moving on a different time scale, namely the variance of the local martingale. To operationalize this theorem, however, is a hard task and usually no explicit solution for this time change can be found. Thus, in principle, one has to attack this problem using approximations or numerical methods. In a multidimensional case, it is not even easy to calculate the local martingale let alone the time change to a multidimensional Brownian motion. The reason is that in order to obtain the local martingale a system of coupled partial differential equations has to be solved, which can be a quite formidable task. Applied literature on these issues is extremely rare which is certainly due to the mostly unsolved associated technical problems. Thus, we do not pursue this issue any further but turn to the next section on diffusion processes.

2.2 Diffusion processes

As in the section before, we restrict ourselves to one-dimensional SDE's and diffusion processes for ease of exposition. The following definition is due to Øksendal (1991, pp. 86):

Definition A.2.1:

A stochastic process x satisfying the SDE:

(A.2.3) $$dx = \mu(x) \cdot dt + \sigma(x) \cdot dB$$

is called a diffusion process (or just: diffusion) where $\mu(x)$ is called 'drift term' or just 'drift' and $\sigma(x)$ 'diffusion term' or just 'diffusion'.

This definition holds also for multidimensional SDE's and thus multidimensional diffusions. It seems rather harmless on first sight but it enables us to study qualitative properties of solutions of (A.2.3) in case that we are unable to explicitly calculate a solution of (A.2.3). 'Qualitative properties' means whether there are boundaries at which the diffusion gets irregular, whether these boundaries can be reached and, if so, whether this will be in finite time, whether a diffusion explodes and so on. Since Karlin/Taylor (1981, chapter 15) is a real bonanza for corresponding theorems and related tools, we will just state a few definitions and lemmas.

Definition A.2.2: Regularity of diffusions

A diffusion process is said to be regular on a definition space Λ if the probability to reach any arbitrary point in Λ from any given starting point in Λ is greater than zero.

Definition A.2.2 is very important for all later theorems and lemmas rely on diffusion processes having this property. What does it mean? Consider for a moment that the diffusion given by the SDE (A.2.3) has a zero diffusion term at x^*, i.e. $\sigma(x^*) = 0$. Then the diffusion at x^* ceases to be a diffusion locally for only the drift term $\mu(x^*)$ is left which is purely deterministic. If this drift term gets also zero, then x^* is an equilibrium point and the question whether it is stable or not is settled by calculating the Lyapunov exponent (since we will not discuss this concept in detail here, see chapter 5 and the references made there). If $\mu(x^*)$ is different from zero, say positive, then the diffusion starting from an initial value greater than x^* can never reach smaller values than x^*. Thus, the probability to reach smaller values than x^* is zero and the diffusion is thus irregular on its definition interval $[-\infty,\infty]$ due to definition A.2.2. If one meets diffusions with points on its definition interval (or definition space for multidimensional diffusions) with zero diffusion terms called 'boundaries', then the first thing one has to do is separating the definition space into areas where the diffusion is regular. On these areas one can then examine the question of whether the respective boundaries can be reached or not. If, for example, it can be shown that a diffusion does not leave a finite interval (or compact subset of the definition space), then one has already ruled out explosive behavior. This is what we have done for our short-term interest rate diffusion in chapter 3. Since the lemma needed to assess whether a boundary is attracting is so important in view of our work, we will state it here again:

Lemma A.2.2: Attraction of a boundary

Be the so called 'scale function' of a diffusion belonging to (A.2.3), S(l, x], given as:

$$S(l,x] = \int_l^x e^{-2\int \frac{\mu(x)}{\sigma(x)^2}dx} \cdot dy$$

A boundary 'l' is then said to be attracting a regular diffusion process defined on an interval [l, r] if S(l, x] < ∞ ∀x ∈ (l, r) holds. This definition holds in a equivalent way for the right boundary, 'r', too.

On first sight, the intuitive meaning of this lemma is not clear. In order to understand it, we have to recall that the local martingale belonging to a diffusion defined by (A.2.3) was given by (A.2.9). The local martingale has therefore exact the same functional form as the scale measure S(l, x]. The lemma A.2.2 thus means that if for a given diffusion a local martingale exists for any point of an interval on which the diffusion is regular, then the boundary confining the regular interval will be reached. This is no longer surprising if we recall the theorem mentioned before, namely that any local martingale can be represented as a Brownian motion under a specific time change. And a one-dimensional Brownian motion is known to be recurrent which means that it 'visits' any point on its definition interval (-∞,∞) at least once in finite time. Thus, it reaches also the boundary and since the local martingale can be represented as a Brownian motion, the local martingale reaches the boundary too. The lemma has therefore a beautifully simple but forceful meaning.

General appendix 3: Stochastic optimization and dynamic programming

In many papers on theoretical finance, the problem of dynamic portfolio selection has been formulated as a continuous-time stochastic dynamic programming problem according to the notion of Richard Bellman. The pioneer in employing this method was Robert C. Merton (1969, 1971). In economics, in contrast, it took remarkably longer until this method found attention. One of the first economic applications were Chow (1979) and Eaton (1981), to be followed by very few subsequent work in the years after, although Malliaris/Brock (1982) had dedicated it a significant part in their well-known book. The (hopefully) final breakthrough, at least in dynamic macroeconomics, came then with the publication of some joint work of Turnovsky/Grinols (1993, 1994, 1996) and the graduate-level textbook by Turnovsky (1995).

As in the appendices before, we will also remain brief here, for there is a large literature on optimal stochastic control theory and dynamic programming. From a theoretical perspective, one should mention the classical work of Fleming/Rishel (1975). Fleming/Soner (1993) is more advanced dealing with recent subjects like viscosity solutions and singular control whereas Chen/Chen/Hsu (1995) is quite easily accessible. For economic (as well as finance and investment) applications, we can recommend Chow (1979), Malliaris/Brock (1982), Dixit/Pindyck (1994) and Turnovsky (1995). Chow (1997) attacks the problem by a heuristically motivated Lagrange method approach. This could probably take away many economists' fears associated with using this seemingly difficult method since economists are used to Lagrange's method from static constrained optimization.

We want to illustrate the method of stochastic dynamic programming in continuous-time by showing the necessary calculations for a simple example with one control and one state variable. It is unnecessary to emphasize that it is no problem to formulate similar problems with arbitrary many state and control variables including algebraic and integral constraints on control and

260

state variables as long as the number of control and state variables remains finite-dimensional. We face the following stochastic control problem:

$$(A.3.1) \qquad V(x(t_0),t_0) = \max_{u \in \Xi} E_{t_0} \left[\int_{t_0}^{\infty} f(u(t),x(t),t) \cdot dt \right]$$

subject to:

$$(A.3.2) \qquad dx(t) = g(u(t),x(t),t) \cdot dt + h(u(t),x(t),t) \cdot dB$$

$$x(t_0) = x_0$$

$u(t)$ denotes the control variable, $x(t)$ the state variable, t is time, Ξ stands for the admissible control space, $f(...)$ denotes the direct target function and $V(...)$ denotes the indirect target function. The goal is thus to choose the control variable $u(t)$ so that the expected value of the whole future target function becomes maximal. The expectation is taken under the probability measure induced by the SDE in (A.3.2) at t_0. Additionally, the control variable $u(t)$ has to be out of some admissible set Ξ which is problem specific[1]. Since we allow the control function to be changed at any time t when we get new information via observing the outcome (i.e. the filtration of) of $x(t)$, we can apply Bellman's principle of dynamic programming. Heuristically, the dynamic programming principle implies for our problem that the optimizer is assumed to choose at every point in time t its optimal choices having observed the whole realization of the stochastic process driving its state variable x. The optimal choices are, technically spoken, adapted to the filtration (i.e. whole story) $\Im_t$ generated by the stochastic process driving x and are thus non-anticipating. Non-anticipating means that optimal decisions are based on past and present information but not on future information. This is important for it allows the use of Ito's Lemma as we saw in the last chapter. Hence, the optimal policies calculated by using Bellman's principle are feedback policies depending on the state variable x.

Applying the method of dynamic programming yields then the so called Bellman equation:

(A.3.3)
$$0 = \max_{u \in \Xi} E_t \left[f(u(t), x(t), t) \cdot dt + dV(x(t), t) \right]$$

Intuitively spoken, (A.3.3) means that an optimal policy at time t is characterized by generating an expected value for 'total target value' of zero over an infinitesimally small period [t, t + dt]. Thereby, 'total target value' consists of the instantaneous value flow of the target function plus a change in the indirect target function which measures all the discounted future target value given the optimal choice of the control variable.

Applying Ito's-Lemma in order to calculate the change of indirect target value, dV, delivers [2]:

(A.3.4)
$$0 = \max_{u \in \Xi} E_t \left[f(u(t), x(t), t) \begin{matrix} \cdot dt + V_t \cdot dt + V_x \cdot dx(t) \\ + \dfrac{1}{2} \cdot V_{xx} \cdot d\langle x(t) \rangle \end{matrix} \right]$$

We plug (A.3.2) into (A.3.4), make use of the fact that the differential of the quadratic variation of the semimartingale x, $d\langle x(t) \rangle$, equals the square of its diffusion term times dt, take expectations, divide by dt and let dt tend to zero. The result is the following so called Hamilton-Jacobi-Bellman (HJB) equation:

(A.3.5)
$$0 = \max_{u \in \Xi} \left[\begin{matrix} f(u(t), x(t), t) + V_t + V_x \cdot g(u(t), x(t), t) \\ + \dfrac{1}{2} \cdot V_{xx} \cdot h(u(t), x(t), t)^2 \end{matrix} \right]$$

The first-order condition of (A.3.5) is:

---

[1] For example, if the control problem deals with portfolio selection where short sales are not allowed and the control variables denote shares of investors wealth, then the control variables have to be out of the interval [0, 1].

[2] In order to simplify future notation, we omit the arguments of the indirect target function V and denote its partial derivatives with subscripts.

$$(\text{A.3.6}) \qquad \frac{\partial f}{\partial u} + V_x \cdot \frac{\partial g}{\partial u} + V_{xx} \cdot h \cdot \frac{\partial h}{\partial u} = 0 \Rightarrow u^* = k(x, t, V_x, V_{xx})$$

and the second-order condition becomes:

$$(\text{A.3.7}) \qquad \left.\frac{\partial^2 f}{\partial u^2}\right|_{u=u^*} + V_x \cdot \left.\frac{\partial^2 g}{\partial u^2}\right|_{u=u^*} + V_{xx} \cdot \left(\left(\frac{\partial h}{\partial u}\right)^2 + h \cdot \frac{\partial^2 h}{\partial u^2}\right)_{u=u^*} < 0$$

As one can see, we have omitted the arguments of the functions f, g and h as well as of the variables u and x for ease of notation. Assuming that the functions f, g and h are well-behaved in some technical sense regarding differentiability, we have used first-order condition (A.3.6) in order to solve for the optimal solution u^*. The optimal control becomes thus a function k of state variable x, time t and the first two derivatives of the indirect target function V with respect to the state variable x. The second-order condition (A.3.7) is self-explaining.

Inserting optimal control u^* back into HJB-equation (A.3.5), we finally get:

$$(\text{A.3.8}) \qquad \begin{aligned} 0 = {} & f\big(k(x, t, V_x, V_{xx}), x, t\big) + V_t + V_x \cdot g\big(k(x, t, V_x, V_{xx}), x, t\big) \\ & + \frac{1}{2} \cdot V_{xx} \cdot h\big(k(x, t, V_x, V_{xx}), x, t\big)^2 \end{aligned}$$

(A.3.8) is generally a nonlinear, functional partial differential equation in the dependent variable V and the independent variables x and t. If it can be solved explicitly, then the optimal control can also be solved explicitly and one can further examine the dynamics of the state variable x after substituting u^* into (A.3.2). Unfortunately, the situations where one can solve (A.3.8) are rather rare.

If the target function f(...) has the economic meaning of a utility function, then a necessary condition to get an explicit solution is that the utility function is time separable and the state variable dynamics (A.3.2) is time autonomous. This implies that the optimal control does not depend on t and the equation in (A.3.8) becomes a nonlinear ordinary differential equation in x which is easier to solve. However, if the economic structure given by

(A.3.2) is rather complicated, then one does not get closed-form solutions, even for time separable preferences. The common proceeding in economics applications is now to use numerical or approximate methods proposed by Chow (1997) or Judd (1998) in order to solve the nonlinear equation (A.3.8)[3]. Another way to pursue could be the search for Lie point symmetries as already briefly discussed in Chapter 4. Since nonlinear PDE's are still an area of heavy mathematical research and the application of continuous-time stochastic programming in economics is still in its infancy (especially concerning complicated models in terms of difficult PDEs to solve), our knowledge about solving dynamic programming problems in continuous-time is still not huge. Yet, it should be a fruitful tool for modeling, especially when economists manage to interest mathematicians for their mathematical problems. The reason is that lots of mathematical research in PDEs was initiated not by mathematical interest alone but by real-world problems of other sciences like physics, chemistry, engineering etc. With this remark, we close the series of general appendices.

---

[3] It has to be emphasized that the purpose of the model should be taken into account when searching for a solution procedure for it could give valuable hints which method to apply.

Bibliography

1. Aghion, P. and P. Bolton, 1991, Government Domestic Debt and the Risk of Default: a Political-Economic Model of the Strategic Role of Debt, in: Dornbusch, R. and M. Draghi (eds.), *Public Debt Management: Theory and History*, Cambridge University Press, 315-345.

2. Ait-Sahalia, Y., 1995, Testing Continuous-Time Models of the Spot Interest Rate, NBER Working Paper 5346, Cambridge: National Bureau of Economic Research.

3. Alesina, A. and A. Drazen, 1991, Why are Stabilizations Delayed?, *American Economic Review*, Vol. 81, 1170-1188.

4. Alesina, A. and G. Tabellini, 1990, A Positive Theory of Fiscal Deficits and Government Debt, *Review of Economic Studies*, Vol. 57, 403-414.

5. Alesina, A., A. Prati and G. Tabellini, 1991, Public Confidence and Debt Management: a Model and a Case Study of Italy, Chapter 4 in: Dornbusch, R. and M. Draghi (eds.), *Public Debt Management: Theory and History*, Cambridge University Press, 94-118.

6. Altig, D., A. J. Auerbach, L. J. Kotlikoff, K. A. Smetters and J. Walliser, 1997, Simulating U.S. Tax Reform, NBER Working Paper 6248, Cambridge: National Bureau of Economic Research.

7. Ariaratnam, S. T., 1994, Some Illustrative Examples of Stochastic Bifurcation, Chapter 21 in: Thompson, J. M. T. and S. R. Bishop (eds.): *Nonlinearity and Chaos in Engineering Dynamics*, John Wiley & Sons, 267-274.

8. Arnold, L., 1973: *Stochastische Differentialgleichungen*, Berlin: Springer.

9. Arnold, L., 1998, *Random Dynamical Systems*, Berlin: Springer.

10. Arrow, K. J. and M. D. Intriligator (eds.), 1990, *Handbook of Monetary Economics*, Vol. 1, Amsterdam: North-Holland.

11. Aschauer, D. A., 1988, The Equilibrium Approach to Fiscal Policy, *Journal of Money, Credit, and Banking*, Vol. 20, 41-62.

12. Aschauer, D. A. and J. Greenwood, 1985, Macroeconomic Effects of Fiscal Policy, *Carnegie-Rochester Conf. Series on Public Policy*, 23, 91-138.

13. Auerbach, A. J. and L. J. Kotlikoff, 1987, *Dynamic Fiscal Policy*, Cambridge University Press.

14. Babbs, S. and N. J. Webber, 1994, A Theory of the Term Structure with an Official Short Rate, FORC working paper, University of Warwick.

15. Barro, R. J., 1974, Are Government Bonds Net Wealth?, *Journal of Political Economy*, Vol. 82, 1095-1117.

16. Barro, R. J., 1979, On the Determination of the Public Debt, *Journal of Political Economy*, Vol. 87, 940-971.

17. Barro, R. J., 1981, Output Effects of Government Purchases, *Journal of Political Economy*, Vol. 89, 1086-1121.

18. Barro, R. J., 1989, The Neoclassical Approach to Fiscal Policy, in: Barro, R. J.: *Modern business cycle theory*, Harvard University Press.

19. Barro, R. J., 1990, Government Spending in a Simple Model of Endogenous Growth, *Journal of Political Economy*, Vol. 98, supplement, 102-121.

20. Barro, R. J. and R. G. King, 1984, Time Separable Preferences and Intertemporal Substitution Models of Business Cycles, *Quarterly Journal of Economics*, Vol. 99, 817-839.

21.   Barro, R. J. and X. Sala-i-Martin, 1995: *Economic Growth*, New York: McGraw-Hill.

22.   Baxter, M. and R. G. King, 1993, Fiscal Policy in General Equilibrium, *American Economic Review*, Vol. 83, 315-334.

23.   Baxter, M. and A. Rennie, 1996, *Financial Calculus*, Cambridge University Press.

24.   Bishop, G., D. Damrau and M. Miller, 1989, 1992 and Beyond: Market Discipline Can Work in EC Monetary Union, London: Salomon Brothers.

25.   Björk, T., Y. Kabanov and W. Runggaldier, 1997: Bond Market Structure in the Presence of Marked Point Processes, *Mathematical Finance*, Vol. 7(2), 211-239.

26.   Björk, T., G. Di Masio, Y. Kabanov and W. Runggaldier, 1997, Towards a General Theory of Bond Markets, *Finance and Stochastics*, Vol. 1(2), 141-174.

27.   Black, F. and M. Scholes, 1973, The Pricing of Options and Corporate Liabilities,*Journal of Political Economy*, 637-654.

28.   Blanchard, O., 1981, Output, the Stock Market and Interest Rates, *American Economic Review*, 132-143.

29.   Blanchard, O. J. and S. Fischer, 1989, *Lectures on Macroeconomics*, Cambridge: MIT Press.

30.   Bluman, G., 1980, On the Transformation of Diffusion Processes into the Wiener Process, *SIAM Journal of Applied Mathematics*, 238-247.

31.   Bluman, G., 1983, On Mapping Linear Partial Differential Equations to Constant Coefficient Equations, *SIAM Journal of Applied Mathematics*, 1259-1273.

32. Bourguignon, F., 1974, A Particular Class of Continuous-Time Stochastic Growth Models, *Journal of Economic Theory*, 141-158.

33. Boyce, W. E. and R. C. DiPrima, 1997, *Elementary Differential Equations and Boundary Value Problems*, Sixth Edition, New York: John Wiley and Sons.

34. Brennan, M. J. and E. S. Schwartz, 1979, A Continuous Time Approach to the Pricing of Bonds, *Journal of Banking and Finance*, 133-155.

35. Brunner, K. and A. H. Meltzer, 1976, The Phillips Curve and Labor Markets, *Carnegie Rochester Conference Series on Public Policy 1*, Amsterdam: North-Holland.

36. Buchberger, B. and F. Winkler, 1998, *Gröbner Bases and Applications*, Cambridge University Press, Cambridge University Press.

37. Bühler, W., 1996, Experiences of the Valuation of Interest Rate Derivatives, Paper presented at the workshop on „Mathematical Finance and Applications" held at Humboldt-University, Berlin, Germany.

38. Buiter, W., G. Corsetti and N. Roubini, 1993, Excessive Deficits: „Sense and Nonsense in the Treaty of Maastricht", *Economic Policy*, 16, 58-100.

39. Buiter, W. H. and K. M. Kletzer, 1997: Debt and Taxes: Ponzi Finance, Dynamic Efficiency and Government Solvency, working paper.

40. Burden, R. L. and J. D. Faires, 1993: *Numerical Analysis*, fifth edition, Boston: PWS-KENT.

41. Calvo, G., 1978, On the Time Consistency of Optimal Policy in a Monetary Economy, *Econometrica*, Vol. 46, 1411-1428.

42. Campbell, J. Y., A. W. Lo and A. C. MacKinlay, 1997, *The Econometrics of Financial Markets*, Princeton University Press.

43. Chamley, C., 1985, Efficient Taxation in a Stylized Model of Intertemporal General Equilibrium, *International Economic Review*, 26, 451-468.

44. Chamley, C., 1986, Optimal Taxation of Capital Income in General Equilibrium with Infinite Lives,*Econometrica*, Vol. 54, 607-622.

45. Chen, G., G. Chen and S.-H. Hsu, 1995, *Linear Stochastic Control Systems*, Boca Raton: CRC Press.

46. Chiang, A., 1992, *Elements of Dynamic Optimization*, New York: McGraw-Hill.

47. Chow, G. C., 1979, Optimal Control of Stochastic Differential Equation Systems, *Journal of Economic Dynamics and Control*, 143-175.

48. Chow, G. C., 1997, *Dynamic Economics*, Oxford University Press.

49. Constantinides, G., 1990, Habit Formation: A Resolution of the Equity Premium Puzzle,*Journal of Political Economy*, 519-543.

50. Courant, R. and D. Hilbert, 1968, *Methoden der mathematischen Physik*, vierte Auflage, Berlin: Springer

51. Cox, J., J. Ingersoll and S. Ross, 1985a, An Intertemporal General Equilibrium Model of Asset Prices,*Econometrica*, 363-384.

52. Cox, J., J. Ingersoll and S. Ross, 1985b: A Theory of the Term Structure of Interest Rates, *Econometrica*, 385-408.

53. Culbertson, J., 1957 The Term Structure of Interest Rates, *Quarterly Journal of Economics*, Vol. 71, 485-517.

54. Delbaen, F. and W. Schachermayer, 1994, The Fundamental Theorem of Asset Pricing, *Mathematische Annalen*, 463-520.

55. Demmel, R., Y. G. Hervé and R. Holzmann, 1995 Implications of the Maastricht Fiscal Criteria on National Fiscal Policy, Working Paper, University of Saarland.

56. Devereux, M. and M. Saito, 1997, Growth and Risk-Sharing with Incomplete International Asset Markets, *Journal of International Economics*, Vol. 42, 453-481.

57. Dixit, A. and R. Pindyck, 1994, *Investment under Uncertainty*, Princeton University Press.

58. Dornbusch, R. and M. Draghi (eds.), 1991: *Public Debt Management: Theory and History*, Cambridge University Press.

59. Dothan, M. U., 1978, On the Term Structure of Interest Rates, *Journal of Financial Economics*, 59-69.

60. Duffie, D., 1992, *Dynamic Asset Pricing Theory*, Princeton University Press.

61. Duffie, D. and L. Epstein, 1992, Stochastic Differential Utility, *Econometrica*, Vol. 60, 353-394

62. Durrett, R., 1996, *Stochastic Calculus: A Practical Introduction*, Boca Raton: CRC Press.

63. Eaton, J., 1981, Fiscal Policy, Inflation and the Accumulation of Risky Capital, *Review of Economic Studies*, 435-445.

64. Eatwell, J., M. Milgate and P. Newman, 1989, *The New Palgrave: Finance*, London: W. W. Norton.

65. Evans, L. C., 1994, Partial Differential Equations, Lecture Notes Vol. 3A and 3B, Mathematics Department, University of Berkeley.

66. Feichtinger, G. and R. F. Hartl, 1986, *Optimale Kontrolle ökonomischer Prozesse*, Berlin: Walter de Gruyter.

67. Feller, W., 1952, The Parabolic Differential Equation and the Associated Semi-Group of Transformations, *Annals of Mathematics*, 468-519.

68. Fisher, I., 1896, Appreciation and Interest, *AEA Publications*, Vol. 3(11), 331-442.

69. Fisher, W. H., 1995, An Optimizing Analysis of the Effects of World Interest Disturbances on the Open Economy Term Structure of Interest Rates, *Journal of International Money and Finance*, Vol. 14(1), 105-126.

70. Fisher, W. H. and S. J. Turnovsky, 1992, Fiscal Policy and the Term Structure of Interest Rates: An Intertemporal Optimizing Analysis, *Journal of Money, Credit and Banking*, Vol. 24, 1-26.

71. Fleming, W. H. and R. Rishel, 1975, *Deterministic and Stochastic Optimal Control*, New York: Springer.

72. Fleming, W. H. and H. M. Soner, 1993, *Controlled Markov Processes and Viscosity Solutions*, New York: Springer.

73. Fritz, J., 1982, *Partial Differential Equations*, fourth edition, New York: Springer.

74. Fudenberg, D. and C. Harris, 1992, Evolutionary Dynamics with Aggregate Shocks, *Journal of Economic Theory*, 420-441.

75. Gallant, A. R. and G. Tauchen, 1996, Which Moments to Match? *Econometric Theory*, Vol. 12, 657-581.

76. Gardiner, C. W., 1983, *Handbook of Stochastic Methods*, second edition, New York: Springer.

77. Gaspar, J. and K. L. Judd, 1997, Solving Large-Scale Rational-Expectations Models, *Macroeconomic Dynamics*, Vol. 1, 45-75.

78. Girsanov, I. V., 1960, On Transforming a Certain Class of Stochastic Processes by Absolutely Continuous Substitution of Measures, *Theory of Probability and Applications*, Vol. 5, 285-301.

79. Hansen, L. and J. Scheinkman, 1995, Back to the Future: Generating Moment Implications for Continuous-Time Markov Processes, *Econometrica*, Vol. 63, 767-804.

80. Harrison, J. M. and D. Kreps, 1979, Martingales and Arbitrage in Multiperiod Securities Markets, *Journal of Economic Theory*, 381-408.

81. Harrison, J. M. and S. Pliska, 1981, Martingales and Stochastic Integrals in the Theory of Continuous Trading, *Stochastic Processes and Their Applications*, 215-260.

82. Heath, D., R. Jarrow and A. Morton, 1992, Bond Pricing and the Term Structure of Interest Rates: A New Methodology for Contingent Claim Valuation, *Econometrica*, Vol. 60, 77-105.

83. Hervé, Y. G., 1998, The Effects of Intergovernmental Fiscal Transfers on the Consumption and Investment Pattern in a Small Open Economy, University of Saarland, mimeo.

84. Hicks, Sir J., 1939, *Value and Capital*, Oxford University Press.

85. Hill, J. M., 1982, *Solution of Differential Equations by Means of One-Parameter Groups*, Harlow: Pitman Publishing Inc.

86. Ho, S. Y. and S. B. Lee, 1986, Term Structure Movements and Pricing Interest Rate Contingent Claims, *Journal of Finance*, 1011-1029.

87. Holzmann, R., Y. G. Hervé and R. Demmel, 1996, The Maastricht Fiscal Criteria: Required but Ineffective?,*Empirica*, Vol. 23, 25-58.

88. Huang, C.-F., 1985, Information Structures and Equilibrium Asset Prices, *Journal of Economic Theory*, Vol. 31, 33-71.

89. Ingersoll, J., 1987, *Theory of Financial Decision Making*, Savage: Rowman & Littlefield.

90. Judd, K. L., 1987, Debt and Distortionary Taxation in a Simple Perfect Foresight Model, *Journal of Monetary Economics*, Vol. 20, 51-72.

91. Judd, K. L., 1992, Projection Methods for Solving Aggregate Growth Models, *Journal of Economic Theory*, Vol. 58, 410-452.

92. Judd, K. L., 1998, *Numerical Methods in Economics*, Cambridge: MIT Press.

93. Kamien, M. I. and N. L. Schwartz, 1991, *Dynamic Optimization*, Amsterdam: North-Holland.

94. Karatzas, I. and S. Shreve, 1991, *Brownian Motion and Stochastic Calculus*, second edition, New York: Springer.

95. Karlin, S. and H. M. Taylor, 1981, *A Second Course in Stochastic Processes*, London: Academic Press.

96. Kliemann, W. and N. S. Namachchivaya (eds.), 1995, *Nonlinear Dynamics and Stochastic Mechanics*, Boca Raton: CRC Press.

97. Kloeden, P. E. and E. Platen, 1992, *Numerical Solution of Stochastic Differential Equations*, Berlin: Springer.

98. Kloeden, P. E., E. Platen and H. Schurz, 1994, *Numerical Solution of SDE Through Computer Experiments*, Berlin: Springer.

99. Kloeden, P. E. and E. Platen, 1995, Numerical Methods for Stochastic Differential Equations, 437-461, Chapter 18 in: Kliemann, W. and N. S. Namachchivaya (eds.), *Nonlinear Dynamics and Stochastic Mechanics*, Boca Raton: CRC Press.

100. Kydland, F. E. and E. C. Prescott, 1977, Rules Rather than Discretion: The Inconsistency of Optimal Plans, *Journal of Political Economy*, Vol. 85, 473-493.

101. Kydland, F. E. and E. C. Prescott, 1982, Time to Build and Aggregate Fluctuations, *Econometrica*, 1345-1370.

102. Lamberton, D. and B. Lapeyre, 1996, *Introduction to Stochastic Calculus Applied to Finance*, London: Chapman & Hall.

103. Lee, B.-S., 1991, Government Deficits and the Term Structure of Interest Rates, *Journal of Monetary Economics*, Vol. 27, 425-443.

104. Léonard, D. and N. Van Long, 1992, *Optimal Control Theory and Static Optimization in Economics*, Cambridge University Press.

105. Lo, A. W., 1988, Maximum Likelihood Estimation of Generalized Ito Processes with Discretely Sampled Data, *Econometric Theory*, 231-247.

106. Lucas, R. E. Jr., 1972, Expectations and the Neutrality of Money, *Journal of Economic Theory*, Vol. 4, 103-124.

107. Lucas, R. E. Jr., 1973, Some International Evidence on Output-Inflation Tradeoffs, *American Economic Review*, Vol. 68, 326-334.

108. Lucas, R. E. Jr., 1976, Econometric Policy Evaluation: A Critique, In: *The Phillips Curve and Labor Markets*, edited by K. Brunner and A. H. Meltzer, *Carnegie Rochester Conference Series on Public Policy 1*, 19-46, Amsterdam: North-Holland.

109. Lucas, R. E. Jr. and N. Stokey, 1983, Optimal Fiscal and Monetary Policy in an Economy without Capital, *Journal of Monetary Economics*, Vol. 12, 55-93.

110. Lutz, F., 1940, The Structure of Interest Rates, *Quarterly Journal of Economics*, Vol. 55, 36-63.

111. Malkiel, B. G., 1966, *The Term Structure of Interest Rates*, Princeton University Press.

112. Malkiel, B. G., 1989, The Term Structure of Interest Rates, in: Eatwell, J., M. Milgate and P. Newman (eds.), *The New Palgrave: Finance*, London: W. W. Norton, 265-270.

113. Malliaris, A. G. and W. Brock, 1982, *Stochastic Methods in Economics and Finance*, Amsterdam: North Holland.

114. Mandl, P., 1968, *One Dimensional Markov Processes*, in: „Die Grundlagen der Mathematischen Wissenschaften", Book no. 151, Prague.

115. Mehra, R. and E. C. Prescott, 1985, The Equity Premium: A Puzzle, *Journal of Monetary Economics*, Vol. 15, 145-161.

116. Merton, R. C., 1969, Lifetime Portfolio Selection Under Uncertainty: The Continuous-Time Case, *Review of Economics and Statistics*, Vol. 51, 247-257.

117. Merton, R. C., 1971, Optimum Consumption Rules in a Continuous-Time Model, *Journal of Economic Theory*, Vol. 3, 373-413.

118. Merton, R. C., 1975, An Asymptotic Theory of Growth Under Uncertainty, *Review of Economic Studies*, Vol. 42, 375-393.

119. Milstein, G. N., 1974, Approximate Integration of Stochastic Differential Equations, *Theory of Probability and Applications*, Vol. 19, 557-562.

120. Modigliani, F. and R. Sutch, 1966, Innovations in Interest Rate Policy, *American Economic Review, Papers and Proceedings Supplement*, Vol. 56, 178-197.

121. Muth, J. F., 1961, Rational Expectations and the Theory of Price Movements, *Econometrica*, Vol. 29, 315-335.

122. Neftci, S. N., 1996, *An Introduction to the Mathematics of Financial Derivatives*, London: Academic Press.

123. Obstfeld, M., 1994, Risk-taking, Global Diversification and Growth, *American Economic Review*, Vol. 84, 1310-1329.

124. Obstfeld, M. and K. Rogoff, 1996, *Foundation of International Macroeoconomics*, Cambridge: MIT Press.

125. Oksendal, B., 1991, *Stochastic Differential Equations*, third edition, New York: Springer.

126. Oseledets, V., 1968, A Multiplicative Ergodic Theorem. Lyapunov Characteristic Numbers for Dynamical Systems, *Transactions of Moscow Mathematical Society*, Vol. 19, 197-231.

127. Persson, T. and G. Tabellini, 1990, Macroeconomic Policy, Credibility and Politics, *Fundamentals of Pure and Applied Economics Vol. 38*, Chur: Harwood Academic Publishers.

128. Pinsky, R. G., 1995, *Positive Harmonic Functions and Diffusion: An integrated analytic and probabilistic approach*, Cambridge University Press.

129. Polyanin, A. D. and V. F. Zaitsev, 1996, *Handbuch der linearen Differentialgleichungen*, Berlin: Spektrum Akademischer Verlag.

130. Pontryagin, L. S., V. G. Boltyanskii, R. V. Gamkrelidze and E. F. Mischenko, 1962, *The Mathematical Theory of Optimal Processes*, Interscience.

131. Press, W. H., S. A. Teukolsky, W. T. Vetterling and B. P. Flannery, 1992, *Numerical Recipes in C: The Art of Scientific Computing*, Cambridge University Press.

132. Richard, S. F., 1978, An Arbitrage Model of the Term Structure of Interest Rates, *Journal of Financial Economics*, 33-57.

133. Risken, H., 1996, *The Fokker-Planck Equation: Methods of Solution and Applications*, second edition, Berlin: Springer.

134. Roll, R., 1970, *The Behavior of Interest Rates*, Basic Books.

135. Roll, R., 1971, Investment Diversification and Bond Maturity, *Journal of Finance*, Vol. 26(1), 51-66.

136. Romer, D., 1996, *Advanced Macroeconomics*, New York: McGraw-Hill.

137. Schöbel, R., 1995, *Kapitalmarkt und zeitkontinuierliche Bewertung*, Heidelberg: Physica-Verlag.

138. Schöbel, R. and A. Yakovlev, 1996, Dynamics and Risk in the Russian Bond Market, Paper presented at the workshop on „Stochastics, Information, and Markets" held at Humboldt-University, Berlin.

139. Schuss, Z., 1980, *Theory and Applications of Stochastic Differential Equations*, New York: John Wiley & Sons.

140. Shiller, R. J., 1990, The Term Structure of Interest Rates, with an Appendix by J. Huston McCulloch, Chapter 13 in: Arrow, K. J. and M. D. Intriligator (eds.), *Handbook of Monetary Economics*, Vol. 1, Amsterdam: North-Holland.

141. Skorohod, A. V., 1989, *Asymptotic Methods in the Theory of Stochastic Differential Equations*, American Mathematical Society.

142. Sobczyk, K., 1991, *Stochastic Differential Equations with Applications to Physics and Engineering*, Dordrecht: Kluwer Academic Publishers.

143. Strickland, C., 1994, A Comparison of Models for Pricing Interest Rate Derivative Securities, working paper, Financial Options Research Centre, University of Warwick.

144. Stroock, D. W. and S. R. Varadhan, 1997, *Multidimensional Diffusion Processes*, second corrected printing, New York: Springer.

145. Tabellini, G., 1986, Money, Debt and Deficits in a Dynamic Game, *Journal of Economic Dynamics and Control*, Vol. 10, 427-442.

146. Takayama, A., 1993 *Analytical Methods in Economics*, Ann Arbor: Michigan University Press.

147. Thompson, J. M. T. and S. R. Bishop (eds.), 1994, *Nonlinearity and Chaos in Engineering Dynamics*, New York: John Wiley & Sons.

148. Tice, J. and N. J. Webber, 1997, A Nonlinear Model of the Term Structure of Interest Rates, *Mathematical Finance*, Vol. 7, 177-209.

149. Todorovic, P., 1992, *An Introduction to Stochastic Processes and Their Applications*, New York: Springer.

150. Turnovsky, S. J., 1989, The Term Structure of Interest Rates and the Effects of Macroeconomic Policy, *Journal of Money, Credit and Banking*, 321-347.

151. Turnovsky, S. J., 1993, Macroeconomic Policies, Growth, and Welfare in a Stochastic Economy, *International Economic Review*, Vol. 35, 953-981.

152. Turnovsky, S. J., 1995a, *Methods of Macroeconomic Dynamics*, Cambridge: MIT Press.

153. Turnovsky, S. J., 1995b, Macroeconomic Policies, Growth, and Welfare in a Stochastic Economy, *International Economic Review*, 953-981.

154. Turnovsky, S. J. and W. H. Fisher, 1995, The Composition of Government Expenditure and its Consequences for Macroeconomic Performance, *Journal of Economic Dynamics and Control*, Vol. 19(4), 747-786.

155. Turnovsky, S. J. and E. L. Grinols, 1993, Risk, the Financial Market and Macroeconomic Equilibrium, *Journal of Economic Dynamics and Control*, 1-36.

156. Turnovsky, S. J. and E. L. Grinols, 1994, Exchange Rate Determination and Asset Prices in a Stochastic Small Open Economy, *Journal of International Economics*, 75-97.

157. Turnovsky, S. J. and E. L. Grinols, 1996, Consequences of Debt Policy in a Stochastically Growing Monetary Economy, mimeo.

158. Turnovsky, S. J. and M. H. Miller, 1984, The Effects of Government Expenditure on the Term Structure of Interest Rates, *Journal of Money, Credit and Banking*, 16-33.

159. Turnovsky, S. J. and P. Sen, 1991, Fiscal Policy, Capital Accumulation, and Debt in an Open Economy, *Oxford Economic Papers*, Vol. 43, 1-24.

160. Vasicek, O., 1977, An Equilibrium Characterization of the Term Structure, *Journal of Financial Economics*, 177-188.

161. Velasco, A., 1997a, Debts and Deficits with Fragmented Fiscal Policymaking, NBER Working Paper 6286, Cambridge: National Bureau of Economic Research.

162. Velasco, A., 1997b, A Model of Endogenous Fiscal Deficits and Delayed Fiscal Reforms, NBER Working Paper 6336, Cambridge: National Bureau of Economic Research.

163. Vetzal, K. R., 1994, A Survey of Stochastic Continuous Time Models of the Term Structure of Interest Rates, *Insurance: Mathematics and Economics*, Vol. 14, 139-161.

164. Vvedensky, D., 1993, *Partial Differential Equations with Mathematica*, Wokingham: Addison Wesley.

Printing: Weihert-Druck GmbH, Darmstadt
Binding: Buchbinderei Schäffer, Grünstadt